W9-BRM-412

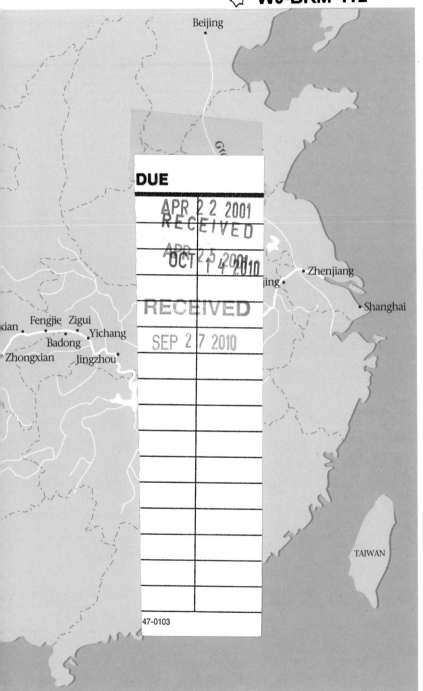

YANGTZE RIVER:
The Wildest, Wickedest River on Earth

YANGTZE RIVER:

The Wildest, Wickedest River on Earth

AN ANTHOLOGY
SELECTED AND EDITED BY

Madeleine Lynn

HONG KONG
OXFORD UNIVERSITY PRESS
OXFORD   NEW YORK
1997

Oxford University Press
Oxford New York
Athens Auckland Bangkok Bogota Bombay
Buenos Aires Calcutta Cape Town Dar es Salaam
Delhi Florence Hong Kong Istanbul Karachi
Kuala Lumpur Madras Madrid Melbourne
Mexico City Nairobi Paris Singapore
Taipei Tokyo Toronto
and associated companies in
Berlin Ibadan

Oxford is a trade mark of Oxford University Press

First published 1997
This impression (lowest digit)
1 3 5 7 9 10 8 6 4 2

Published in the United States
by Oxford University Press, New York

© Oxford University Press 1997

British Library Cataloguing in Publication Data
available

Library of Congress Cataloging-in-Publication Data

Lynn, Madeleine, date.
    Yangtze River: the wildest, wickedest river on earth / an anthology
selected and edited by Madeleine Lynn
    Includes bibliographical references.
    ISBN 0-19-586920-6 (alk. paper)
    1. Yangtze River (China)—Description and travel. 2. Yangtze River
(China)—Description and travel—Literary collections.
3. Chinese literature—Translations into English. I. Title.
DS793.Y3L96   1996
895.1'008032512—dc20   96-44698
                                                CIP

Printed in Hong Kong
Published by Oxford University Press (China) Ltd
18/F Warwick House, Taikoo Place, 979 King's Road,
Quarry Bay, Hong Kong

Many people have helped and encouraged me on the long journey to complete this book. Special thanks to Edward Stokes, Deirdre Chetham, and Jane Ram; also to Chao Mei Wah, Bill Hurst, and Simon Winchester.

ACKNOWLEDGEMENTS

The Editor and Publisher wish to thank the following publishers and agents for permission to reproduce copyright material:

Alfred A. Knopf Inc. and Brook Hersey for an excerpt from *A Single Pebble* by John Hersey, copyright John Hersey, 1956; 'Alarm at First Entering the Yangtse Gorges' and 'On Being Removed from Hsun-yang and Sent to Chung-Chou', from *One Hundred and Seventy Chinese Poems*, by Arthur Waley, trans, copyright 1919, and renewed 1947 by Arthur Waley, reprinted by permission of Alfred A. Knopf Inc and Constable Publishers; Chinese Literature Press for 'Water Town', 'Where Apes Howl Endlessly', excerpts from *A Ballad of Algae* and *The Angry Waves* and poems 'A Visit to Jinshan Monastery', 'Thoughts in Beigu Pavilion at Jingkou', 'Song of Inspector Ding', 'Thoughts When Travelling at Night', and 'On Women Selling Firewood'; Columbia University Press for 'The Merchant's Joy', 'A Trip to Shu', and 'Drunk Song' from *The Old Man Who Does As He Pleases* by Burton Watson, copyright © 1973 by Columbia University Press. Reprinted with permission of the publisher; The Commercial Press (HK) Ltd for the poem 'Struggling up the Three Gorges' from *Li Po: A New Translation*; from *Twentieth-century Chinese Poetry* by Kai Yu Hsu, translated by Kai-yu Hsu, Translation copyright © 1963 by Kai-yu Hsu. Used by permission of Doubleday, a division of Bantam Doubleday Dell Publishing Group, Inc. Foreign Languages Press for the interview 'Captain on the Yangtze River' from *Portraits of Ordinary Chinese*, and the poem 'Swimming'; HarperCollins Publishers and David F. White for an excerpt from *In Search of History: A Personal Adventure* by Theodore H. White, copyright © 1978 by Theodore H. White. Reprinted by permission of HarperCollins Publishers Inc; Houghton Mifflin Co. and Aitken, Stone & Wylie Ltd for an excerpt from *Sailing Through China*, text copyright © 1983 by Paul Theroux; Tom Hilditch for 'The Plight of the Baiji' first published in the *South China Morning Post*; IMG–Bach Literary Agency, copyright © 1995, and the Putnam Publishing Group, copyright © 1979 by Noel Barber, for an extract from *The Fall of Shanghai* by Noel Barber; The John Day Company for 'A Second Song of Chang Kan', 'Meditation at Red Cliff', and 'Leaving White Emperor City at Dawn' from *The White Pony*; John Murray (Publishers) Ltd for an excerpt from *The Forgotten Kingdom* by Peter Goullart; Jonathan Cape for 'The Red Cliff' from *Selections from the Works of Su Tung-P'o*, translated by Cyril Drummond Le Gros Clark, 1931; Penguin Books Ltd for the poem 'Sadness of the Gorges' from *Poems of the Late T'ang* translated by A. C. Graham (Penguin Classics 1965) copyright © A. C. Graham, 1965. Reproduced by permission of Penguin Books Ltd; Reed Consumer Books Ltd and Harold Ober Associates Inc., copyright © 1969 by The John Day Company, Inc., for an excerpt from *Pearl S. Buck: A Biography*; Reed Consumer Books Ltd, for an excerpt from *Behind the Wall* by Colin Thubron; Moss Roberts for 'K'ung Ming Borrows Some Arrows' from *Three Kingdoms*, translated by Moss Roberts; Harriet Sergeant for an excerpt from *Shanghai*, by Harriet Sergeant, 1979.

Photo credits: David B. Youtz, pp. 17, 28, 38, 41, 51, 56, 67, 88, 116, 129, 133, 143, 164, 182, 188, 199, 204, 210, 225, 229, 232, 266, and cover (centre); Rebecca Lloyd and Peter Hookham, pp. 121, 161, 169, 217, 253, and cover (bottom); from *Thomson's China* by John Thomson, Hong Kong: Oxford University Press, 1993, pp. 71, 135, 247, 263.

The Editor and Publisher have made every effort to discover which excerpts included in this anthology are subject to copyright, and in those cases, to track and secure the permission of the copyright holders for their inclusion. In a few cases these efforts have not been successful, and the Editor and Publisher offer their apologies to the copyright holders (if any), trusting that they will accept the will for the deed.

CONTENTS

Acknowledgements   vii

Introduction   xiii

Glossary of Place-names   xix

Yangtze Facts and Figures   xxiii

PROLOGUE: UP FROM THE SEA: SETTING OUT FROM SHANGHAI   1

1. 1890s Shanghai   3
  Isabella Bird
2. Birth and Paralysis of a Great City   9
  Harriet Sergeant
3. Captain on the Yangtze River   15
  Chen Kexiong

PART 1: THE LOWER AND MIDDLE REACHES: SHANGHAI TO YICHANG   21

Zhenjiang, Meeting of the Waters   26

4. A Visit to Jingshan Monastery   27
  Su Dongpo
5. Thoughts in Beigu Pavilion at Jingkou   29
  Xin Qiji
6. Ship Aground and a Scene of Desolation   31
  Laurence Oliphant
7. The Wildest, Wickedest River   37
  Pearl S. Buck

River Journeys, River Lives   44

8. Thoughts When Travelling at Night   45
  Du Fu
9. A Second Song of Chang-Kan   46
  Li Bai

10. Song of Inspector Ding   48
    Li Bai

11. Looking for Li Bai   49
    Colin Thubron

12. A Ballad of Algae   53
    Mao Dun

13. Water Town   61
    Zhao Pei

14. A Trip to Shu   65
    Lu Yu

15. Dodging Demons and Fast-moving Islands   69
    Thomas Woodroofe

16. The Plight of the Baiji   76
    Tom Hilditch

17. Flooding and the Value of a Life   82
    William Spencer Percival

18. Beacon Fire   87
    Chen Shixu

19. Drunk Song   92
    Lu Yu

20. The Trials of Travel   94
    Augustus R. Margary

21. The Red Cliff   98
    Su Dongpo

Battle Strategies   102

22. K'ung Ming Borrows Some Arrows   103
    Luo Guanzhong

23. Crossing the Yangtze   107
    Noel Barber

Dreams of the Past, Visions of the Future   117

24. Meditation at Red Cliff   118
    Su Dongpo

25. Swimming   120
    Mao Zedong

PART 2: THE UPPER REACHES: YICHANG TO CHONGQING 123

The Three Gorges 127

26. Struggling up the Three Gorges 128
   Li Bai
27. Leaving White Emperor City At Dawn 129
   Li Bai
28. Setting out in a Houseboat 130
   Isabella Bird
29. Through the Gorges in a Wuban 139
   Edwin J. Dingle
30. Alarm at First Entering the Yangtze Gorges 142
   Bai Juyi
31. On Being Removed from Hsun-Yang and Sent to
   Chung-Chou 144
   Bai Juyi
32. Through Ch'ing-Tan Rapid and Other Stories of
   the Gorges 145
   William Gill
33. A Yangtsze Dragon 151
   William Ferdinand Tyler
34. The Sadness of the Gorges 158
   Meng Jiao

Bitter Strength 159

35. The Trackers 160
   Marion H. Duncan
36. Old Pebble, Head Tracker 162
   John Hersey
37. Where Apes Howl Endlessly 168
   Captain Zhang

The Steam Age 174

38. The Advantages of Steam 175
   Archibald J. Little
39. Perils of the Yangtsze 177
   H. G. W. Woodhead
40. Down the River on the Dollar Line 185
   Tan Shi-hua

41. Upriver on a Merchant Ship   190
    David W. Swift

Scenes of Sichuan   197

42. Crossing into Sichuan   198
    Thomas W. Blakiston
43. On Women Selling Firewood   201
    Du Fu
44. A Yangtze Childhood   203
    Tan Shi-hua
45. Life in Wanxian   209
    David W. Swift
46. Entrance to Hades   216
    Archibald J. Little
47. Chongqing   221
    Theodore H. White
48. Crossing the Yangtse in the Mist   227
    Robert Payne
49. Past, Present, & Future   230
    Paul Theroux

PART 3: THE UPPER REACHES: BEYOND CHONGQING   235

50. The Yangtse in its Real Home   237
    Samuel Pollard
51. Nakhi Mountain Wedding   245
    Peter Goullart
52. Slipping into Tibet   251
    Marion H. Duncan
53. Frozen   258
    Evariste-Regis Huc

EPILOGUE: IN PRAISE OF THE RIVER: A NEW INSPIRATION   263

54. The River   264
    Tsou Ti-fan

Bibliography   267

INTRODUCTION

Eastward runs the Great River
Whose waves have washed away
All the talented and courteous men in history.

Su Dongpo (1036–1101), Meditation on Red Cliff.

To most Chinese, the word 'Yangtze' means nothing. That was merely the local name for the last 200 miles of the river on its way to the sea, where it ran through the ancient fiefdom of Yang. The majority of nineteenth-century Westerners never ventured beyond that section, so to them the river was the Yangtze. But the wide delta mouth that they knew is only a tiny fraction of this mighty river. In fact, there is a local name for every stretch of its almost 4,000 miles. Each name reflects either one of its many different personalities, or the name of those living along its banks. The Wild Yak River, River of Golden Sand, Beautiful River, the Ba River (named after the ancient Ba nationality, now extinct): all are the Yangtze. When referring to the river as a whole, the Chinese call it simply *Chang Jiang*—'Long River', or *Da Jiang*—'Great River'. And so it is: the words resonate with associations for all Chinese. The dividing line between North and South both geographically and culturally, the river is central to Chinese history and to the Chinese sense of themselves. It has been lived along, fought over and written about for over 2,000 years. From childhood onwards, Chinese are familiar with its wealth of history, poetry, and legends.

Since history began, the Great River has been of crucial strategic and commercial significance. Time after time as dynasties rose and fell, the fields and cliffs along the Yangtze were the scene of decisive struggles. It is easy to see why these lands are so important. The rice paddies of the river basin are the main granary of China, while the wilder, more inaccessible regions upriver have provided the ideal refuge for many an army in retreat. Crossing the country from west to east, the river is a natural conduit for goods, whether traditional ones such as silk, tea, and salt, or in the nineteenth and early twentieth century, a more sinister product: opium. Indian 'foreign mud' was brought upriver by the British as far as Wuhan; but the bulk of the drug was home-grown and came downriver from Yunnan and Sichuan.

Western travellers along the Yangtze were to find that distance was calculated differently there. On his voyage in 1861, the British naval officer Blakiston eventually realized that a Chinese b*— officially the equivalent of half a kilometre (0.3 of a mile)—was a loose term often used not just as a measure of distance, but taking into account the difficulty of the terrain. Thus a day's journey was always reckoned as one hundred b*, whether the traveller actually covered one hundred b* or only ten. In Wanxian in 1923, American businessman David Swift noted that distance was generally measured not in b* or miles but in travel time; thus Wanxian was said to be fifteen days from Shanghai.

Time there has a different meaning also. Often it appears simply to stand still. After all, until very recently, little changed along the Yangtze. Boatmen and peasants led the same hard and dangerous lives their ancestors did. Their troubles were the same: wrecks, floods, wars, taxes, or conscription and the supernatural creatures that haunted the river.

Where little changes, the past can seem very close. For the Chinese from eleventh-century poet and warrior Xin Qiji, to Mao Zedong in the 1950s, the river was alive with ancient heroes. A recurrent theme running through writings on the Yangtze is the story of the Three Kingdoms. It took place in the third century AD, when three rival leaders struggled to succeed the dying Han Dynasty. The decades-long drama was played out in epic battles up and down the river. Often hugely outnumbered, the principal hero Liu Bei's best weapon was his cunning, as demonstrated in the extract 'K'ung Ming Borrows Some Arrows' and in the story of the Battle of Red Cliff. Not only the educated, but every boatman knows these tales, immortalized by generations of story-tellers and poets, and the subject of numerous operas.

The fourteenth-century novel *The Three Kingdoms*, based on this period, was one of Mao's favourite books. As he planned his own Yangtze campaigns, without doubt those brave and wily warriors were in his thoughts. In 1949, his brilliantly executed crossing of the lower Yangtze (as described in 'Crossing the Yangtze') was a turning point in the civil war.

Until recently only a tiny minority were literate, older written accounts of the Yangtze come from scholars (usually government officials) who spent time along the river. They include some of China's most renowned poets, Su Dongpo, Li Bai, Du Fu, and Bai Juyi. To be stationed in a government post in one of the gay cities along the lower reaches could be pleasant, but to be posted to the wild upper reaches was considered a miserable fate. Many were sent there in exile or disgrace. The journey to Sichuan up through the narrow gorges was extremely dangerous. As the Shanghai-based journalist H. G. W. Woodhead reported, as late as the 1920s and 1930s, steam ships were often wrecked, while junks were even more at risk. Those eighth- to twelfth-century poems of the terrors of travelling the river ('Struggling up the Three Gorges', and 'Alarm at Entering the Yangtze Gorges', for instance) have a raw immediacy and power unsurpassed by anything written since.

Once upriver, the scholar endured an isolated existence, largely among minority tribes, many of whom spoke only their local dialect. In 'On Being Removed to Hsunyang and Sent to Chung-chou' Bai Zhuyi compares the Ba people of the gorges to apes, saying how glad he would be to meet anyone remotely human. Sichuan was as foreign to him as later, all of the Yangtze beyond the safety of the foreign concessions would be to Western travellers.

Although early rivermen and women could not write, their sufferings and pleasures survive in scholars' poems, and in their rich, and often frightening folklore. Yangtze tales and superstitions have been handed down orally and were also recorded by both Chinese and Western writers. As many of these extracts show, the Yangtze was peopled not only with heroes, but also goddesses, dragons, and demons. Later, leftist writers like Mao Dun were to describe the harshness of peasant life in works such as 'Ballad of Algae'. In the 1980s, Chinese reporters travelled the country to give ordinary people a voice, interviewing them about their lives. 'River Captain' and 'Where Apes Howl Endlessly' are two of those accounts. With the revolution, peasants were to gain not only a voice, but a new sense of possibilities. Banished were the river demons, and with them the traditional, passive sense of fatalism. Mao Zedong's poem 'Swimming' and also the final piece in this anthology 'The River', reflect this new attitude.

What of the first Westerners to travel the Yangtze? Although a rare few came before the nineteenth century, it was the Opium Wars of the mid-1840s that forced the Chinese to open certain ocean and river ports to foreigners. For the first time, non-Chinese were allowed to travel freely up the Yangtze. From then on until 1949, Western military and government men, traders, missionaries, adventure seekers, and plant and animal hunters were to travel upriver to the interior.

With supreme confidence they came, equipped with tea, rice, and curry powder (to kill germs) and prepared to deal with any eventuality. Lone stalwarts like sixty-four-year-old Isabella Bird in 1896 had to contend not only with tiny, uncomfortable boats, but with anti-foreign sentiments. Mrs Bird was pelted with mud several times, and on one occasion attacked and injured for the indecency of travelling in an open sedan chair. Just a few years before in 1891 there had been a wave of anti-missionary demonstrations throughout the Yangtze basin, while the 1900 Boxer rebellion against all foreigners was only a few years away.

Others, like Lord Elgin in 1858, brought British soldiers and some home comforts with them, although all their expertise could not prevent them from running aground. His Lordship's private secretary paints an unforgettable picture of Elgin and his men supping on sherry and sandwiches, as they survey the devastation wrought by the Taiping rebels. They were at the very spot where seven hundred years previously, the warrior Xin Qiji had reminisced about heroes who had fought there centuries before his own time. Numerous poets in fact, had gazed at the river over their wine and mused over long-ago battles, and the transience of life. Lord Elgin, however, over his sherry, was concerned about trading opportunities, and the difficulties of thoroughly mapping the river. To men like these, Chinese stories of a valiant past were irrelevant.

Most Western travellers at that time knew little of China's long history. Moreover, they were seeing the country at its lowest ebb; first came the long-drawn-out death of the very last imperial Dynasty, followed by the chaos and war of the years leading up to the 1949 revolution. Many foreigners saw themselves as the bearers of progress and Christian salvation to a once-great, but now backward country.

Yet certain themes stand out in travellers' accounts, whether Chinese or foreign, ancient or contemporary: the sheer terrifying power of the river and the majesty of the rugged scenery of the upper reaches, particularly in the Three Gorges, with their treacherous rapids and towering cliffs; the perils and discomforts of travel; and the precarious lives of poverty, sweat, and back-breaking labour of the river's people. There are the trackers painfully dragging the boats step by step through the Gorges, the farmers cultivating each available inch of land by hand and battling the frequent floods, and the ubiquitous coolies, their backs scarred by years of carrying goods by shoulder-pole.

We are indebted to missionaries such as Abbé Huc, Samuel Pollard, and Marion Duncan for descriptions of the remote regions beyond Chongqing. To read their descriptions of their travels through the lands of Tibetans and 'Mantsz' tribesmen is to marvel at the dogged perseverance and courage of these men. Then there were men like Peter Goullart, a loner who found a paradise in the mountains of Yunnan in the 1930s and 1940s.

While a utopia for wildlife may still be found in the remoter parts of Yunnan and Tibet, the inexorable increase of the human population below Chongqing in the last hundred years has stripped the river and its banks of almost all other living creatures, and polluted its waters. Travel writer Paul Theroux has little hope for the future and the article by Hong Kong journalist Tom Hilditch bears him out.

Man intends to alter the landscape even further. Pearl Buck described the Yangtze as the 'wildest, wickedest river upon the globe.' The gigantic Three Gorges Dam, begun in 1993, promises finally to harness the river. Those in favour of the project say that it will bring an end to the floods of the lower reaches, and bring greater prosperity to the region through its hydro-electric power. Those against it predict that it will be a costly environmental disaster. Whoever is right, without question, the Yangtze will be changed irrevocably.

This book approaches the Great River as did most foreigners a century ago, arriving by sea at Shanghai, a new city by Chinese standards and largely a Western creation. The journey continues deep into Central China, through the densely populated Yangtze basin. It braves the rapids of the Three Gorges and ends in territory unknown and alien to most Chinese, rugged highlands sparsely inhabited by minority ethnic groups.

No single book could ever claim to give a complete chronicle of events and people along the Yangtze. Chinese history is far too long and complex for that. This is merely a personal selection of writings, which I hope readers will enjoy, and which may inspire them to travel the Long River for themselves.

There are several different systems of romanizing Chinese characters, and some of the early foreign visitors followed no particular method, but simply reproduced the Chinese sounds as best they could. In addition, not only have many place-names been changed over the years, but also the Yangtze passes through many different regions each with its own local dialect, so that the same place-name may be pronounced in several slightly different ways. This easily leads to some confusion. Although I have used the *Pinyin* romanization of Chinese words in the introductions, I have kept the traditional spellings of 'Yangtze'. I have retained the original old spellings in the excerpts, and here provide a glossary of the most common place-names mentioned in this book.

GLOSSARY OF PLACE-NAMES

'Water' words occur repeatedly in place-names. *JIANG* and *HE* both mean river, as in 'Jiujiang', nine rivers; 'Lijiang', beautiful river; and 'Henan', south of the river. *CHUAN* is also an ancient word for river, as in 'Sichuan', four rivers. *HU* means lake, as in 'Hubei' and 'Hunan', north and south of the lake respectively (referring to Lake Dongting). *XIA* means gorge and *TAN* is rapids.

Shanghai place-names and those not along the river are listed in alphabetical order, while as far as possible the rest are listed in order going upstream.

MODERN PINYIN NAMES	*OLD SPELLINGS, OTHER NAMES*
Shanghai	Shanghae
Hongkou	Hongkew
Huangpu	Whangpoo
Jiabei	Chapei
Pudong	Pu-tung Point/Pootung
Suzhou Creek	Soochow Creek
Wusong	Woo-sung
Lower and Middle Reaches	
Jiangsu Province	Kiangsu, Kiang-su
Jiangyin	Kiangyin
Zhenjiang	Chin-kiang/Chinkiang/Jingkou
Jinshan	'Golden Mountain' referred to as 'Golden Island'/Chin Shan
Yangzhou	Yang-chow/Yangchow
Danyang	Yunyang
Chang Gan	Chang-kan
Nanjing	Nanking/Jinling or Chinling
Anqing	Anking
Poyang Lake	P'oyang Lake
Jiujiang	Kiukiang
Liuguan Point	Liu-kuan Point
Qizhou	Ch'i-chow/Chi-chou/Chi-mouth
Hubei Province	Hupeh/Hu-pei/Hoopeh
Kingdom of Chu (part of today's Hubei)	Ch'u

Lin Gao	Lin Kao
~~Huangzhou~~	~~Huang-chou~~
Xiakou	Hsia-K'ou

Wuhan, *made up of three towns:*

Hankou	Hankow
Hanyang	Hanyang
Wuchang	Wu-Ch'ang

Dongting Lake	Tungt'ing Lake
Jingzhou	Chiang-ling/Kiangling
Yichang	I'Chang/Ichang

Xiling Gorge, *made up of seven gorges including:*

Yichang Gorge	Ichang Gorge
Huang Niu Xia	Yellow Ox/Cow Gorge
Niugan Mafei Xia	Niu-kan/Ox Liver and Horse Lungs Gorge
Micang Xia	Mitan/Rice Granary Gorge

Rapids

Xiang Tan	Hsiang-tan
Xin Tan	Hsin-tan/Ch'ing Tan/Ch'in Tan/ New Rapid

Wu Gorge   Witches Gorge

Qutang Gorge   Chutan/Ch'ut'ang/Wind Box/ Feng-hsiang

Yenyu Rock   Yen-yu

Upper Reaches

Guandukou	Kwan-du-kow
Baidicheng	White Emperor City/White King City
De Jian	Teh Chien
Xianshi	Hsien-Shih
Ba River, Kingdom of Ba	P'a/Pa
Zigui	Kwei/Tse-kwei
Badong	Pa-tung
Fengjie	Kwei Fu/Kwei-Chou/Kuizhou
Sichuan Province	Szechuan/Szecheun/ Sze Chuan/Szechwan/ Sse-Tchouan/Sz'chuan/ Kingdom of Shu
Xinlongtan	Hsin-lung-tan/New Dragon Rapid
Wanxian	Wan Hsien/Wanhsien

Zhongxian	Chung-Chou
Fengdu	Fêng tu
Tianzishan	T'ien tze Shan
Jialing River	Chialing river
Chongqing	Chungking/Chung-king
Yibin	Suifu
Lijiang	Likiang
Jinshajiang	Kin-Cha-Kiang/Ching-sha-chiang/'
River of Golden Sand'
Tibet	Thibet
Bayan Shan	Bayen-Kharat Mountains
Murui usu	Mouroui Oussa/Winding Water

Other Places in China

Beijing	Peking/Pekin
Chefoo	Zhefu
Chengdu	Chengtu
Guangdong Province	Kwangtung
Guangzhou	Canton
Hangzhou	Hang-chow
Huang He	Huang-Ho/Yellow River
Kaifeng (Northern Song capital)	K'ai-feng
Lhasa	Lha-ssa
Ningbo	Ningpo
Shaanxi Province	Shensi
Shandong Province	Shantung
Tianjin	Tientsin
Zhefu	Chefoo

YANGTZE FACTS AND FIGURES

The third longest river in the world after the Nile and the Amazon, and the longest in all of Asia, the Yangtze flows for some 6,300 kilometres (3,900 miles). It winds through eight Provinces: Tibet, Yunnan, Sichuan, Hubei, Hunan, Jiangxi, Anhui, and Jiangsu.

For navigational purposes the Yangtze is usually divided into three parts:

Lower reaches: The mouth to Wuhan, about 900 kilometres (560 miles).

Middle reaches: Wuhan to Yichang, about 1,000 kilometres (620 miles).

Upper reaches: Yichang to the source in Qinghai Province, 4,400 kilometres (2,700 miles).

The river is navigable by boats of up to 5,000 tons as far as Wuhan in the Middle Reaches, 3,000 tons to Yichang, 1,500 tons to Chongching, and 500 tons to Yibin, a total distance of about 2,700 kilometres (1,700 miles). Small boats can continue for about 100 kilometres (62 miles) beyond that. When the water is particularly low in the summer, boats run aground quite frequently all along the river. On the completion of the Three Gorges Dam, boats of up to 5,000 tons should be able to sail as far as Chongqing.

The Yangtze has a drainage area of an estimated 1,127,000 square kilometres (700,000 square miles), which is about one-fifth of China's total land area. It affects the lives of more than 400 million people—nearly one out of every thirteen on earth.

The Yangtze Valley produces about two-thirds of China's grain and over 30 per cent of its cotton.

Water levels fluctuate tremendously. In the winter the water is low, while in the summer it is swollen by the melting snows of the mountains of Central Asia and by the monsoons from the South.

At Wuhan, there is a seasonal variation of about fifteen metres (fifty feet), while at Chongqing, it can rise by as much as thirty metres (one hundred feet) in the summer.

In summer, the water in the Gorges is between 150 to 180 metres deep (500 to 600 feet), making it the one of the deepest stretches of river in the world.

The Three Gorges Dam will raise the water level permanently by 100 metres (328 feet), from Sandouping inside the first gorge above Yichang, up to Chongqing.

The river carries approximately 1,000 billion cubic metres of water to the sea annually, and discharges 500,000,000 tons of yellow silt into the Yellow Sea.

UP FROM THE SEA:
SETTING OUT FROM SHANGHAI

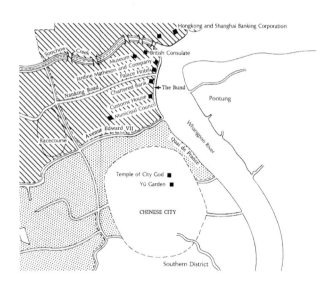

A medium-size domestic trading port and fishing town for centuries, Shanghai ('above the sea' or 'up from the sea') changed dramatically after the establishment of foreign concessions there, as a result of the 1842 Opium Wars. It quickly grew into China's most important—and most exciting—commercial hub. The key was its location. Serving as both a sea and river port, it is the gateway outwards to the Pacific and inwards, not only to the lands around the city itself, but also to the entire Yangtze basin, a vast area whose population today is about 200 million people.

Until the revolution in 1949, Shanghai teemed with activity. From its docks along the Bund, Chinese luxuries such as tea, silk, and porcelain were loaded on to ships bound for the West, while foreign opium and textiles were unloaded to be sent up river and all over China. Men and women from surrounding provinces flocked here looking for work, some making good, others destined to die in the gutters. Many overseas banks had offices here and there was a busy Shanghai Stock Exchange. For those with money, pre-1949 Shanghai was the gayest city, not only in China, but in all of Asia. To this day its very name evokes a certain rather wicked glamour and sophistication. The Chinese say that even if a Shanghainese lives in a hovel, he or she will always emerge dressed in style and ready to out-talk and usually out-smart anyone else in business dealings.

After 1949, however, the city's fortunes changed. Although trade and industry continued to prosper, there was little money to invest in infrastructure. As author Harriet Sergeant describes in the second extract, the 1980s city landscape remained frozen in the 1940s. The once grand buildings became shabby and neglected and, as the population soared, the problems of overcrowded housing and congested traffic grew worse. But since 1988 Shanghai has been allowed to keep more of her revenue. The city has embarked on an ambitious building programme and is courting foreign investment. Shanghai is making a comeback.

1

1890S SHANGHAI

ISABELLA BIRD

A clergyman's daughter who suffered from poor health all her life, Isabella Bird seemed an unlikely candidate to become an explorer. Yet she proved to be one of the most intrepid of all nineteenth-century travellers, and her books enjoyed tremendous popularity. She began travelling in her forties for the sake of her health, and set off for China at the age of sixty-four.

This account of her arrival in Shanghai is taken from the story of her voyage up the Yangtze during 1896 and 1897. Today's travellers can still identify with her lively description of the water's dramatic change of colour and the myriad boats of all shapes and sizes. But the opium hulks and their foreign masters are long gone.

Many hours before reaching port, the deep heavenly blue of the Pacific gradually changes into a turbid yellowish flood, well named the Yellow Sea, holding in suspension the rich wash of scarcely explored Central Asian mountain ranges, the red loam of the 'Red Basin' of Sze Chuan, and the grey and yellow alluvium of the Central Provinces of China, all carried to the ocean by the 'Great River', according to a careful scientific estimate, to the extent of 6,428,858,255 cubic feet a year, solid stuff enough to build an island ninety feet in depth and a mile square annually.

Countless fishing-boats roll on the muddy waste; sailing vessels, steamers and brown-sailed junks of every build show signs of convergence towards something, and before long a blink of land is visible, and a lightship indicates the mouth of the Yangtze Kiang and a navigable channel. It is long even then before anything definite presents itself, and I confess to being disappointed with the first features of the Asiatic mainland—two long, thin, yellow lines, hardly more solid-looking than the yellow water stretching

along the horizon, growing gradually into low marshy banks, somewhat later topped with uninteresting foliage, through which there are glimpses of what looks like an interminable swamp. Then Woo-sung appears with its new railroad, godowns, white-washed buildings, and big ships at anchor discharging cargo into lighters and native boats, and then the banks of the narrowing Huang-pu, the river of Shanghai, are indicated by habitations and small fields and signs of small industries.

Within four miles of Shanghai the vivacity of the Huang-pu and its banks becomes overpowering, and the West asserts its ascendency over the slow-moving East. There are ranges of great godowns, wharves, building yards, graving docks, 'works' of all descriptions, filatures, cotton mills, and all the symptoms in smoky chimneys and a ceaseless clang of the presence of capital and energy. After the war with Japan there was a rapid increase in the number of factories.

4

The life and movement on the river become wonderful. The channel for large vessels, though narrow, shifting and intricate, and the subject of years of doleful prophesies as to 'silting up' and leaving Shanghai stranded, admits of the passage of our largest merchantmen, and successful dredging enables them to lie alongside the fine wharves at Hongkew. American three- and four-masted and other sailing vessels are at anchor in mid-stream, or are proceeding up or down in charge of tugs. Monster liners under their own steam at times nearly fill up the channel, their officers yelling frantically at the small craft which recklessly cross their bows: great white, two-storeyed paddle arks from Ningpo and Hankow, local steamers, steam launches owned by the great firms, junks of all builds and sizes, manageable by their huge rudders, sampans, hooded boats, and native boats of all descriptions, lighters, and a shoal of nondescript craft make navigation tedious, if not perilous, while sirens and steam whistles sound continually. 'The plot thickens'. Foreign hongs, warehouses, shipping offices and hotels are passed in Hongkew, the American settlement, and gliding round Pu-tung Point, the steamer anchors abreast of the bund in a wholesomely rapid flow of water 2000 feet wide.

I arrived in Shanghai the first time on a clear, bright autumn day. The sky was very blue, and the masses of exotic trees, the green, shaven lawns, the belated roses, and the clumps of chrysanthemums in the fine public gardens gave a great charm to the first view of the settlement. Two big, lofty, white hulks for bonded Indian opium are moored permanently in front of the gardens. Gunboats and larger war-vessels of all nations, all painted white, and the fine steamers of the Messageries Maritimes have their moorings a little higher up. Boats, with crews in familiar uniforms, and covered native boats gaily painted, the latter darting about like dragon-flies, were plying ceaselessly, and as it was the turn of the tide, hundred of junks were passing seawards under their big brown sails.

On landing at the fine landing-stage, where kind friends received me and took me to the British Consul's residence in the spacious grounds of the Consulate, I was at once impressed with the exquisite dress of the ladies, who were at least a half of the throng, and with the look of wealth and comfort which prevails.

Naturally, Isabella Bird describes the European city of Shanghai—that 'model settlement', with its Western clubs and amusements, its mounted Sikh policemen, its modern drainage and water systems. In sum, the Shanghai that 'in spite of dark shadows, is a splendid example of what British energy, wealth, and organising power can accomplish'.

Yet Mrs Bird does not fail to point out that to her surprise, even in the foreign settlements, the Chinese are much in evidence. Wealthy Chinese own grand shops not far from the Bund and their richly dressed wives and children ride in some of the handsomest carriages along Bubbling Well Road (now Nanjing Xi Lu or Nanjing West Road), 'the fashionable afternoon drive of Shanghai'. Because of their ignorance of the Chinese language, foreign merchants are utterly dependent on their Chinese compradores.

Nor does she fail to venture beyond the European settlement to peer inside the walls that surround Shanghai the Chinese city, a place that few of her contemporaries cared to visit or even think about:

To us the name Shanghai means alone the superb foreign settlement, with all the accessories of western luxury and civilisation, lying grandly for a mile and a half along the Huang-pu, the centre of Far Eastern commerce and gaiety, the 'Charing Cross' of the Pacific—London on the Yellow Sea.

But there was a Shanghai before Shanghai—a Shanghai which still exists, increases and flourishes—a busy and unsavoury trading city, which leads its own life according to Chinese methods as independently as though no foreign settlement existed; and long before Mr. Pigou, of the H.E.I.C., in 1756, drew up his memorandum, suggesting Shanghai as a desirable place for trade, Chinese intelligence had hit upon the same idea, and the port was a great resort of Chinese shipping, cargoes being discharged there and dispersed over the interior by the Yangtze and the Grand Canal. Yet it never rose higher than the rank of a third-rate city.

It has a high wall three miles and a half in circuit, pierced by several narrow gateways and surrounded by a ditch twenty feet wide and suburbs lying between it and the river with its tiers of native shipping as crowded as the city proper. This shipping, consisting of junks, lorchas, and native craft of extraordinary rig, lies, as Lu Hew* said, 'like the teeth of a comb'.

To mention native Shanghai in foreign ears polite seems scarcely seemly; it brands the speaker as an outside barbarian, a person of 'odd tendencies'. It is bad form to show any interest in it, and worse to visit it. Few of the lady residents in the settlement have seen it, and both men and women may live in Shanghai for years and leave it without making the acquaintance of their nearest neighbour. It is supposed that there is a risk of bringing back small-pox and other maladies, that the smells are unbearable, that the foul slush of the narrow alleys is over the boots, that the foreigner is rudely jostled by thousands of dirty coolies, that the explorer may be knocked down or hurt by loaded wheelbarrows going at a run; in short, that it is generally abominable. It is the one point on which the residents are obdurate and disobliging.

I absolutely failed to get an escort until Mr. Fox, of H.M.'s Consular Service, kindly offered to accompany me. I did not take back small-pox, or any other malady, I was not rudely jostled by dirty coolies, nor was I hurt or knocked down by wheelbarrows. The slush and the smells were there, but the slush was not fouler nor the smells more abominable than in other big Chinese cities that I have walked through; and as a foreign woman is an everyday sight in the near neighbourhood, the people minded their own business and not mine, and I was even able to photograph without being overborne by the curious.

Shanghai is a mean-looking and busy city; its crowds of toiling, trotting, bargaining, dragging, burden-bearing, shouting, and yelling men are its one imposing feature. Few women, and those of the poorer class, are to be seen. The streets, with houses built of slate-coloured, soft-looking brick, are only about eight feet wide, are paved with stone slabs, and are narrowed by innumerable stands, on which are displayed, cooked and raw and being cooked, the multifarious viands in which the omnivorous Chinese delight, an odour of garlic predominating. Even a wheelbarrow—the only conveyance possible—can hardly make its way in many places. True a mandarin sweeps by in his gilded chair, carried at a run,

---

* Lu Hew (usually written Lu Yu) was a twelfth-century poet-official. See 'A Trip to Shu' and 'Drunk Song'.

with his imposing retinue, but his lictors clear the way by means not available to the general public.

All the articles usually exposed for sale in Chinese cities are met with in Shanghai, and old porcelain, bronzes, brocades, and embroideries are displayed to attract strangers. Restaurants and tea houses of all grades abound, and noteworthy among the latter is the picturesque building on the Zig-Zag Bridge*.... The buildings and fantastic well-kept pleasures of the Ching-hwang Miao, which may be called the Municipal Temple, the Confucian Temple, the Guild Hall of the resident natives of Chekiang, and the temple of the God of War, with its vigorous images begrimed with the smoke of the incense sticks or ages of worshippers, its throngs, its smoke, its ceaseless movement, and its din are the most salient features of this native hive....

On returning to the light, broad, clean, well-paved, and sanitary streets of foreign Shanghai, I was less surprised than before that so many of its residents are unacquainted with the dark, crowded, dirty, narrow, foul, and reeking streets of the neighbouring city.

* This building is the the famous Huxinting Teahouse on the Bridge of Nine Turnings, which many Europeans imagined to be the model for the teahouse on 'willow pattern' crockery. It still stands today.

2

BIRTH AND PARALYSIS OF A GREAT CITY

HARRIET SERGEANT

Visiting Shanghai at the end of the 1980s, writer Harriet Sergeant charts the course of the city's rise to greatness. 'The Yangtze made Shanghai', she says. The Huangpu, Shanghai's river, leads into the Yangtze, connecting it to half of China; it leads also to the ocean, linking it to America, Asia, and Europe, and making Shanghai one of the foremost ports in the world. Yet what Harriet Sergeant finds in the 1980s is a town whose vital juices have dried up, a desiccated mummy of a city.

On a sunny afternoon I took the lift up Shanghai's tallest pre-war building. Broadway Mansions, now renamed Shanghai Mansions, stands at the confluence of the Soochow Creek and the Whangpoo. From across the old Garden Bridge, it looms over the Bund, a sixteen-storey cliff face of red brick with terraces rising in uneven steps up its sides. In the 'thirties the Foreign Correspondents' Club occupied the top floors. Drink in hand, journalists watched from its heights the bombing of Shanghai. During the war the Japanese made it their headquarters after they had conquered the city. The lift stops in a glass corridor opening on to a terrace. I walked out, looked around and understood something of the excitement of the Japanese generals. Shanghai extends to the horizon in every direction. Distance bestows a sense of intimacy and power on the onlooker. I felt I only had to stretch out my arm, pry open a window or lift off a roof to understand Shanghai.

It is a grey city: grey slate, grey stone, grey scuttling figures and the wide, lazy loop of the grey Whangpoo river. It is a busy city. On the river floats every shape and size of boat down to the smallest tug equipped with a clothes line, charcoal stove, wife and children. Directly below me and bordering the Whangpoo curved the Bund, Shanghai's most important street and as busy as the river with bicyclists breaking in waves around cars and buses, the persistent tinkling of their bells rising through the hooting of the motorists and the deeper boom of the ships' horns. Away to the south-west ran the French Concession, its tree-lined avenues gashes of green through the grey roofs. Between it and the river lay the misshapen circle of the old Chinese City of Nantao, the city wall long since gone, the narrow, stone streets now clean of the beggars, pimps and street-hawkers that used to infest its gloom. To the north of Soochow Creek stretched Hongkew and Yangtzepoo, once part of the International Settlement and home to the poorer foreigner before it was destroyed by Japanese and American bombs. Between the modern buildings I could still glimpse areas of grey-tiled, Chinese roofs curling at the corners like burnt paper. Beyond was the working-class district of Chapei and to the east, across the river, Pootung. They reached the horizon in a botched landscape of factory and dockland; grey and very busy.

In the 'thirties Shanghai covered 20 square miles, $12\frac{1}{2}$ square miles of which was under foreign control. It was a small, densely packed city. In 1932 its population stood at over 3,000,000. At the same time Greater London contained $7\frac{1}{2}$ million people spread over 70 square miles. Shanghai was almost three times as crowded.

Most of all Shanghai is a river port. The Whangpoo dominates the city. All Shanghai's grandest foreign firms and banks built their offices along the Bund, looking out over the Whangpoo. In autumn when fog shrouded the Bund, the sound of fog-horns echoed between the buildings and reverberated up and down the streets to join with the low, muted note of a conch shell blown from a junk or the thrash of propellers. The smell of Whangpoo, a mixture of sewage, seaweed and coal, infiltrated the city. It caught people unawares as they left nightclubs or restaurants, reminding them that however big and sophisticated Shanghai had become, it was still a river port.

The river always appeared busy. Small ships travelled fussily, letting off steam, their sirens screaming. Steam launches chugged back and forth dragging six or seven barges. Bobbing in and out among the liners, sampans propelled by an *ulow* [a large oar] took passengers and sailors to and from their ships. Junks with sails spread wide drifted past on the current. Foreign cruisers, moored midstream, gleamed in the sun, guns protruding beneath their awnings. Further down, against a backdrop of factories and godowns, dredgers churned slime from the river bed. In the wet docks men, balancing on sampans while holding brushes several yards long, splashed the side of a passenger liner orange. Dirty, old coasters, trailing black smoke but still jaunty under names like *Amelia* and *Aphrodite*, made their way out to sea.

A few minutes' walk from the East Gate of the Chinese city lay the junk anchorage. Here junks crowded up against each other in different shapes and sizes. Some were built to cross the ocean. Others worked just one river. All shared square bows, brown sails patched in bright colours and poops painted with a gigantic eye. On every poop you might catch a glimpse of potted plants, perhaps a cat asleep, washing hanging on a bamboo pole, a bird in a cage and someone fanning the charcoal while the rice boiled.

Wharves lined the river right through the centre of the city. On the Bund itself ships loaded and unloaded, their hatches open wide while cranes ground overhead. Coolies rushed back and forth across gangplanks, loads of cargo on their heads. As they ran, they half-sang and half-called together, the foreman shouting out whatever inspired him: 'Look at that fat, white foreign woman coming past now'; the others taking up the chant: 'Oh, look at her, look at her'. The foreman continuing, 'Imagine getting lost up her Jade Gate'; the others replying, 'What a fate! What a fate for a poor man!' Country people loaded up flat-bottomed boats with jars of soya sauce, baskets of chickens, rolls of mats and then turned to make their way back up the river and into the interior.

You could not escape the river. At the end of every east-bound road, out of every window on the Bund, there it was, an open expanse in a city with no open spaces, reflecting the sky, catching the light and coiling its way around Shanghai like a great, silver snake. 'If it were not for this river there would be no Shanghai', mused a local paper in 1931:

The inhabitants would not be able to breathe in the smoky atmosphere without the fresh sea breezes: there would be no money to build her houses, her hotels, and her firms, if it were not for this stretch of water that spells commerce and links her

11

with the outside world. The river flowed between these banks long, long before anybody ever thought of building a city and calling it Shanghai.

The river had attracted Shanghai's very first Western visitor. Mr Hugh Lindsay, an agent of the East India Company, arrived in Shanghai in 1832. Since 1757 the Chinese government had restricted the foreign trader to Guangzhou and business to one small guild of merchants, the Cahong. Mr Lindsay was on the lookout for an alternative to Guangzhou. He found it, he was sure, in the small, walled city of Shanghai.

What Mr Lindsay saw were junks. He counted an average of four hundred entering Shanghai weekly in one July which, if representative of the whole year, made Shanghai one of the leading ports in the world. Some junks came from Guangdong and Manchuria, a few from Java, Indochina and Siam but the majority arrived down the Yangtze. This great river, as Mr Lindsay quickly appreciated, was the reason for Shanghai's importance. The Yangtze Watershed drains half of China reaching one-tenth of the world's population. Ocean-going vessels travelled inland as far as Hankou, river steamers to Suifu and smaller craft still further, not only up the Yangtze, but also to its tributaries, providing almost thirty thousand miles of waterway. In Mr Lindsay's time rafts transported most goods. They carried up to twenty tons, stayed afloat in one foot of water and transported whole villages including the local barber and tinsmith down to the city.

Shanghai is a great city because it stands at the tip of the fertile and populated, lower Yangtze basin. The Chinese had been building waterways across the area for two thousand years. Goods travelled to and from Shanghai by an estimated half a million miles of artificial waterways. Almost no roads existed. The Chinese erected single-span, humpbacked bridges in order to allow boats to pass under rather than anything more than a wheelbarrow to go over. When the British arrived Shanghai was China's largest native port. 'The advantages which foreigners would derive from the liberty of trade with this place are incalculable', mused Mr Lindsay.

Shanghai offered the foreigner position. It stood midway on the coast between north and south China and near to Japan with which the West began to trade in 1853. Barely a hundred miles east lay the great circle route of ships travelling between the west coast of North America, Japan, China and south-east Asia. Shanghai formed the natural centre of Far Eastern shipping and was midway between Atlantic Europe and America. It was to become, as Mr Lindsay foresaw, the seaport of the Yangtze River and the principal emporium of Eastern Asia.

The Yangtze made Shanghai. Nowhere else in the world did such a vast area and so many people depend on one river and one city for their trade. It meant opportunities for foreign importers as well as exporters and set Mr Lindsay to dreaming of the Chinese snug and happy in Lancashire textiles.

The city depended on the interior for its wealth but could not control it. Shanghai never became a state city. The Shanghai businessman showed little interest in administration. Within his city he could do what he liked because in the nineteenth century the Chinese government was inept, and, after 1911, non-existent. Beyond the city limits Shanghai's influence proved diffuse rather than direct and about progress rather than politics or power. Shanghai became the centre and disperser of novelty. Winding slowly up into the smallest tributaries went stories of what the floating villagers had seen and heard; kerosene street lamps, the first rickshaw, unbound feet, bobbed hair, escalators and communism.

Reluctantly I took the lift down from the top of Shanghai Mansions and joined the flow of Chinese pressing home from work. In the aqueous light of dusk, the crowds spread over the pavements and on to the roads silent but for the swish of bicycle wheels and the tinkling of bells. Most had moved into the city from the countryside during the 'fifties. They showed little curiosity about Shanghai's past or the foreign buildings they lived and worked in. Some even suggested the city should be razed and started again. They represented the vast indifference of the country to Shanghai's qualities and reminded me that Shanghai's development depended as much on its relationship with China as with the Whangpoo.

The one hundred years that saw Shanghai emerge as an international port witnessed the disintegration of the Middle Kingdom (as the Chinese referred to their country). Shanghai's independence relied on China's weakness. This swung both ways.

The revival of a strong, central government in China put an end to Shanghai. . . .

When Shanghai fell in 1949 to the Chinese communists a door was shut. During the Cultural Revolution the door was bolted for good. A world had gone. I first went to Shanghai just after the Cultural Revolution and was planning my last trip when the tanks arrived in Tiananmen Square. Nothing appears to have altered since the pre-war era. Shanghai is bigger, there are more people and a few new skyscrapers but otherwise communism has fallen on the city like a sandstorm, burying and preserving. The street names are different but not the buildings, from the office blocks and hotels on the Bund to the villas in the suburbs. Even the interiors are untouched. The marble lobbies and art-deco swimming pools are pre-war as are the light switches. Communism has mummified Shanghai's appearance in a manner inconceivable to a Westerner, Shopping centres, over-passes and subways are all missing. So, despite the carefully preserved wrappings, is Shanghai's spirit.

3

CAPTAIN ON THE YANGTZE RIVER

CHEN KEXIONG

Leaving Shanghai, the voyage up the Yangtze begins. In an interview in the late 1980s, Captain Chen Kexiong describes a life spent on the river. He began sailing at seventeen, and worked his way up to become captain of Jiangyu No. 2, a 3,500-ton state-owned ship, capable of carrying over 1,000 passengers—the majority crammed into tiers of bunks in fourth and fifth class. His route is the 2,399 kilometres between Shanghai and Chongqing, a voyage of seven days going upstream and five downstream back to Shanghai. As he points out, although the river is not as dangerous as it used to be, accidents can still happen.

I grew up in a small village by the Jialing River, a tributary of the Yangtze. When I was a child, I loved to play by the river. I'd sit there, gazing at the vast expanse of water that flows eastward. As my eyes would follow the seagulls gliding over the water and the boats navigating up and down the river, I often wondered where the water came from and where it flowed to, why seagulls always flew behind the boats, and why the ship sometimes sounded one whistle and sometimes two, and what these whistles meant.

These questions made a sailing career seem fascinating to me, then the son of a farmer, and they have been answered over the years. Seagulls trail a ship because they're hungry and are looking for food. The ship blows one whistle to signal that it's going to pass another ship on its starboard, and two whistles to show that it's going to pass its port.

The Yangtze River has three sections. Each has its own characteristics. In the lower reaches, the river bed is full of dirt and sand, and the river is wide. In the middle reaches, the river also is wide, but there are quite a number of shoals, and the water level is only several meters in some places. It's so shallow

15

that sometimes the bottom of the ship almost touches the river ~~bed. In the upper reaches, the river course is narrow and tortuous,~~ and full of rocks and abrupt turns.

The most dangerous part is the upper reaches, especially the section known as Chuanjiang. The section begins at Yibin, a city down from Chongqing in Sichuan Province, and ends at Yichang in Hubei. It's more than 1,100 kilometers long, and is noted for a world-famous attraction, the Three Gorges.

Each year, thousands of people come here from China and abroad, especially in the summer, to take a boat trip through the Three Gorges. For them, the gorges are a scenic wonder, while for us boatmen, however, the place is hell.

The Chuanjiang section has many high, steep mountain gorges and is full of twists and turns, some of them so abrupt that you almost have to turn the ship 90 degrees. The river's very narrow, with the narrowest point being no more than 40 meters in width. It would be impossible for another ship as large as ours to pass. The current is rapid during the flood season, three meters a second. Also, there are about 2,000 rocks and reefs in the section between Chongqing and Yichang, which could prove to be quite dangerous.

The Three Gorges used to be the worst part of this section. No one has counted how many lives have been lost in this hell. Because it was so difficult to navigate boats on this part of the river, in the past the boats had to be towed by boat-trackers, who worked like coolies. They walked on the bank and towed the boats using ropes. It was a misery for these people.

That was in the past. You don't see boat-trackers now since the government has transformed the course of the river and blasted away many of the big rocks that used to block the way. But the water level remained shallow for many years. However, after the Gezhouba Dam was built in 1981 near Yichang, the water level in the Three Gorges rose by about 20 meters. Sailing down the gorges is no longer as dangerous as it used to be.

Still sailing on the Chuanjiang and the gorges is often a battle. You must always be on the alert. A small mistake can turn into disaster. And accidents, such as hitting a reef, or colliding with another boat, do occur from time to time. Not long ago, we collided with a private cargo boat that was ferrying goods across the river.

The owner of that ship was in such a hurry to get the job done that he had his men move before we'd cleared. Their boat hit on us on the stern. We suffered no damage, since our ship was made of steel, but the cargo boat was severely damaged. They asked us to pay damages. Since it wasn't our fault, we refused. But they threatened not to let us pass until we had given them money. Blocking our way, they refused to budge. In the end we paid them 1,000 yuan just to get going.

Nowadays there are more and more such boats sailing on the Yangtze. They're small in size, pay little attention to regulations, and cause us a lot of trouble. Each year our company chalks up anywhere from 300,000 to 400,000 yuan in losses on account of accidents of this sort.

There's another type of incident that's very distressing. Some people try to kill themselves on the trip. Last year, a young lady at midnight jumped over the side of the ship. When I learned of this, I ordered the ship to stop immediately, and we started a search. We searched up and down the river for several hours, but couldn't find the woman. Those who attempt to commit suicide always seem to choose to do so at midnight, probably because they don't want to be seen and saved.

On board here you see many things, such as quarreling, fighting, and stealing. In this sense, life on a passenger ship is no different from that on land. There are a few policemen on our ship as a

17

security measure, and we've a special department that mediates conflicts among passengers, all of which save me a lot of trouble.

I graduated from a navigation school. I was a sailor, helmsman, third mate, second mate, and first mate. I worked on a cargo vessel for ten years, then was transferred to a passenger ship. I've been on four ships, one cargo, and three carrying passengers. I became a captain in 1985, after studying a year at a navigation management school in Chongqing.

My greatest ambition when I was young was to become a captain, which was the most prestigious position on the river. I had a quick temper before. But the river has changed me. I think even the most restless person can become patient after sailing so many years on the Yangtze. But we aren't like those seamen whose horizons are broader. We sail a narrow course and we must be very prudent and cautious.

We've a TV room on the ship. To offer more entertainment to our passengers we recently opened a ballroom. But what's most important to the passengers is safety. That's why my cabin is by the bridge. Although I've three associates—first mate, second mate, and third mate—and although we could, in principle, rotate shifts, I am always on duty when we're sailing through the Three Gorges, passing the Gezhouba Dam, going under bridges, or approaching a port. There are four bridges across the river, and a dozen ports. We seldom assign the third mate to be on duty when we're sailing at night, or in the upper reaches, because he's young and less experienced. There are at least three people on duty on the ship's bridge each shift: a helmsman, a signal man, and an officer in charge. Each shift lasts four hours and each of them works two shifts a day.

My sailing experience has enabled me to see a lot of things that I'd never seen before, hear a lot of things that I'd never heard about, know a lot of interesting people, and learn a lot of worthwhile things. For instance, I'm now able to forecast changes in climate in advance just like a weather man, since our sailing is greatly influenced by weather. Sometimes we've to anchor for days because of unfavorable weather.

But there are problems, too, with this kind of life, for example, a sailor doesn't get much good food or leisure time. Moreover, he's to be so devoted to his work that he has little time to spend with his family. A married sailor spends more time with his colleagues than with his wife and children. And his folks have to pay if they want to take a boat trip. His family gets no special privileges. That's why so many young sailors have difficulty in finding a marriage partner. There are also more divorces among the sailors than there used to be.

I'm lucky. I've been married for more than twenty years, when being a sailor was a much more admired occupation. My wife is a saleswoman and we get along very well. Only I often feel guilty that I haven't taken good care of her and our children. I couldn't be with her even when she was ill. Every year I've been at home for only a total of three months. I've decided that after I retire, I'll stay at home and be with my wife. I owe her so much.

One complaint I have is that our government is investing too little in harnessing the Yangtze. The problems of silt and pollution are terrible. I know in the United States they've spent a lot of money to tame the Mississippi River. The Yangtze is as important to China as the Mississippi is to the States, or maybe even more so. I hope the government will pay more attention to the Yangtze.

I'm a heavy smoker. Everyday I consume about two packs of cigarettes. Each month I spend nearly thirty yuan on smoking. My monthly salary is 190 yuan.

I've two children, a daughter and a son. My son works as a helmsman on my ship. When he decided to become a sailor after graduation from high school, my wife was against it. But I supported him. Although a sailor's life is hard, someone has to do the work.

PART 1

THE LOWER AND MIDDLE REACHES:

SHANGHAI TO YICHANG

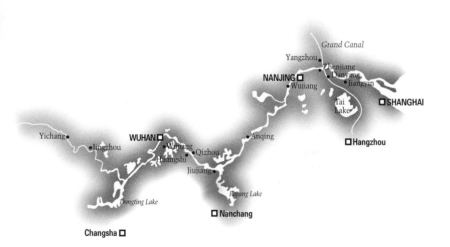

The wide wide Yangtze, dragons in deep pools;
wave blossoms, purest white, leap to the sky.
The great ship, tall-towered, far off no bigger than a bean;
my wondering eyes have not come to rest when it's here before me.

Lu Yu (1125–1209), *The Merchant's Joy*

Truly, the most overwhelming impression of the lower and middle Yangtze is the sheer expanse of it. As it nears its mouth at the Yellow Sea, the river estuary sprawls over fifty miles wide across the flat plain, like an endless brown ocean. Travelling hundreds of miles up stream to Wuhan, British naval officer Thomas Woodroofe noted with amazement that the river there was still nearly two miles across. Wuhan marks the end of the lower reaches, the place to change ships, since vessels over 5,000 tons can sail no further. The middle reaches, from Wuhan to Yichang, are navigable by boats of up to 3,000 tons.

The lower reaches are the despair of navigators and chart-makers. They bear along a volume of silt so great that the shore near the mouth is growing at the rate of a mile every seventy years. Sand bars can rapidly become islands, islands sometimes join with the shoreline and once-deep channels are transformed into shallows.

The green-brown delta of the lower reaches is one of the most fertile and prosperous regions in China. Known as 'the Land of Fish and Rice', it is a landscape dominated by water. Acres of paddy fields are criss-crossed by canals and streams and dotted with lakes and fish ponds. Mulberry trees and tea bushes are grown in profusion, for this is also a land of silk and tea. Another source of wealth is the miles of salt flats, which lie between the dykes and the sea. According to thirteenth-century Marco Polo, salt was the chief article of commerce on the *Kiang* ('river'), which he described as the largest river in the world. The total volume and value of the shipping carried on this river, he said, exceeded that of all of the rivers of the Christians put together, and their seas into the bargain. He was told by the Imperial Customs Collector that about 200,000 craft went up stream every year, not counting those that returned down stream. Today's railway network, however, has brought about a sharp decline in the numbers of boats since Marco Polo's time.

While ship-owners, merchants, and landlords could make great profits, for many ordinary people life along the river was mostly drudgery and dread, as Li Bai (701–762) and Mao Dun (1896–1981) make clear. Moreover, the 'Golden Waterway', as it is called, sustainer of so many livelihoods, is also a frequent bearer of disaster.

As a farmer along the lower reaches said to explorer How Man Wong in the 1980s: 'We can't do without it and we can't deal with too much of it', for the people here live under the annual threat of floods. Their prosperity and very lives depend on a great wall of dykes and embankments, which contain the river for almost 2,000 kilometres all the way up to Yichang. Despite all precautions, the region is still prone to flooding, even in a normal rainy season. The Yangtze and its vast network of tributaries and lakes need only a few weeks of heavy rainfall to overflow and merge into a giant sea. Gentleman and sportsman W. S. Percival describes a flood of 1887, while almost exactly a hundred years later author Chen Shixu tells the story of a more recent one, probably based on the terrible flood of 1983.

Many catastrophes were man-made, however. Some of the region's worst devastations took place in the 1840s and 1850s, when the weakening Manchu empire was beset from both without and within. The British realized that admittance to Shanghai and the right to go up the Yangtze were the keys to increasing their China trade. In 1842, during the first of the Opium Wars, they captured Shanghai and then Zhenjiang, almost 200 miles up river. The latter was bombarded by British gunboats carrying a formidable 7,000 troops. This victory led to the end of the war and the Treaty of Nanjing, actually signed on board a British warship at anchor near Nanjing's city walls. Among other concessions, the treaty opened up Shanghai to foreign trade.

Yet the British seemed mere gadflies compared to the internal threat facing the Manchus. As the Emperor's brother put it, 'The rebels menace our heart. . . . The British are merely a threat to our limbs.' The Taiping Rebellion (1850–64) was a revolt on such a scale that it has been called the worst civil war the world has ever seen. The movement started far south of the Yangtze in Guangdong, led by Hong Xiuquan, who believed he was the younger brother of Jesus Christ. His aim was to overthrow the

Manchus and establish his own Heavenly Kingdom (*Taiping Tianguo*). In 1852, thousands of rebels took to the water in a ragged fleet of any boats they could muster and sailed along the southern waterways until they reached the Yangtze. Battling and winning territory, followers and loot as they proceeded up river, they finally reached Nanjing in 1853 and established it as their capital. At one point they held almost half of China, but at the cost of bitter fighting, with some Yangtze cities changing hands as many as three times. Laurence Oliphant, Lord Elgin's Private Secretary, describes the situation in Zhenjiang in 1858 during the midst of the rebellion, comparing the ruins to those of Pompeii.

After only eleven years did the Imperial forces finally defeat the Taipings, by a siege of Nanjing in 1864. It is said that not one Taiping surrendered, preferring to fight to the death or to commit suicide. An estimated twenty to thirty million people died as a result of this warfare, with the lower Yangtze region suffering the most. A 1950 government census found that the population of the area was still twenty million lower than it had been in 1850.

While the Manchus tried vainly to cope with the rebels, the British continued to press for more access to the interior. The Treaty of Tianjin, which the Manchus signed reluctantly at the end of the second Opium War in 1858 gave the British a host of concessions, some of which were to greatly affect the lives of those along the Yangtze. The British finally got their way and were allowed to travel to all parts of the interior, while their ships were given authority to sail the Great River. The Chinese managed to stall for a little longer on actually opening Yangtze ports to trade however, arguing that the region was in turmoil because of the Taipings. The Treaty stipulated that Zhenjiang would be opened a year from the date of signing and that as soon as peace was restored, British ships would be permitted to trade further up river at such ports as Hankou (formerly spelt Hankow, one of the three cities that make up today's Wuhan). From then on the Customs offices for both sea and river ports were to be run by foreigners; the opium trade was declared legal; and missionaries were entitled to protection from the Chinese authorities.

For almost a century from the signing of this Treaty, a steady trickle of foreigners made their way up the Yangtze, to do business, to preach, to explore. Foreign gunboats patrolled the river to protect their right to do so. Some visitors made a single journey, others settled for years in towns along the way. Despite the dangers, it must have seemed that a foreign presence, while usually not welcomed, was well established and permanent. But this was all to change in 1949 and for many, the first premonition came when the Communists had the temerity to shell a British warship, the *Amethyst*, which was on its way from Shanghai to Nanjing. As Noel Barker describes, the Communists were preparing to attack the Nationalists. The *Amethyst* was in the way, and the Communists had no compunction in breaking what they considered to be unequal treaties. Few foreigners were to sail the river again until after 1978, when China opened to the West. But this time they came as tourists, in Chinese-owned boats.

Zhenjiang: Meeting of the Waters

Zhenjiang ('guard the river'), although not a large city, occupies a key position, at the point where the Grand Canal meets the Yangtze. Even before the Canal was built in the fifth century AD, this was an important ferry crossing. For over 2,000 years there has been a town on this spot, fought over countless times, both for its strategic significance and its commercial value as a transportation hub.

Famous for the beauty of its temples and wooded cliffs overlooking the water, it was known as 'the best scenery under heaven'. During the Song dynasty (960–1279), it was an important source of silk for the court. The two poems which follow were written in Zhenjiang—then called Jingkou—during the Song dynasty.

4

A VISIT TO JINGSHAN MONASTERY

SU DONGPO (1037–1101)

A gifted poet, essayist, and painter, Su Shi seemed destined for a brilliant career. But his very intelligence and habit of speaking his mind led to his downfall. Throughout his life he was repeatedly banished, dismissed from official posts, and even imprisoned at one point. Released from jail in 1080, he was exiled to Huangzhou, a small town on the Yangtze's middle reaches. Here he built a little hut on the eastern slope of a hill, and took the name that he is usually known by, Su Dongpo: 'Dongpo' means 'Eastern Slope'. He loved drinking and talking all night long with friends, and he wrote many poems during his years spent along the banks of the Yangtze. Su's home district was far upriver in Meishan, Sichuan. In his day, Jinshan (Golden Mountain) was an island in the middle of the river, but sometime in the nineteenth century, the ever-shifting and increasing sands caused it to join with the river bank.

The Yangtze has its source in my home district,
Serving the state I have followed its waves to the sea;
Tides here, they say, may rise a full ten feet;
On this cold day the sand still shows the traces;
This massive boulder south of Zhongling Fountain
Has been engulfed from of old to emerge again;
I climb to its top, gaze back towards my old home,
Yet see only green ranges north and south of the river.
Longing for home, I look for my boat to return,
But the monk makes me stay for sunset:
Countless ripples in the breeze seem creases in leather,
The ragged clouds in the sky are like red fish-tails;
The moon is a fragile crescent above the waves;
By the second watch it sinks, the sky turns black,
Then it seems as if a torch flares in midstream,
Its flames lighting up the hills, startling the crows . . .

I go sadly to bed, not knowing
What this can be, the work of ghost or man?
Glorious river and hills—I should have retired!
The River God is shocked by my tardiness.
I apologise to the god: Don't get me wrong.
I vow by your river to return to my farm!

5

THOUGHTS IN BEIGU PAVILION AT JINGKOU

XIN QIJI (1140–1207)

In 1127 the Jin (Golden) Tartars, a fierce nomadic tribe from north of the Great Wall, captured the Song Dynasty capital of Kaifeng. One of the Emperor's sons escaped and fled south of the Yangtze, eventually setting up a new capital in present-day Hangzhou. His dynasty, known as the Southern Song, managed to keep control of the Yangtze valley and the southern regions; but all the rest of China was held by the Tartars. Still, during this time the South flourished as never before. The trade of Yangtze valley products such as silk, tea, and porcelain greatly increased; industry, craftsmanship, and the arts all thrived; life in the capital of Hangzhou and in Yangtze cities like Jingkou was gay and luxurious.

But there were those who longed to recapture the northern lands lost to barbarians. As a young commander of twenty-three in 1162, Xin Qiji had fought against the Tartars and then led his troops south across the Yangtze to join the Southern Song court. His plan for renewing the struggle against the Tartars was not adopted, as the Song Emperor decided it was better to make peace with them and at least be sure of holding on to the South. Thus Xin was forced to remain a civilian for the rest of his life.

At the age of sixty-six he was appointed governor of Jingkou. At the tower on Beigu Shan (Northern Hill) overlooking the Yangtze, he muses regretfully on the region's martial past, looking back to the Three Kingdoms period (AD 220–280). The 'young king' he refers to is Sun Quan, founder of the Kingdom of Wu, which occupied the lower Yangtze, and whose capital city was on Beigu Shan. Sun Quan's rivals for power over the whole of China were Liu Bei, who ruled over Shu, in the Upper Yangtze valley, and Cao Cao, Duke of Wu, in northern China. Unlike Xin Qiji's sovereign, these three heroes fought to the end. The poem's last line is a quotation from Cao Cao: even though Sun Quan was his enemy, Cao Cao admired him.

Where can I see our northern territory?
Splendid the view from the Beigu Pavilion.
How many dynasties have risen and fallen
In the course of long centuries
And history goes on
Endless as the swift-flowing Yangtse.
A young king with a host of armoured men
Held the south-east and fought with never a moment's respite;
Two alone of all the empire's heroes could match him—
Brave Cao Cao and Liu Bei.
'How I long for a son like Sun Quan!'

6

SHIP AGROUND AND A SCENE OF DESOLATION

LAURENCE OLIPHANT

*Lord Elgin was responsible for negotiating the Treaty of Tianjin of 1858
which forced the Chinese to allow the British to travel and trade upriver.
In November that year he and his convoy made a triumphant expedition
up the Yangtze as far as Hankou. Here is a description by Elgin's private
secretary, Laurence Oliphant, of their unexpected landing at Jinshan
Island and of the terrible destruction wrought by the Taipings, whom he
calls the rebels or insurgents. They were to find similar scenes all the
way along their journey: deserted villages, ruined cities, and a river
almost empty of boats.*

16 th.—At seven o'clock this morning the thermometer stood
at 37°. Shortly after getting under weigh we passed Keunshan
Pagoda, perched upon a hill overhanging the river. At this
point the banks become very picturesque—high rocky bluffs rise
precipitously from the water's edge, and behind them a range of
irregular pointed hills form a complete amphitheatre. On the
left bank the shores are wooded and populous, occasionally
extensively cultivated, and groups of peasants collect upon the
water's edge to look at us, as the five ships progress steadily in
line against both wind and stream. Here, too, we remarked
extraordinary changes in the course of the river. At one place it
divides; one channel, at least half a mile in width, surrounding
a populous island, which, at the date of the chart, had been part
of the mainland.

The sharp exhilarating air, our steady progress, and the increasing
interest of the river-banks, all combined to raise our spirits.
Presently we sweep round a bold projecting bluff, and Silver Island
opens to view, with its quaint temples embowered in autumnal
foliage; their white walls are gleaming, and their frowzy priests
are basking in the mid-day sun. Beyond, a noble reach of the

river curves beneath the swelling hills which rise from its margin, their summits crowned with the irregular wall of Chinkiang, and their slopes strewn with the debris of that once populous city; while in the distance, as though rising from mid-stream, stands a precipitous rock called Golden Island, with its tall pagoda pointing to the skies.

The scene is one of such surpassing interest and beauty that it rivets our gaze. We are just lamenting that we cannot stop for a moment to appreciate more fully its merits, when—crash, our wishes are gratified—the old ship gives a heave and a lurch. It is too late now to 'stop her', and go 'full speed astern'. We are irrevocably pinnacled on the top of a rock; the *Cruizer* has barely had time to avoid running into us, and shaves cleverly past us as she sheers off. The *Retribution*, panic-stricken, has let go her anchor. With her gunboats swinging in mid-stream astern, she looks like a kite with a tail. The current sweeps and eddies past with impetuous velocity, and gradually succeeds in jamming us broadside on to the rock, converting us into a sort of breakwater, so that we have quite a little sea on one side, and a dead calm on the other.

We have ceased to enjoy the view now, that pleasure being transferred to our friends the priests who are apparently much interested in the spectacle. We are within easy hailing distance of them: they afterwards told us they were perfectly aware of the danger that awaited us; but they gave us no warning. The whole British fleet, consisting of several ships of the line, besides smaller craft, had passed through this channel fifteen years before, without discovering this fatal rock, and sixteen fathoms were marked above it. We were by no means proud of our discovery, but nobody was to blame except the priests, and we were too amiable to quarrel with them, so we landed and paid them a visit. The island had been visited by the rebels at a comparatively recent date. A great part of the very handsome temple had been destroyed, and the idols cast into the river by them. A celebrated vase, reputed to be more than two thousand years old, was kept here; but on the rumoured approach of these iconoclasts, those who were intrusted with the safe keeping of this precious relic buried it in time to insure its safety, and it has not since been exhumed. A temple, which formerly stood on the highest part of the island, had been burned, more, according to the Bonzes, for the purpose of terrifying the neighbourhood than from fanaticism. . . .

As in nature the most exquisite flowers are generally inhabited by slimy caterpillars, so in China the most lovely retreats are invariably tenanted by grimy ecclesiastics. We are bound to remember, however, that we are indebted to them for picturesque buildings, which harmonise admirably with the scenes in which they are situated; while the priests themselves, in their long ash-coloured robes, are an agreeable addition, so long as they are kept in the background of the picture. These gentry informed us that the tidal influence extended beyond this point, but was not regular in its operations. They led us to expect, however, a rise of two or three feet,—and this we trusted would be sufficient to float us off. Meantime, in order to be the better able to take advantage of any favourable change which might occur, we commenced, for the second time, to lighten the ship, divesting her of shot, guns, spars, coal, &c., and working all through the night.

17th.—Landed on the right bank, and walked to Chinkiang over about two miles of plain, intersected by the remains of rough earthworks. This strip of level ground, which intervenes between a range of hills and the river, was until recently the abode of a thriving and industrious population. Scarce a year has elapsed since it was a scene of violence and bloodshed, the theatre of an action between the Rebel and Imperialist forces. The devastation is now widespread and complete. A few of the peasantry have crawled back to the desolate spots which they recognise as the sites of their former homes, and, selecting the heaps of rubbish which still belong to them, have commenced to construct out of them wretched abodes,—roughly thatching in a gable-end that has escaped the general destruction, or replacing the stones which once composed the walls with strips of matting. Miserable patches of garden were being brought into existence between the crumbling, weed-covered walls; but the destitute appearance of the scanty population served rather to increase than diminish the effect which this abomination of desolation was calculated to produce.

We entered the city by the north gate, and might have imagined ourselves in Pompeii. We walked along deserted streets, between roofless houses, and walls overgrown with rank, tangled weeds;

heaps of rubbish blocked up the thoroughfares, but they obstructed nobody. There was something oppressive in the universal stillness; and we almost felt refreshed by a foul odour which greeted our nostrils, and warned us that we had approached an inhabited street.

At a spot where were a few chow-chow shops, and two partially inhabited streets crossed each other, was the most lively place in the town. We obtained a small share of interest here from a mob of hungry, ragged boys; but the people generally seemed too much depressed even to stare at a barbarian, and we strolled unmolested in any direction our fancy led us.

On our way to a fort which crowned a bluff overhanging the river, we passed under some handsome stone arches, which were still standing conspicuous amid the desolation by which they were surrounded. From our elevated position we commanded an extensive view over the area enclosed by the walls of the city, and which was thickly strewn with its ruins.

Chinkiang was first taken by the Insurgents, almost without resistance, on the 1st of April 1853, and was held by them against a continued Imperialist siege up to the commencement of 1857, when it was evacuated in consequence of the failure of supplies. It has been held by the Imperialist forces ever since. To judge, however, from the reluctance manifested by its former inhabitants to return to it, confidence is but partially restored. Only the very poorest class of traders and shopkeepers have ventured into its dilapidated streets; and although efforts are being made by the Government to give some stimulus to its repopulation, by rebuilding some of the public buildings, such as the Government offices, the Confucian Temple, the Drum Tower, &c., the results are by no means encouraging. The rebels have, during their occupation, considerably enlarged the boundaries of the city, having carried a wall over the heights to the east of it, and down nearly to the water's edge on the bank of the river, enclosing a large space beyond the old wall in both directions. The population of Chinkiang was formerly estimated at about 500,000; it does not now probably contain above 500 souls.

18th.—We have painted a water-line on the rocks, so as to be able to detect the variations of the tide at a glance. As, however, there were no indications of a rise to-day, and the ship seemed immovable, we chartered a small native boat, and started off on an expedition to Golden Island, distant about five miles. As we approached it we discovered, to our astonishment, that it was no longer an island. Flourishing cabbage-fields now occupied the space marked on the chart as a channel with four fathoms of water in it.

We landed on this recently-formed peninsula, and walked across it to the Rock. Climbing up the steps hewn out of the living stone, we reached the base of the Pagoda, shorn now of those external decorations which once rendered it celebrated, but still standing, a battered monument of its own departed glory, and of the beauty by which it was surrounded. . . .

Now, with the exception of the dilapidated pagoda, there is not one stone left upon another of the remaining buildings. Though so recently destroyed, a remarkable air of antiquity seems to pervade this sacred spot. The rock-cut steps are worn and crumbling, and the ruins generally look as though centuries had passed since the destroyer's hand had been ruthlessly at work. A line of wall with a few wretched guns in the embrasures, a few wretched soldiers in some mat tents in rear, and a quantity of gay flaunting flags, indicate that this is a military post. These banners and embrasures are apparent on numerous hill-tops, and surround the city of Chinkiang. If we were to judge by them, the preparations for defence would seem extensive indeed; but it is scarcely too much to assert that there are more flags than embrasures, more embrasures than guns, and more guns than men. We sat down on the top of the rock to discuss a sandwich and a glass of sherry, and enjoy the view. It was one of melancholy beauty. On our right the skeleton houses of the city clustering up the hillsides, and filling the whole amphitheatre with their ruins—the straggling wall running along the ridges, gay with gaudy banners when all around is sad, and defending, as though in mockery, a dreary waste of rubbish; beyond, the irregular outline of distant hills, with the broad river spreading itself proudly out upon the fertile plains to the north and east; fronting us Silver Island, its bright colouring toned down by distance, and its soft outline contrasting with the precipitous bluffs beside it,— all combined to form a picture upon which it was pleasant to gaze in that mild autumnal afternoon.

We could discern the ships anchored in midstream: one which was broadside on, and leaning very much over, was a feature in the scene we could have gladly dispensed with. In the situation of Chinkiang, its ruined state and the nature of the surrounding country, I was a good deal reminded of Kertch after its evacuation by the Russians. We walked through it on our way back, and found on our arrival at the ship some excitement existing at the prospect of getting off. The paddle-wheels were revolving violently; hawsers and stream-cables were out in sundry directions; those who were not hauling at something were jumping or rolling the ship. At last a happy and combined effort proved successful, and she seemed literally to tumble off her perch into deep water. The event was signalled by three hearty cheers from all hands, which had no sooner subsided than, to our astonishment, we heard them faintly echoed from the shore. We were wondering whether the Chinamen were mocking us when they were repeated, and we then discovered that Lord Elgin and a small party of walkers were thus heartily testifying their satisfaction. The singular stillness of the evening air rendered sounds audible at a great distance. Two hundred and sixty tons in weight had been removed from the ship before she had been sufficiently lightened to float off the rock.

THE WILDEST, WICKEDEST RIVER

PEARL S. BUCK

How dim and far away the Taiping destruction seems from the ordered world of Pearl Buck's childhood, spent in a tiny house overlooking Zhenjiang's British concession. Yet it was only about forty years earlier that the Tianjin Treaty had allowed the creation of the British settlement at Zhenjiang, and also given missionaries such as Pearl Buck's father the right to preach and live in the interior.

Her upbringing was a curious mixture of East and West: bilingual in Chinese and English, she had a Chinese Amah and Chinese playmates, but American clothes and schooling, and scones with jam for tea. As she says, 'In those years I slipped instantaneously out of one life into another, depending upon the geography of the moment.' She describes the lives of the Chinese around her with sympathy and keen observation, yet nevertheless her frame of reference is that of a Westerner. The heroes she recalls when thinking of the Yangtze are not the many Chinese associated with the region, such as the legendary warriors of the Three Kingdoms, but foreign visitors—Marco Polo and the American flier, Charles Lindbergh.

Here she talks about her Zhenjiang childhood and the deep impression made on her by the Yangtze.

When I return to the earliest world I can remember it is of a window opening upon the Yangtze River in the river port of Chinkiang, that old city of the Chinese province of Kiangsu. It lies facing another old city on the opposite bank of the river, Yangchow, a city made famous by Marco Polo. They have not yet altogether forgotten Marco Polo in Yangchow, for he was governor there for three years. Five hundred and more years after that and about twenty years ago, wandering among little curio shops in the crooked streets, I found a small alabaster figure of a man dressed in Venetian garb. Cut

into the base of the figure were four Chinese characters which said, 'An honorable foreign heart'. . . .

Below the window lay the street called the Bund, because it ran along the river. The strip upon which we looked down was in the British concession, that piece of land like many others which England wrested from China after the Opium Wars to form bases for shipping and trade centers. Hour after hour during the day and the night steamers crept and sidled up to the squat hulks that lay offshore and discharged their cargo. Causeways connected the hulks to the shore and down these causeways all day and sometimes all night endless lines of coolies trotted with bags upon their bare backs, bags of sugar from Java, and rice from Kwangtung and jute and rape seed and tea and spices.

Every coolie had his queue wrapped around his head and his blue trousers knotted about his hard waist and in his hand a strip of blue cotton or a gray towel with which to wipe away his sweat. They were always sweating, these coolies, summer and winter, and their thighs and knees quivered under their heavy loads. Their eyes bulged, their faces wore horrible grimaces of strain, and their breath came out of them in singsong grunts and they kept step with each other and swung into rhythm to lighten their intolerable loads. Stuck into every queue was the bamboo tally stick that each man was given with the sign of this load. This he must hand to the tally man in the godown as he threw down his load.

Sometimes when we went out to walk we stopped and looked in the shadowy caverns of the vast godowns which held stored the wealth that poured into the port from all over the world, to be sent out again into inland China upon the backs of donkeys and mules and camels and men. There was always the same smell in the godowns, a mixture of hemp and peanut oil and the acrid sweetness of crude red-brown sugar . . .

I suppose if I had at that time of my life, when I was about six, been given my choice of all the places in the world, I would have put aside Buckingham Palace and the White House and chosen a hulk on the bank of the Yangtze River. The gala days of my years then were when my mother went to call upon Cap'n and Mrs. Swan. The Swans were a stout Scotch couple who lived on the Jardine Matheson Hulk. They had comfortable rooms which had been the saloon and captain's quarters of the coast-going vessel which once the hulk had been. Cap'n Swan himself had been a captain on this very ship, but now he was a river master, and managed the comings and goings of the English company's steamers at the port.

We always chose a day and an afternoon when no steamer was tied to the hulk. Steamer days were impossible for visiting. In the first place Cap'n Swan was always in a swearing bad temper on those days and Mrs. Swan, who was a staunch Scotch Presbyterian, preferred not to have visitors, since it left Cap'n Swan more at liberty. The coolies did not understand Scotch swearing, but to have to check himself in the presence of visitors put a fearful strain on the Cap'n. Besides, on steamer days the hulk was a hurly-burly of grunting coolies and dust and hustle and yelling. The coolies were implacable in their march. They swept over anyone in their way. I can remember being whirled aside by their sinewy brown legs as if I had been whirled away by wheels of machinery.

So we waited for calm afternoons and then at the decent calling hour of four we put on our best clothes and with Wang Amah along in a clean blue cotton coat to keep my little brother and me from climbing ropes and railings, we crossed the causeway to the hulk. The causeway was a terror in itself. The heavy boards were laid three or four inches apart, far too close, my reason told me, for children of four and six to fall through. But those spaces seemed to grow wider as we stepped over them and opened to show the swift wicked brown river beneath. My head swam as I stared down at that current. I was transfixed by the smooth evil movement of implacable water, so that to this day I cannot see the gathering of an ocean wave without knowing it cruel and having to fight against yielding to its power. And once in my own country when I stood at the head of Niagara Falls and watched the turn of the river over the great ledge beneath it, awful in its smooth power, I was caught back into the supreme terror of my childhood, the terror of the Yangtze River, so smooth, so swift, so dimpled with whirlpools and eddies that it was taken as fate that any who fell into those waters never came up again, even for rescue. . . .

For all her empathy with individual Chinese whom she knew and loved, Pearl Buck still looks back with nostalgia on the times of the foreign concessions when the Chinese 'knew their place'. In these memoirs written in 1970, she reflects ruefully on how much has changed since those colonial days of her childhood. Nowadays she says, English ships no longer ply the river and 'the park benches along the Bund, once kept freshly painted and only for white folk, were peeling and decaying and cracking under the load of any Chinese loafer, beggar, student, or coolie who chose to sit upon them'. And yet there is the Yangtze:

But that river keeps rolling along. It has not changed a whit. I learned to know its every mood during the hours I spent at the window. On a crisp spring morning it looked as innocent as beauty itself, the sun caught in all its pointed yellow wavelets and shining upon brown and white sails and painted junks and bobbing sampans. Ferries plied safely back and forth, laden with people, and gunboats from America and France lay quiet with only their flags astir. Along the shores farmers, while they plowed or manured their green cabbages with the watered night soil they saved in great vatlike jars, kept their fishnets deep in the water. Whenever they stopped to rest they sauntered over to the riverbank and pulled a rope and the nets came swinging up out of the water. There was nearly always a fish in those nets. Then the farmer took a long-handled wooden dipper and dipped up the shining twisting silver shapes and had fish to eat with his cabbages or to sell at the market.

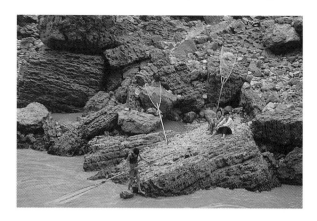

But there were other days when the river boiled like a muddy cauldron. Storms could beat upon it as fiercely as though it were a sea, and in the rough waters I have seen a ferry ease over upon its side and slide hundreds of people off as though they were insects, and turn still farther until it floated bottom up. Those black bobbing heads were visible only for a moment and then the river sucked them down. Nobody went to their rescue. A strange superstition locked men's hearts so that seldom was a hand put out to pull up even a child who fell into the river. It was believed that the gods decreed who was to drown, and if any human being defied the gods and saved a drowning man that man would live only to do evil. He would kill someone or commit a crime and the one who saved him would be responsible, and few dared to take the responsibility. Even the boat folk who lived in the mat sheds upon their flat-bottomed wooden boats let the river keep what went into it. And fair weather to foul, the restless river kept gnawing at its farther banks. On that side the land was good farmland and the river bit it off, foot by foot, so that in a few generations a family could lose its entire farm. And then on the other side, where the city was, the river threw up a wide flat of mud that was a nuisance because the hulks had to be continually moved farther and farther away and the overloaded coolies had that much farther to walk.

That was the way the river was, and is, forever. The Yangtze River is the wildest, wickedest river upon the globe, and the most beautiful. It was as wide as an inland sea where our window looked

41

across it. The farther shore was a gray-green line. For a thousand miles the river is wide and deep and full of fierce and changing currents. Then it grows narrow and runs between rocky cliffs, and is fiercer than ever. It is an open, frank sort of fierceness, though, in the gorges. The fierceness that is horrible is the smooth dimpling golden spread of the lower Yangtze, which looks so amiable and still when one stands upon the shore and sees the waves lapping innocently at one's feet. But from an airplane you can see the real beast, for the river is never still. It moves with a long slow rush to the sea, a torrent as implacable as Niagara and more awful because it is so long, so slow. . . .

Such is the Yangtze, and there is no other river to equal it for beauty and cruelty. The loveliest scenery in the world is to be found along its curving shores. Islands feathery with bamboos and studded with exquisite temple roofs tiled with porcelain, farmlands rich with alluvial deposits, little villages with cobbled streets running straight down to the river, cities whose walls guard them on three sides and the Yangtze is the fourth, cliffs and mountains, the Yangtze has them all. It has spoiled me for any other river in the world. Even my own Father of Waters seems mild and small to me in comparison. I have seen Mississippi floods, and they are terrible and death-dealing, but I am grateful that they are nothing like the gargantuan Yangtze floods that swallow up valleys for miles inland and make islands of distant mountains. I stood once on Purple Mountain in Nanking, many miles distant from the river, and it was a great island, and lapping at its base, fifty feet deep over farmhouses and fields, were yellow Yangtze waves. . . .

One of the most memorable events of Pearl Buck's childhood was the visit to China of Charles Lindbergh and his wife, during the flood of August 1931. This terrible flood killed over 140,000 people and left another twenty-eight million homeless.

[They] flew over the floods and did the splendid reconnoitring of destitute, water-surrounded towns and villages that formed the basis for relieving and saving thousands of lives. And just as they were leaving, their plane taking off from the Yangtze, a wing tipped and they were thrown into the river. The Chinese said the river reached up and pulled at the plane in revenge. By all Chinese experience and belief they should have drowned, but they kept up until they were rescued, to the awe and astonishment of everyone, and most of all the Chinese. A touch of magic went into all Chinese reminiscence about the Lindberghs thereafter.

'The old demon couldn't pull them under,' the people said. 'That's because they were American.'

River Journeys, River Lives

Today, traditional junks have been replaced by engine-powered boats and Confucian scholar officials by Party cadres. Yet whether written in the twelfth or twentieth century, much of what is described in these pieces would be recognizable to Yangtze folk of any era. Most construction and farm work is still done by hand, using methods unchanged since people first settled here. Moreover, as shown in 'Beacon Fire', written in 1984, floods continue to take lives and wreak destruction. Human emotions have not changed much either.

What has changed dramatically, however, is the pollution of the river and the huge growth in the human population along it. As Tom Hilditch reports in 'The Plight of the Baiji', the blue Yangtze the poets sang of is gone forever, and very soon the dolphins unique to the river will be gone too.

THOUGHTS WHEN TRAVELLING AT NIGHT

DU FU (712–770)

Throughout his life, the great poet Du Fu (Tu Fu) wandered from one province to another, a victim of war and bouts of misfortune, illness, and poverty. He held a series of minor, badly paid government posts, including several along the Yangtze, but was often without employment. These poignant lines were written towards the end of his life, as he travelled down the Yangtze. In just a few words, they evoke the vastness of the river and sky by night and Du Fu's feelings of despair and insignificance, intensified by his surroundings.

Between soft, grassy banks in the light breeze
A lone, tall-masted boat sails through the night;
Stars hang low above the wide, flat plain,
And up rides the moon as the mighty river flows on.
Since I have not in truth won fame by writing,
In old age and illness I should retire from office.
Drifting along, to what can I liken myself?
A lonely beach gull between heaven and earth.

A SECOND SONG OF CHANG-KAN

LI BAI (701–762)

Although Du Fu's friend Li Bai (Li Po) also led a precarious existence, he revelled in it. He was an eccentric genius, the model of the wild, drunken poet. Li spent much of his life wandering from place to place, spending long periods in the mountains and in areas along the Yangtze. Although at one time he was appointed as one of the court poets, he was the only well-known poet of the period who never attempted the Civil Service Exams. Unlike many of his friends, he was never given an official government post, although he kept hoping for one. However, he could never have fitted the mould of government servant. He leaned towards Daoism (Taoism) and had no patience with the dull and rigid Confucian texts on which both the exams and the government system were based. One of his poems begins: 'I am the madman of the Ch'u country/Who sang a mad song disputing Confucius'. It is hardly surprising that he was never considered government material.

In this poem a young wife is left in the village of Chang-kan, near Nanjing, while her husband sails upriver to the wild Three Gorges region. This is a journey of about 1,500 kilometres (almost 1,000 miles), through treacherous rapids, far from the wide placid waters of the lower reaches. Xiang-tan must be one of the rapids that rush through the gorges. Here is her lament.

I was a young girl hidden deep in her chamber;
I did not know the dust and smoke of the world.
Because I have married a man of Chang-kan,
Daily I go to the sands and look at the winds.

In May the south wind blows.
I think of you sailing down from Pa-ling.
In September the west wind whirls.
I dream of you coursing down the Yangtze river.

You came, you went away, and I shall always sorrow.
We were often parted, and rarely met.
When did you arrive at Hsiang-tan?
In wind and storm my dream follows you.

Last night the wind raged furiously,
And broke the trees on the riverbank.
The river flooded over, the waters were boundless and dark:
Where were you then, O my beloved?

Your wife mounts the saddle of a flying cloud,
Desiring only to meet you east of the Orchid Island.
Then we shall be happy as mandarin ducks among green reeds,
Or as the sporting halcyons embroidered on a silk screen.

There was a time—I was just fifteen—
My face was as red as a peach flower.
Why should I be a river merchant's wife,
Thinking always of water and wind?

SONG OF INSPECTOR DING

LI BAI (701–762)

For much of China's history, there was a 'corvée' labour system, whereby each district had to provide the government with conscripts to work on public works projects, such as building dikes. This poem describes the hard lives of some of these men, quarrying stone, dragging it to the river, and then hauling the laden boats upstream. In this region the summers are so hot day and night, that the buffalo are said to mistake the moon for the sun. Yunyang, in Jiangsu Province, is now called Danyang, while Mang and Dang are two hills famous for their good quality stone.

Yunyang sends conscript labour to the Yangtze,
Both river banks are alive with men and trade;
When the buffaloes of Wu pant beneath the moon,
It's weary work hauling boats!
The river water's too muddy to drink,
Thick silt fills half the pot;
When workmen chant the Inspector's Song,
Hearts break, tears fall like rain,
Ten thousand slave in the quarries,
But who will haul the stone to the river bank?
Look yonder at rocky Mang and Dang—
What tears have fallen here since ancient times!

LOOKING FOR LI BAI

COLIN THUBRON

In his collection of Chinese poems, The White Pony, *Robert Payne writes that Li Bai's heart's desire was 'to go rowing in a boat with my hair down'. According to Payne, he had all Shelley's delight in water and loneliness, and never felt entirely human or at ease in the world. And though the story is certainly untrue, it is significant that for centuries many believed he died at the summons of the angelic hosts who suddenly appeared to him on a moonlit night when he was drinking in his boat. Two children of immortality came carrying banners, and dolphins arrived, standing on their tails, waiting to carry him to the celestial palaces.*

But it is more probable, as Liu Hsu relates in the Old Book of Tang, *that Li Bai died in 762 from overdrinking, and was buried near the river.*

Po Chu-i (Bai Juyi) visited the grave fifty years later, finding only a small mound in an endless plain of grass.

Over a thousand years later in the mid-1980s, the travel writer Colin Thubron also goes in search of Li Bai.

My favourite Chinese poet, Li Bai, was drowned in the Yangtze forty miles south-west of Nanjing while leaning drunkenly overboard trying to embrace a reflection of the moon. After hearing that his grave lay on the river bank near an obscure town named Caishiji, I had a sentimental desire to visit it, and from there to circle south a hundred miles to one of the loneliest of the Buddhist holy mountains.

By his contemporaries in eighth-century China, at the zenith of the Tang dynasty, Li Bai was regarded with superstitious wonder. He passed his life in vagabondage, shockingly free from the civic duties expected of educated men, and flung off the domestic bonds of four successive marriages in favour of concubines or solitude. His poetry is filled with the desolate mountains and waterfalls of his journeying. It is the poetry of darkness and of the spirit-voyage. When he was drunk—which was often—he composed at supernatural speed, and his startling shrillness of voice and the possessed glitter of his eyes only enhanced the spell which he cast on those who met him. They believed him an immortal banished from heaven.

I did not know if Caishiji was open to foreigners, and it seemed wiser not to ask. At the central bus depot in Nanjing I was turned away, but a garrulous young salesman adopted me in the small railway station outside the southern gate, bought me a ticket and followed me on to my train in mixed fascination and concern. He had taken my quest to heart. He, also, desired to locate the tomb of Li Bai, he announced, and ensconced himself delightedly in my carriage. His name was Jianming, he said, which meant 'Build the Splendour', but there was no telling what splendour this might be. Dressed in shorts and sandals, and carrying only what appeared to be a large washing-bag, he looked unheroically nomadic. He was meant to be visiting the regional offices of his firm—an electrical trading company from the coastal province of Fujian—but he waved all this into the air. He would go wherever I was going, he said. He would protect me. He grinned at me with ugly, boyish charm. His protruding lips and shelving brows turned him into Peking Man. I was his new friend, he said.

Our train crept painfully up the Yangtze valley. The carriage was full of soldiers, wretchedly equipped—shapeless fatigues, plimsolls, no insignia but the red star on their caps. They looked infinitely expendable. After two hours we left them and took a series of one-jangling buses over the paddy-fields towards Caishiji. The heat was intense. My companion negotiated our itinerary in complicated bouts of enquiry, while I sank into passivity.

I started to despair of finding Li Bai. Our buses degenerated into trotting hearses bursting with peasants spitting and retching out of the broken windows. I had a deepening sense of burning my boats. Whenever we trudged between bus-stops, my rucksack bowed me like a congenital hump. But Build-the-Splendour was thrilled. He had never been in these parts, he said. We were seeing life. It slowly dawned on me that he was as lost as I was. From time to time he would turn and beam at me with a mouthload of crooked teeth, and say: 'Only one more bus!'

But where was Li Bai? The drunkard seemed to be laughing at me. He was shifting about. Some said he was in one place, some in another. Ubiquitous but unspecified, he had returned to being a god.

But beyond Caishiji we left our last bus and entered a parkland where trees grew young from the pale soil, and a temple stood under hills. Far below us, barges were hooting on the Yangtze. When we peered into the temple, expecting to encounter the obese calm of the Buddha, we saw instead—stark on a scroll-painting—the vagabond-poet toasting the moon from a mountain-top (with a pretty girl and a picnic nearby). We went in. The whole temple was dedicated to him. In hall after statued hall he stood or lolled in earthy ecstasy, wine-cup in fist, his chin tufted defiantly by a Mephistophelean beard, glaring in furious challenge at the sky.

We climbed through galleries and into courts. Where was his tomb? The pilgrimage had become a stubborn point of honour now. I imagined him wilfully eluding me. We reached the apex of the enclosure, but found only a restaurant where two waitresses lay asleep in immodest postures, as if Li Bai had positioned them.

But behind the temple rose a steeper hill, where we circled up a stone stairway roaring with cicadas. The heat groaned and throbbed in my ears. The feeling that Li Bai was playing a practical joke intensified. Then the steps hoisted us into solitude, up to the summit under a blue tent of sky. I felt a light sense of triumph. The place was perfect: crowned with a tiny tumulus like the grave of a dwarf emperor. In front of it, an inscribed stone. The Yangtze rolling yellow beyond. Nobody there, but a few old men sunning themselves.

I asked Jianming to read out the inscription. He squatted in front of it and declaimed:

'"Here lie the cap and clothes. . . ."' He stopped.

'What?'

'". . . the cap and clothes of the Tang poet Li Bai."'

'Just his clothes? A tomb for clothes?'

'Yes.'

Sweating and bewildered, I consulted the conclave of old men. Dimly I remembered that in the poet's final song he described himself faltering into death but leaving a part of himself behind:

A garment that he hung upon the rocks
when he wandered to the Islands of the East.

But was that all? And had he really died here?

Yes, said one of the patriarchs, he had been under arrest and died of grief on his way back to the capital. He had received a pardon, said another, and just died of disease. But most of them repeated the time-honoured story that Li Bai had drowned in wine and the Yangtze while trying to cuddle the moon. His body had been disinterred at some unknown time and buried. . . . But they disagreed elaborately on where, or on how I might reach the place, and only concurred in evoking an inferno of five or six more bus-drives.

From far away down the slope near the river, rose the sound of shrill laughter.

12

A BALLAD OF ALGAE

MAO DUN

Mao Dun, considered one of China's greatest modern literary critics and writers, was born in 1896 near Shanghai. He was a political and social activist all his life, and one of China's first writers of 'revolutionary literature', that is, fiction written from a Marxist standpoint. He and his contemporaries wanted to get away from the Chinese tradition of writing for a small, highly educated audience and write accessible and educational literature for everyone.

Yet, as can be seen in this extract from one of his short stories written in 1936, his characters are real people, not mere propaganda figures. While the narrative teaches the reader about conditions along the Yangtze, the meat of the story is a classic love triangle. Set in the 1930s in a river village, Caixi lives with his wife and his sickly nephew Xiusheng. As Xiusheng is well aware, Caixi and Xiusheng's wife are having an affair, and she is pregnant, probably by Caixi.

When the northwest wind had blown for two days on end you could scarcely hear a dog bark in the tiny village. A leaden sky met the gaze everywhere, except where at the eastern horizon a strip of vague yellow appeared weakly yet wilfully to be attempting to melt away the sky's leaden cover.

Seven or eight low houses crouched like beetles on the ground. The stacks of fresh rice straw resembled withered wild fungi; close beside them and on the riverbank some distance away tallow trees denuded of leaves reared their newly snapped forked branches in dignified contention with the northwest wind. These kindly mothers to the peasantry generally needed no laborious tending, and when winter came and their black nuts burst into white tips, they gave up their covering of slender fingers and submitted to a thousand knife wounds to make good the peasants' lives with those oil-rich nuts.

Twisting westwards like a black python, the river crawled past paddy-fields criss-crossed with dykes and past irregularly shaped mulberry orchards, widening towards the west until it merged with the horizon. As summer turned into autumn, this merry, goodly stream became sewn over with coin-like, floating duckweed and threads of waterweed, but had now been swept clean of both by the northwest wind, and its naked torso wrinkled in the bitter cold into waves fragmented like fish scales, turning black with fury.

Caixi, a strapping fellow approaching forty, came out of one of the low houses, strode to the east end of the threshing ground and looked up at the sky all around. The vague yellow on the eastern horizon was now hidden under the great, chinkless lead cover of the sky. Caixi looked then sniffed to test the humidity of the air.

'It's going to snow, damn it!' he mumbled to himself and went back indoors. . . .

'Xiusheng!' Caixi's manly tones at once set the air in the house ringing. 'The weather's changing. Get in the hornwort—today!'

The dingy black object wriggling in the corner was Xiusheng, the 'householder', for all that he was Caixi's nephew. Ten years younger than Caixi, he looked a great deal older. A tiller of the soil, he had been afflicted with jaundice from childhood. He was engaged in filling two sacks with ground rice, checking that the weight was even.

'Today?' he replied, straightening up. 'I was going into town to sell the rice.'

'You can do that tomorrow! What are you going to do if there's a heavy fall of snow? And what about the money from selling the tallow nuts the time before last? All gone, is it?'

'Ages ago. It was your idea to redeem the winter clothes. Now we've no oil, we're out of salt, and yesterday the headman was round dunning us for Master Chen's interest, one yuan fifty; I said at the time, pay him back his interest and we can redeem the clothes bit by bit later, didn't I? But no, you two—'

'Ah!' shouted Caixi irritably. 'In any case, if we miss today our share of the hornwort will be lost, won't it?' And he retreated bellowing into the back of the house.

Xiusheng shot a dubious look at the sky outside. He too expected snow, and the hornwort would be piled up already in the narrow bends of the stream after the past two days of northwest wind, and snow or no snow, if he waited another day the others would have got to it before him; yet he couldn't forget the village headman's 'Have the money ready tomorrow or I'll have the rice as security, all right?', and once the headman got his hands on the rice, three yuan worth would be down to one fifty.

'The rice has to be sold, and the hornwort has to be got in,' thought Xiusheng as he tentatively hefted the sacks on the carrying pole. Putting them down, he decided to ask if any of the neighbours was going to town and could take the rice along and sell it for him.

Hornwort was collected to prepare fertilizer for the coming spring. On the lower Yangtse this was applied once in spring when the seedlings were transplanted and again in July or August when they had reached waist height. In the region where Xiusheng lived, the second application was thought more important, and for this bean cake was necessary. One year there had been an 'incident' in the area that produced bean cake, and prices rose every year, outstripping peasants' means and bankrupting the dealers.

Poor peasants had then had to rely on a single application, the earlier one that they called the 'first spreading', the best material for which was held to be the river waterweed referred to locally as 'hornwort'.

Hornwort had to be gathered in winter when a northwest wind had been blowing; it was easiest then, when the wind had piled it up together. But winter was hardly the pleasantest time to be out in the severe cold.

Deprived of bean cake, the peasants had no choice but to wrestle doggedly for their lives.

Caixi and Xiusheng propelled their boat in a westerly direction. They knew from experience that the most hornwort was to be found in a fork some twenty *li* from the village, but also that two village boats had set out ahead of them, so that to reach their goal they would have to go ten *li* west then turn south for ten more at double speed. This was Caixi's idea.

They made their way downstream against the still powerful northwest wind, Caixi poling and Xiusheng rowing.

The wind played with the free end of Caixi's blue cloth belt, wrapping it around the bamboo punt pole again and again. He grasped it without breaking rhythm and wiped the sweat from

his face, then with a brushing noise the pole met the frozen earth of the bank and the lip of the boat sputtered with silver spray. With a powerful and long drawn out, deep chested cry, Caixi whirled the pole nimbly through the air into the water on the other side of the boat, leaned on its end for a two-handed thrust, heaved it out again and whirled all twelve feet of it dripping over his head once more.

The pole danced with ever greater animation as Caixi, seeming to seek an object for his anger, trickled all over with the hot sweat of victory.

The river began to widen out after something like ten *li*. Endless expanses of harvested paddy-fields stretched before the eye. The branch stream snaked through the intricate chessboard of the tilled earth like a glittering belt studded here and there with the thatched housings of waterwheels. The sparse grey mounds were hamlets from which rose vague white smoke.

And near and far across this simple farmland rose the proud, verdant cemeteries of the rich.

Waterfowl rose fluttering from the dry reedbank and scattered abruptly to land far out of sight.

Caixi, holding his pole across the bows of the boat, was struck with the novelty of this familiar scene. Mutely, nature was communicating with him. He felt something in his breast that wanted to get out.

He gave a long cry for the bleak land.

His cry was dispersed by the northwest wind. Slowly, he put the pole down. Dry reeds rustled along the bank. The strokes of the oar from the stern were sharply audible though sluggish and listless.

Caixi went aft and gave Xiusheng a hand with the oar. Water, as though defeated, hissed past.

Before long they had reached their destination.

'Now let's get on with it! They'll be here in no time, and there'll be no peace with everybody grabbing for it.'

As he spoke, Caixi lifted the massive clamp used to gather the hornwort. They stood one on either side of the bows holding the clamps open, stabbed down into the thick bank of weed, closed the clamps, then with vigorous twists hauled them up and tossed the mess of weed and mud into the bottom of the boat.

As though woven together, the weed of the river resisted the strength of the men tearing at it. Mud and splinters of ice added to the weight. Caixi's protruding chin knotted forcefully as he stirred and twisted with determination. He shouted with triumph every time it came up, and the thick clamp of bamboo creaked and bent like a bow.

'Harder, Xiusheng! Faster!' Caixi spat on his hands, rubbed them and full of beans applied himself to raising his weed clamp.

Xiusheng's puffy face was oozing with sweat too, though he was moving at only half Caixi's rate and got only half the weed that Caixi got with each sweep of his clamp. Still, his shoulders ached, his heart pumped wildly in his chest and from time to time he whimpered softly.

The hornwort, with its accompaniment of mud and ice, gradually built up in the bottom of the boat, which settled lower in the water; whenever Caixi planted his feet firmly to bring up another full load, the boat veered outwards and icy water washed over the bows to soak his straw-shod feet. He was in shirtsleeves, having removed the torn jacket, but the blue belt stayed tightly around his waist; from head to waist he gave off heat in billows like a kitchen steamer.

The creaking of oars and the sound of voices were borne gradually nearer on the wind. A felt hat flashed from the clump of dry reeds not far ahead. Then a small boat made its laborious way out, then another.

'Aha, there you all are!' cried Caixi merrily, as he strained to heave a clampful of weed into the boat; then with a sly smile he raised up the bamboo clamp, smashed it down into a thick clump that he had had his eye on for some time, opened it as wide as it would go and stirred as hard as he could.

'Well, I'm blowed! Where did you come from? How come we didn't bump into you on the way?' shouted a man in the newly arrived boat as it ploughed into the bank of hornwort.

'Us?' said Xiusheng, knocking off and panting. 'We—' But Caixi butted in with vitality ringing in his voice.

'We flew down from the sky, didn't we? Ha, ha!'

As he spoke, he brought his clamp down a second and a third time.

'Don't talk so big. You're old hands at bog-trotting, as we all know,' laughed the newcomer, clumsily extracting his thick hornwort clamp of bamboo.

Caixi continued hurriedly to lay into his selected area without replying, then put up his clamp and looked first into his boat then at the stream with its carpet of tatters, which his experienced eye told him was only a surface layer mixed mostly with duckweed and fine liverwort.

Putting down the clamp, he hoisted up the end of his belt, wiped away the sweat that covered his face and went nimbly aft.

The mud that had splashed on to the stern was frozen almost solid, and Caixi's torn padded jacket was stuck firmly to the planks; he prised it up, slung it round his shoulders and squatted down.

'We're done,' he said. 'It's all yours, the whole streamful.'

'Tchah! It's all very well to be gracious when you've skimmed the cream off,' retorted one of the newcomers as he set to work.

The calm backwater was bustling in no time.

Xiusheng lifted a plank and took out the coarse flour rolls they had brought with them. They too were frozen as hard as stones. He bit bravely into one. Caixi ate too, though reflectively with his face to the sky; he was reckoning whether any of the nearby waterways had a lot of hornwort on them.

Dark cloud gathered thickly, and the northwest wind dropped somewhat. A distant steam whistle announced the passage of the passenger packet on the main stream.

'It can't be noon already, surely? Wasn't that the steamboat?'

There was a hubbub as the weed gatherers looked up at the sky.

'We'd better be off home then, Xiusheng,' said Caixi standing up and grasping the oar.

This time Xiusheng took the pole. Caixi gave a wild laugh as they emerged from the sidestream. 'North, go north! There's bound to be some in the Dead End.'

'There too?' said Xiusheng, surprised. 'We'll have to spend all night in the boat.'

'Never mind that. Can't you see the weather's going to change? If we fill the boat today we shan't have to worry!' replied Caixi decisively and with a few thrusts of the oar directed the boat into a small cross-stream.

Xiusheng went silently aft and helped him row. But he had used up what strength he had and did not so much row as allow himself to be rowed by the oar, which in Caixi's hands became a living dragon. The water slapped and splashed, and some unplaceable birds started up from the bleached, withered reeds with a wailing call.

Caixi's iron arms moved along as regularly as a lever; sweat drenched his face, and there was joy in his eyes. He began a song that the villagers often sang:

> She was eighteen or nineteen with tits nice and plump
> That quivered and shook when she wiggled her rump
> As she set off to market while dawn was still cold,
> And her hubby was hung on one end of her pole.
> It was twenty-five *li* there and twenty-five back,
> But her fancy man stopped her, though she didn't slack.
> It was by the sheep shack
> That he grabbed her and rolled her right on to her back.*

Xiusheng took the entire song as meant for himself. His puffy face went ashen, and his legs trembled a little. Suddenly he crumpled at the waist, his hands lost contact with the dragon-like oar, and he subsided backwards and sat down on the planking.

'What? Xiusheng!' asked Caixi in surprise, halting in the middle of the song without stopping his hands moving in the slightest.

Xiusheng hung his head and did not answer.

---

* A satire on rich peasants who married their infant sons to older wives who would work for them but tended to look elsewhere for male companionship.

'You're a useless lad,' said Caixi pityingly. 'Have a rest, then.' Caixi seemed to remember something and levelled his eyes at the horizon; in a while the song welled up again from his throat.

'Caixi!' Suddenly Xiusheng was on his feet. 'Do you have to? I may be useless, I may be sickly, and I may get nothing done. but while there's a breath in my body I'll starve to death before I stand by while my wife cheats on me!'

Never before had he displayed such openness or decision. Caixi was momentarily at a loss. He looked at Xiusheng's face livid with anger and pain, and was smitten with remorse; it was true that the song, though current for ages, came sufficiently close to the circumstances of their particular triangle for it to grate understandably on Xiusheng's ears. He felt that he should not have sung with such gusto in front of Xiusheng as if purposely to taunt him and put him down. But hadn't he said about starving to death first? In fact, Caixi put in a great deal of work living with Xiusheng. Was Xiusheng now exerting his position as head of the family and telling him to go? At this point in his train of thought Caixi became angry himself.

'Right then, if I go I go!' said Caixi coldly, and his rowing slowed involuntarily.

Xiusheng, who seemed not to have expected such a reaction, squatted down again dejectedly.

'But,' added Caixi, again coldly but more seriously, 'don't you go hitting your wife any more! A woman like that, and you still don't appreciate her? And she's carrying a child that'll carry on our name.'

'You keep out of it!' Xiusheng leaped up wildly, his voice so shrill that it seemed on the verge of being lost. 'She's my wife, and if I kill her it's me that'll get the chop!'

'Would you? Try it!' Caixi rounded on him sharply, his fists tightly balled and his eyes fixed on Xiusheng's face.

Xiusheng seemed to be trembling all over: 'I will, if I want. I'm fed up with life. From one year's end to the next they're pressing you for grain, collecting your taxes, dunning you for debts, running you into the ground. You eat for today, and there's none for tomorrow. You pawn your summer clothes and you can't get your winter ones out of hock. And you haven't even got your health. I'm fed up with it! Life is misery!'

13

WATER TOWN

ZHAO PEI

This essay, written in the mid-1980s, describes scenes typical of many sleepy little towns along the lower Yangtze. The room devoted to silk culture in each small house is where the family raises silk worms. Racks from floor to ceiling contain flat paniers of the white grubs, chomping steadily and swiftly on beds of green mulberry leaves. At the turn of the century, the 'tiger bones' on sale could well have been genuine, and the hookahs in the teahouse would probably have contained opium rather than tobacco as they do today.

Most towns and villages on the lower Yangtse are scattered along the river, under whose bank is a slope of flagstones and above it grey brick houses with tiled roofs, their thick walls forming the boundary between households. Some people drive rows of stone or wooden posts into the beach and then put up a little stilt house with planks. Downstairs are two rooms: one for silk culture, the other for a cooking stove painted with florid patterns, and upstairs another two rooms, one a living room, the other a family bedroom. The projecting wall resembles a bird's nest overlooking the river. The six lattice windows are covered with gossamer paper. On summer evenings when the sunlight streams into the building and turns it into a food steamer, the humid breeze from the river disperses the heat.

The households along the river like to grow loofahs, lentils and gourds. When the creepers crawl along straw ropes up the walls and cover the roofs with their dark green leaves, the rooms seem hidden in the shade of a balmy spring, nice and airy.

Serried roofs and jagged buildings by the river and the numerous black-canopied boats lying under the bank make the river into a tranquil lane with only a beam of light overhead and a line of green in the water visible. When the river is in spate and the flagstones are submerged, the streets and alleys seem to be islets floating on the green water. The residents in the stilt houses need only let down baskets to buy any kind of fish and vegetables from the fishermen and peasants. If the water is rapid in the narrow channels, the boatman, holding a pole against his bronzed, sinewy shoulder, will bend it into a bow, pushing the boat through against the current as he chants rhythmical cries from his heaving chest to synchronize his movements. If the water is not polluted with filthy waste from factories, there will be frogs to be found lying on emerald duckweed, croaking at the ripples. Mischievous fish shake the duckweed, and the alarmed frogs flop into the water.

Few of the channels can be dated. The locust, plane and sponge trees twisting out of the crevices in the river bank have grown two arm-spans round, and houses scattered here and there are advanced in years, some like hump-backs, others with knotty arms of distorted features. When a black-canopied boat in full sail slides through the shadowy channels, it seems to be a winged cherub who will carry you to the remote future. But for the television aerials glittering in the sunshine like the wings of dragonflies and the sweet music floating from records in flower-decked rooms, you would think it a deserted corner forgotten by the world.

On either side of the channels stand quays with a flight of seven or eight steps every few dozen yards. No one knows when some skilful sculptor in the township of Lili in Wujiang carved the mooring holes so exquisitely. The elaborate compositions, elegant in shape and meticulous in execution are not inferior to the stone sculptures of the Tang era. One of them is in the shape of an ox horn entwined with ribbons, another shaped like a miniature anchor, and another like an 'S'. It is obvious that the craftsman assimilated techniques from the brick carving and folk scissor-cuts of the Yangtse Valley. Probably coming from the family of a boatman helped him make them so vivid and graphic.

Under the quays there are always women with their trousers rolled up standing in the water washing rice and vegetables. Peasants' motorboats loaded with fragrant, sweet watermelons, musk-melons and thin-skinned, juicy peaches pass by. The peasants on deck, their heads held high and chests thrown out, look around smugly. They seem to hold not the engine bar but the lever of the times. The boats swish past like helicopters in flight. The spray churned up by the motorboats wets the breasts of the women and ripples their baskets, but they merely frown at the trick and murmur, 'Rascals!'

Over the channels stand arched bridges overgrown with ivy. When the river is lulled, the shadows of the bridges and the arched spans falling on the water form a dim moon, over which the boats seem to sail, while the boatmen sing their folk-songs cheerfully down the wind.

At the end of every bridge is usually a teahouse dignified with the name of 'The Moon-reaching Tower', 'The Star-plucking Pavilion' or 'The Orchid-viewing Hall'. In reality it is nothing but an ordinary stilt house, on whose roof yowling cats in heat scurry about. When it rains, fine raindrops from outside glimmer in the hazy smoke. Townsfolk who are tea addicts reck little of the structural condition of the teahouse. Some, backs hunched, creep in before daybreak jabbering like garrulous old women and bustle around the smoke-blackened stove to help the staff do this and that. By the time the burning husks in the stove give off a greenish flame and the water in the pots on top is bubbling, there is no unoccupied seat in the L-shaped building, and the white steam impregnated with the fragrance of tea spreads throughout the ill-lit house.

Apart from peasants who have just sold their produce at the early fair, most customers are old-age pensioners. They have their accustomed seats and know each other very well. One of them could even say how many wrinkles another has on his forehead. In the teahouse you hear humorous stories, absurd legends, good-humoured jokes and philosophical proverbs. Sometimes a wisecrack splits their sides with laughter.

Many of them like keeping cage-birds. They bring them here for fresh air when the stars are still overhead in the early morning and hang them from the eaves like lanterns at festivals. The canaries, white-eyes, thrushes and mynahs chirp and twitter as the customers happily talk and laugh inside. The teahouse also provides nickel-copper hookahs for those who smoke. Puffing away, they narrow their eyes as if listening to a famous singer. Not until the lyrical aria is finished will they blow to the ceiling the cloud of smoke they have kept in their mouths so long that their faces have turned red as fire.

The teahouse is very busy with many people going in and out. Women from the countryside bring baskets or trays of sunflower seeds or fried food to sell here. A quack doctor is making wild boasts about his skills and at the same time soliciting buyers for his sham tiger bones. In fact they are bones of an ox browned by smoke. Occasionally some girls from a cultural centre come here with their faces rouged red as strawberries and florid aprons round their waists and sing a song about the scenery around Lake Tai then perform an excerpt from a local opera before giving a slide show on changes in the countryside. At these times the whole teahouse is so quiet that even the moaning of a fly entangled in a spider's web can be heard.

14

A TRIP TO SHU

LU YU (1125–1209)

In the summer of 1170, Lu Yu set off from his home in Shaoxing near Shanghai for the city of Kui-zhou, just west of the Three Gorges, and now known as Fengjie. Kui-zhou was the capital of Shu, the ancient name for what is now the province of Sichuan. Lu Yu was to take up the post of Vice-Governor there, but a position in the wilds of Shu was not a plum posting. Like his contemporary Xin Qiji ('Thoughts in Beigu Pavilion at Jingkou'), Lu Yu believed that the southern Song dynasty should fight against the Jurchen invaders. This was an unpopular stand and Lu Yu's enemies at court persecuted him throughout his career.

To reach far-away Kui-zhou, Lu travelled by boat along the Grand Canal and then up the Yangtze. The trip took about five months, including side-trips, and delays for boat repairs or because of bad weather. Lu Yu's diary, provides a fascinating picture of everyday life along the river.

This diary extract was written after a side-trip to the famous Lushan Mountain, on a tributary of the Yangtze near Jiujiang (known then as Xunyang or Hsunyang), on the Yangtze's middle reaches. With Poyang Lake to the east and the Yangtze to the north, the views from the top are spectacular, and to this day Lushan is a favourite summer retreat. This excerpt describes the voyage as far as the little backwater of Huangzhou, a distance of about 100 kilometres (62 miles). It took them three days, as the wind was against them and coolies had to tow their boat.

14th day: It rained at dawn. Moving out into the big river, we met a raft made of wood and measuring over ten or more chang across and over fifty chang long.* There were thirty or forty houses on it, complete with wives and children, chickens and dogs, mortars and pestles. Little paths ran back and forth and there was even a shrine—I've never seen anything like

---

* A *chang* (now spelt 'zhang') is 3.3 metres (3.6 yards) long.

it. The boatmen tell me that this is actually a rather small raft. The big ones sometimes have soil spread over the surface and vegetable gardens planted, or wine shops built on them. They are unable to enter the coves but travel only on the big river.

Today we had the wind against us and the boat had to be pulled along. From dawn to sunset we barely managed to go fifteen or sixteen li. We tied up at the side of Liu-kuan Point. We have reached the border of Ch'i-chou. The boys went ashore, and when they got back, they said they had found a little path that led around behind the mountains, where they came upon a man-made lake, very wide, with many lotuses and water chestnuts. There were numerous water mallows growing along the bank. Several houses basked in the late sun, with rush hedges and thatched roofs—truly a rare and picturesque spot, yet lonely and with no sound of human voices. They saw some large pears which they wanted to buy, but could find no one to buy them from. There was a little boat out on the lake gathering water chestnuts which they called to, but got no answer. They were about to press on farther when they saw some traps at the side of the road and, fearing that there might be tigers or wolves around, they didn't dare go on.

In the evening we saw a big turtle bobbing up and down in the water.

15th day: Somewhat overcast. The west wind is getting stronger and it is extremely difficult to tow the boat. From Rich Pond west we've been following the south bank of the river—nothing but big mountains rising and dipping like billows. There are people living here and there at the foot of the mountains. From time to time we see them crouching in sheds they've made, holding bows and arrows and watching for a tiger to go by. We passed Dragon's Eye Point, a mere fist of stone in the river. On the mountain beside the point there is a dragon shrine. Sometime after four in the afternoon, the wind shifted around behind us. We stopped for the night at Ch'i Mouth Garrison, where there are many houses crowded together and a large number of boats bound for Shu tied up at the embankment.

In the evening I climbed up on the bank with my sons and looked out over the great river, enjoying the moonlight. The

surface of the river stretches far off to the horizon and the reflection of the moon falls across the water, rippling and swaying and never coming to rest, like a golden dragon—a sight to amaze the eye and move the heart.

Today I bought prepared medicine at the Ch'i Mouth market. In the medicine shops are all the things one needs for simmering and decocting such as peppermint and black plum preparation. Such ingredients are hard to get hold of suddenly when one is on a journey—that the medicine shops were thoughtful enough to stock them is very commendable.

18th day: We finally got started at mealtime and by four in the afternoon reached Huang-chou. It is an out-of-the-way and backward place where there is little to do. But because Tu Mu and Wang Yü-ch'eng were once its governors and Su Tung-p'o and Chang Lei* lived here in exile, it has ended by becoming a famous town. We tied up at the Lin-kao Pavilion, where Su Tung-p'o once

---

* Tu Mu (803–852) was a famous T'ang poet-official; Wang Yü-ch'eng (954–1001) a poet-official of the Northern Sung; Su Tung-p'o (1037–1101) was a famous poet-official; Chang Lei (1054–1114) a scholar-official.

stayed, the place of which he said in a letter to Ch'in Shao-yu,*
'a few steps out the gate and you are at the great river.' The misty
waves stretch far into the distance and the spot has an open and
spacious air.

I called on the governor Yang Yu-i and the vice-governor Ch'en
Shao-fu. The governor's office is extremely shabby—the reception
room barely holds four or five visitors—though the building his
assistants are in is somewhat better.

In the evening we shifted the boat to Bamboo Garden Port.
There was too much wind and rough water at Lin-kao—it's no
place to tie up for the night.

21st day: We passed Twin Willow Cove. Looking back over the
river, we could see distant mountains piled on top of each other,
jagged and steep. Since leaving Huang-chou, we've been going
through a series of coves, but all of them broad and open. The
land along the river is gradually getting higher and is planted
mostly in crops such as beans, millet, and buckwheat. In the
evening we tied up at Willow Row Landing—a big embankment
with tall willows and many people living crowded together. Fish
are as cheap as dirt—a hundred cash will buy enough to satisfy
twenty mouths. What's more, they're all large fish. I tried to find
some small fish to feed to my cat but couldn't.

* Ch'in Kuan (1049 – 1101), disciple of Su Tung-p'o.

15

DODGING DEMONS AND FAST-MOVING ISLANDS

THOMAS WOODROOFE

It is 1919, and Toby, a young British sub-lieutenant, is on his maiden voyage up the Yangtze aboard the gunboat Beetle. *This passage from Thomas Woodroofe's semi-autobiographical novel describes the journey between the treaty ports of Zhenjiang, and the impressive city of Hankou.*

Although they may no longer believe in them, and certainly no longer take the precautions described in this extract, even today, older boatmen are familiar with the superstitions about demons. Nor have they forgotten about the foreign gunboats, which patrolled the river right up until 1949. Writing in 1984, travel writer Paul Theroux quotes one captain: 'Before Liberation, this river was different. The foreigners were very careless. They ran rampant. The Chinese people hated and feared them, because they had a reputation for not stopping for a junk or sampan, or they might swamp a small boat in their wake. It made them unpopular. The gunboats were worst of all.'

The memories are still there. In 1994, I told the farmers in a small Yangtze village that I lived in Hong Kong, and was amazed to find that they were very nervous about the handover of Hong Kong to China in 1997. 'But why should it affect you?' I asked. 'We know that the British will not give up Hong Kong without a fight,' they answered, 'and British gunboats will sail up the Yangtze just like before.'

The raft of logs that Toby mistakes for an island is similar to that mentioned in the previous passage by Lu Yu, on his voyage over 700 years earlier. Such rafts were still a common sight until the middle of this century.

They left in the cool freshness of the dawn and steamed up a river that had narrowed to more normal proportions. That morning Toby caught his first sight of the China of his dreams. He saw a pagoda.

It stood on the river bank like a lighthouse, isolated and lonely, far from anywhere. It towered up for seven storeys and they passed so close to it that he could see tiles missing in its roof and creepers twining their way up its slender length. It seemed to have no purpose, standing there all alone; perhaps the architect had said to himself: 'I shall now build a beautiful thing' and for once could concentrate on sheer beauty without worrying his head about utility. In all probability it had never been used; perhaps it had been built as a tribute to the majesty of the river which flowed ceaselessly past its foot. But whatever the reason of its erection, the architect intended it to stay there; it was securely anchored to three anchors out in midstream by cumbrous, rusty iron cables. He was taking no chances with demons who might remove it in the night.

'But why', asked Toby when Blair told him of this, 'should demons who are capable of removing a seven-storied pagoda bodily in the night, be baffled by a few anchors?'

'You don't know demons,' replied the captain, 'and anyhow, there it is.' And there it was. After centuries the pagoda still towered over the river, unremoved by demons, so perhaps there was something in those anchors after all.

It was not long after this that Toby had his first actual experience with a demon. The ship was steaming up a long straight reach and Blair told him to take over.

'Keep a cable or so off this bank and you'll be all right,' he said. 'I'm going down for some breakfast but I'll be up again before we get to the corner.'

It was a delightful moment. It was the first time Toby had been in charge of anything larger than a picket boat, but, though he was childishly thrilled, in front of the quartermaster he tried to give the impression that he was merely bored. He leaned over the dodger and yawned. And in a few moments he was bored. He wanted something to happen, to give orders, to swing the ship round. He wanted to be something more than an ornament, only there to see that the quartermaster kept on his course and did not go suddenly mad and try and ram the bank. He glanced round, but that stolid individual was spinning the wheel carelessly a spoke or two at a time, now to starboard, now to port, while he gazed out ahead and occasionally loudly sucked his teeth. He was showing no signs of lunacy.

Toby lit a cigarette, and then, across the glare, he saw a junk in the distance—fairly large she looked and coming down towards him. He would have to alter course. There was oceans of room so he wouldn't call the skipper.

'Port ten,' he ordered gruffly.

'Port ten, sir,' repeated the quartermaster.

Toby experienced a delightful feeling of omnipotence as the bows swung round, just because he wanted them to.

'Midships.'

'Midships, sir.'

'Starboard ten. Steady on that tree, d'ye see it?'

'Steady, sir, on the tree, sir. Aye aye, sir.'

He gave another glance at the junk and was surprised to find that she also had altered course, so that once again their paths were converging. 'They must be mad,' he thought and held on for another minute.

They were approaching rapidly and it looked as if the junk were trying to impale herself on the *Beetle*'s stem.

He altered hard over the other way. The junk followed suit. Toby started to sweat. Just his luck to strike a raving lunatic his first time on the river—the junk skipper was obviously suffering from suicidal mania. He put the helm hard over once more and just managed to scrape under her stern, missing her by a few feet.

As she shot past he could see her skipper standing up on her high stern, grinning; while the crew were beating gongs and letting off fire-crackers. Instead of looking shaken, however, at their narrow escape, they appeared to be highly delighted.

'Celebrating, I suppose,' thought Toby, 'but it was a damn close shave,' and he brought the *Beetle* back to her course.

'Did you see that lunatic, sir?' he burst out when Blair came back on to the bridge, 'the fellow must have been stark, staring mad! And I altered in tons of time, too!'

Blair laughed. 'You've got to expect that from every junk you meet. He was only planting his devil on you.'

Every junk, or sampan even, is followed by a demon, much as a yacht tows a dinghy astern. If, however, you scrape across the bows of another junk, or better, the knife-like stem of a foreigner, this invisible tow-rope is cut, and the demon uncomplainingly attaches itself to the ship or whatever did the cutting. As it is always uncertain how far astern the demon may be, to be on the safe side you want the operating craft to pass as close under your stern as possible, while you speed the demon on his way and wish him luck in his new situation by beating gongs and firing crackers.

When Toby learned this, he started to collect demons, and by the end of the day had collected so many that the *Beetle* was like a Thames tug towing a long string of barges.

Before they anchored for the night, he told his skipper about the load they were towing.

'Let's get rid of 'em,' suggested Blair, 'good practice for you. Cut across this fellow's bows.'

He pointed to a large junk that was carrying out some sinister manoeuvres some way ahead.

Toby waited until the junk was nearly on top of him and then altered course. 'The bows of the junk slid past his own stern, while her crew danced about in a frenzy of excitement and he could see her skipper up on his high poop waving his arms and chattering with rage—or perhaps terror.

The *Beetle* anchored that night free of devils.

However malignant, a demon is luckily also singularly obtuse. If this were not so, the life of a Chinaman would be almost unbearable. A demon hates a noise, but he is also incurably inquisitive. At marriages and funerals, at festivals or family gatherings, even at the start of a journey, these malignant creatures arrive unbidden in swarms. They gate-crash weddings; throng the graveside at funerals; try and get in to the feast on someone's birthday, and jostle round the station like a crowd greeting a film star, if precautions are not taken. Therefore the celebrants on these occasions annoy the delicate ear-drums of the unwanted guests by a terrific gonging or heroic fusillade of fire-crackers. For this reason also, the wheelbarrow coolie is able to go his way unmolested as long as his wheel is making a hideous din.

Whenever a cluster of junks get under way and leave their mooring place under the bank near a village—and they always moved an hour before dawn, Toby noticed—the gonging starts while the preparations are being made. A Chinese gong is always cracked—the more hideous the cacophony the more the demon objects. Just before shoving off, crackers are brought in to help, so that almost every dawn on the river was heralded in by a mad frenzied gonging and a popping and spitting of crackers that suggested a trench raid, while the upper air, presumably, was thronged by an exasperated mob of demons. . . .

Toby was amused to find that the matter-of-fact Wang was a firm believer in demons. All day, while he was up on the bridge, Wang squatted just below, patiently waiting for the orders of his master. If the *Beetle* anchored still with a string of demons attached, Wang would look at him reproachfully, and they would be held responsible for all the minor accidents of life that followed: a broken cup, a lost sock, a cut finger, a stomach-ache. Wang would shrug his shoulders and announce dogmatically: 'Belong devil. Makee plenchee bobbery.'

From that decision there was no appeal. . . .

The day before they reached Hankow Toby had been left alone on the bridge and had been looking at villages they were passing, when he glanced out ahead and was amazed to see an island that his skipper had not mentioned. He did not know which side to pass it, and rather than take a chance, sent down for Blair.

'What is it?' said the latter when he arrived on the bridge.

'That island, sir. Which side shall I pass it?'

'Island? What the—I don't see any—oh! my God!'

Blair broke off into a roar of laughter. 'Leave it on your starboard hand,' he ordered solemnly.

The island was flat and low-lying with a few mean huts huddled together in its centre.

'Aye aye, sir,' said Toby and accordingly altered course.

Blair stood by his side, grinning.

Quickly they came up to it and Toby felt a fool. His island was a huge raft of logs, floating down on the current.

'Slow both,' ordered Blair. 'Let's have a look at them. They look as if they were going to ground on that spit. And they will, too, if they can't tow her out a bit. There goes their boat.'

A boat had pushed off from the raft towing a thick fibre rope. The crew of this boat yuloed madly off towards midstream, being incited to further efforts by an ecstatic drumming from the raft. The *tempo* of the drumming slowed down and the party in the boat lessened their stroke. Then the drum seemed to be beating out some signal, for the crew of the sampan left their yulo and crowded round an unwieldy wickerwork contraption in the bows. The drumming ceased for a second or two. Then there were three sharp taps: 'rap tap tap', and over went the affair from the bows.

'Sea-anchor,' said Blair.

At once the drumming started up again, more excited than ever, and those left behind on the raft manned a capstan to which the rope had been brought, and started to heave round. In addition to the drummer was a kind of cheer-leader. He had long flapping sleeves which he whirled madly about as he did a sort of war-dance. Women came out of the huts and screamed encouragement, hens fluttered out of the way, pigs squeaked and the dogs set up a tremendous barking. The cheer-leader had clappers in the end of his sleeves, which helped to swell the din. Faster and faster went the drum, round and round spun the coolies at the capstan, sweating and panting. Just as the noise had worked up to a wild, hysterical crescendo, and Toby was expecting the cheer-leader to collapse from his frenzy at any moment, the sea-anchor appeared at the side of the raft.

At once the drum and the noise ceased. The sampan secured alongside and its crew jumped out. Apparently all was well: the course of the raft had been altered by a few yards and she was swinging well clear of the spit into midstream. If she had grounded she would have broken up, with ruin for all concerned—the logs would have escaped singly, the livestock have been drowned and the crew homeless. The *Beetle* went on and as Toby looked back over the stern all was peace in the floating village, which had sheered out into midstream. The coolies were gathered round a huge pot with their bowls; the cheerleader had removed his cloak of office; the women had returned inside the huts leaving their children to play outside; the dogs were selecting cool places for themselves in the shade.

Next morning the *Beetle* rounded a bend and in the haze ahead was a large city. First the round grey tanks of the oil companies; then a Japanese cruiser anchored in midstream; the mast of an ocean-going cargo steamer with a blue funnel; a succession of tall buildings along the bund, and far beyond, a smoky haze over the Chinese city. They had come eight hundred miles and still the river was nearly two miles across. Blair went alongside a hulk that lay just under the towering Hongkong and Shanghai Bank, an imposing building of marble and shining white stone, with massive wrought iron doors.

Toby felt as if they were anchoring in Threadneedle Street.

16

THE PLIGHT OF THE BAIJI

TOM HILDITCH

Until recently, the river teemed not only with demons, but also with friendly, benevolent creatures. The baiji, white flag dolphins, were believed to be goddesses, or girls transformed into mermaids. Even in the 1980s they could be seen frolicking around boats in the river's lower and middle reaches; generations of riverfolk and travellers spun stories about them. Yet today only a handful survive. Since Tom Hilditch wrote this report, a late 1994 survey estimated that there were fewer than one hundred baiji left alive.

The most astonishing thing about baiji dolphins is not that they still cling to life in China's Yangtze River despite pollution, heavy traffic and ruthless fishing. Nor that they are 'living fossils' almost unchanged by two million years of evolution. Nor that they will almost certainly be the first dolphins to become extinct in human history. The most astonishing thing about the baiji is that the species could be saved today for HK$3 million, or the price of 17 couture Chanel suits.

When the Yangtze was formed 30 million years ago as the Himalayas were forced up by clashing continental plates, the 6,300-kilometre river was a paradise for the primitive dolphin; a Garden of Eden, rich in shrimps, fish, lush water-weeds and vast areas to play in. While other primitive dolphins had to struggle and adapt to survive in the sea, the baiji flourished in the lower reaches of the Yangtze, from the Three Gorges to the sea, and in more than 1,000 tributaries and dozens of major lakes. Biologists estimate they numbered over 5,000. They had no natural enemies, no parasites and no reason to evolve.

Today the last 150 baiji differ little from the fossils of their ancestors. Their paradise, however, *has* evolved. It has turned into hell.

At first, developments along the river bank posed no threat to the dolphins. Another hairless mammal arrived, settled along the Yangtze, made experiments with sticks and stones but lived in relative harmony. As early as 200 BC, Han Dynasty scholars mention that the Yangtze was teeming with baiji. But instead of hunting them, the ancient Chinese deified them. Countless poets and scholars were charmed by their human qualities—their whistling speech, their habit of standing vertically in the water when the atmospheric pressure was low, the way their young were breast-fed—and almost always perceived them as transformed maidens. Fishermen went further. They viewed them as 'goddesses of the Yangtze', believing they were standing up to warn them of storms (like many fishwives' tales this is true: low atmospheric pressure always precedes a storm). The area's folk history and art is full of references extolling the baiji as a 'galloping white horse' capable of flying across rivers and lakes with silk-gowned divinities riding on their backs.

Fishermen in Anhui and Jiangsu provinces still tell the Song Dynasty tale about the kidnapping of a beautiful young maiden. She was being ferried across the Yangtze to be sold into slavery when the boatman tried to rape her. To escape his clutches and preserve her honour she jumped into the river. The boatman jumped after her. Seeing this, God took pity on the maiden and turned her into a baiji. She became the 'goddess of the Yangtze', in charge of protecting fishermen. The rapist boatman was turned into a finless porpoise, known locally as a 'river pig'.

I am taking a boat to the Wuhan Institute of Hydrobiology to see the only baiji in captivity, meet with marine biologists and discuss how the dolphins can be saved for the price of 1,811 pairs of Fogal tights.

The Yangtze, the planet's third greatest river, is still awesome. But for the baiji it is paradise lost. Trash floats on its surface and scales the river banks. The 'azure blue' noted by sixth-century poets has turned to a 20th-century brown, a thick gravy of silt and mud caused by massive deforestation up-river and massive construction everywhere. The banks appear to be one continuous dock. Commercial culture has replaced folk art. Poetic and mythical references to the baiji have given way to the Baiji Furniture Store, the Baiji Hotel and the Baiji Beer Company. I saw many fishermen wearing black rubber boots made by the Baiji Shoe Company. But I didn't see any baiji.

Wuhan is in Hubei province. This is the centre of China and yet 5,000-tonne vessels pass by heading towards Nanjing, Shanghai and the East China Sea. Ships of 1,000 tonnes head the other way to Chongqing in Sichuan province. Scuttling between them day and night are thousands of power boats, passenger ferries, tug boats, barges and sampans. About 150 million people live on the banks of the Yangtze and the river is the country's most vital artery flowing through the provinces of Sichuan (the 'land of abundance'), Hunan (the 'granary on earth'), Jiangsu (the 'land of fish and rice') and the city of Hangzhou ('heaven on earth'). Since new laws opened the 'golden water-way' to privately owned boats in 1981, freight has tripled and will continue to grow. The dolphins, effectively blinded by the silt and disorientated by propeller noise, have died like hedgehogs on a highway.

Dams block the baiji's migratory routes to breeding grounds. Pollution is suffocating the water. The Yangtze's annual fishing haul has decreased by an estimated two thirds over the last decade. The baiji are starving and when they find food it is often toxic. An even bigger threat to the dolphins is fishermen.

When Mao launched the Great Leap Forward in the autumn of 1958 and announced, 'There is no Heavenly Emperor or Dragon King', the baiji lost its greatest protection. The goddess of the Yangtze became lunch. A leather factory opened, using the dolphins' skin as material to make bags and gloves. Its meat was sold for five cents a kilo. Its fat was bottled as a fine oil to treat burns. The species never recovered.

While famine still wracked China, the leather factory had to close: there weren't enough dolphins any more. Today, facing depleting fish stocks and no longer restrained by superstitious beliefs, Yangtze fishermen use lines threaded with vicious 15-centimetre 'rolling hooks' spaced five or eight centimetres apart. The lines are trawled from boats. A fish snags on one hook. It writhes and twists to escape and rolls into more and more hooks. Official records state that in the last 20 years, 22 baiji have died on rolling hooks. But as killing baiji is now illegal, the true number is probably many times that.

Mummified corpses of dolphins which fell victim to rolling

hooks are on display in a museum at the Wuhan Institute of Hydrobiology, their silver-grey skins slashed in the torturous death of a thousand cuts. 'Fishermen get in touch with us when they find dead baiji,' says Dr Wang Ding, an American-educated marine biologist and one of the institute's six experts in cetaceans. 'Most of the fishermen have good hearts and are very upset to see the baiji dying. They know it means the river is dying too.'

When he is feeling optimistic Wang estimates there are 150 baiji left in the Yangtze (compared with, say, 1,000 pandas in the mountains of Sichuan). He bases the numbers of reports he receives from his network of fishermen and boat operators and from what surveys the institute can afford to run. 'But,' he says, 'the numbers have now got so low, the population so separated and conditions so bad that their numbers will fall faster than ever. Time is against us because dolphins will not breed when they are under so much stress.'

How much stress? As stressed as, say, a stockbroker at 2.30 pm on Black Monday?

'Worse,' says Wang. 'Some female dolphins have died simply because of stress.'

The Chinese Government has made huge strides towards preserving baiji in recent years. Through the Chinese Academy of Sciences, the institute now has an $8 million oceanarium capable of holding baiji for research and breeding. There have been a couple of research grants and, recently, a new jeep. But money remains scarce and while the authorities offer what they can spare, their priorities remain the preservation of 1.2 billion human beings rather than 150 dolphins.

Just how scarce money is becomes clear when Dr Stephen Leatherwood, chairman of Ocean Park's Conservation Foundation, arrives from Hong Kong and Wang presents him with the institute's wish list. It includes the kind of hardware even an amateur naturalist would take for granted. 'We could do with a new pair of binoculars and some video tape . . . and camera film.'

Before he leaves, Leatherwood finds himself handing over his personal underwater camera and a wide-angle lens.

Leatherwood is here to offer his support for a plan to save the baiji. 'It is a desperate last measure,' he says. 'But it is the only hope for the survival of the species until a time when the Yangtze can support dolphins again.'

The proposal is to take five speedboats to the stretches of the Yangtze where it is hoped dolphins still exist. When, or if, a baiji is spotted the boats net the area, put the mammals in the back of the boat and race at top speed to a prepared semi-natural reserve.

The reserve, near Shizhou in Hubei province, is an ox-bow lake; a bend in the Yangtze which was eventually cut off from the river to become an isolated lake some 20 kilometres long and two kilometres wide. Here the water is cleaner, there is little construction around the edge and, most importantly, the Chinese Government has pledged to ban fishing when the first baiji arrives. The reserve has already been tested. In 1990, 10 finless porpoises (river pigs to you and me) were put in as an experiment, and so far six calves have been born. It is believed the reserve could hold up to 50 baiji for as long as the Government upholds the ban on fishing.

Two years ago the plan was just a dream, but now everything is in place. Leatherwood, who is also the chairman of the International Union for Conservation of Nature and Natural Resources' Cetacean Specialist Group, has examined and approved the reserve and pledged support from an international team of vets and dolphin handlers. The mission will take 90 days and it must start in March at the latest.

All it needs now is $3 million.

While to Hong Kong people that might seem an outrageously small price for saving the world's most ancient species of dolphin, to Wang and his colleagues in Wuhan it is an impossible sum. 'Our only hope for the future of the baiji rests with our friends abroad,' says Wang.

Before leaving, I help Leatherwood and Wang take underwater pictures of Qi Qi, a 16-year-old male baiji that had been brought to the institute in 1980, after being caught in rolling hooks and almost bleeding to death. After a few technical problems we eventually pull the camera out of the water and examine the footage. At first there is a long stretch of green nothingness but suddenly Qi Qi materialises, a dot of silver growing as he swims over from the other side of the pool. Following a little twisting and rolling and uncertain showing off, he comes right up to the camera and fixes the lens with his black bean-shaped eye:

'Is this is the first time any baiji has ever been filmed underwater?' asks Leatherwood.

'You think we can afford a camera?' says Wang.

And then it strikes me how strange it is to be present at the making of what may become the only film record of a lost species—as mysterious and compelling and pointless to future generations as an accidental video of a UFO or that black and white clip of the Abominable Snowman disappearing into the trees. I look at the screen again and Qi Qi has gone. All that is left is the green nothingness of the automatic camera searching in vain for something to focus on.

17

FLOODING AND THE VALUE OF A LIFE

WILLIAM SPENCER PERCIVAL

Two bluff English gentlemen, William Spencer Percival, a long-time resident of Shanghai, and his friend Sir Roderick Runnimede went on a shooting excursion up the Yangtze in 1887 'for health and pleasure combined'. Here is Percival's description of a visit to Hankou, with a report of a flood earlier that year, as told to him by a certain Captain Tod. Percival also airs his views on the Chinese attitude to life and death, and the cynical way in which the value of a life was sometimes determined. As Pearl Buck mentions in an earlier passage, the Chinese were traditionally fatalistic about being claimed by the river god, and accepted their fate if they fell into the river. In addition, if someone altered a drowning person's fate by saving his life, then the rescuer became responsible for that person forever. The thought of having another mouth to feed was enough to discourage most from making any rescue attempts. After 1949, however, the Communists encouraged people to take a more aggressive stance towards nature, rather than passively accepting their destiny.

On the fourth day after leaving Shanghai, we reached Hankow, and, fortune being good to us, we arrived there just in time for the races. It seems curious to talk about races in the interior of China, a sport the Chinese never heard of till it was introduced to them, like many other things, by the hateful 'foreign devil'; but here were races sure enough, by well-trained, well-fed, and well-groomed ponies, conducted and managed by a body of European residents, with the same rules and laws that govern the race-courses in the old country.

No matter what part of the world Britishers and Europeans generally find themselves landed in, there are four amusements never wanting, a race-club, a cricket-club, a lawn-tennis club, and—what seems to be as necessary as a dinner-table—a billiard-table.

On the outskirts of Hankow, nearly all the so-called Chinese houses—or, more correctly speaking, all the most miserable shanties, letting in both wind and rain—on the bank of the river, are raised well up on piles, thirty to forty feet above high-water mark; narrow wooden pathways, running between the rows of houses, and small bridges connecting these pathways where the houses are not continuous. In these wretched dwellings live some hundreds of families, to all appearance without a care, and in the greatest state of contentment. Their business, whatever it may be, is mostly connected with boats and junks, for each house possesses either a sampan or a small, home-made, flat-bottomed boat, mostly rotten and leaky, which is continually bringing its occupants to grief, and when not in use is moored to the lower end of the piles. The owners ascend and descend by means of some iron spikes, driven in alternately on either side of one of the piles.

There is in times of flood the greatest distress among the riverside population. When the water rises twenty-five, thirty, or more feet above its ordinary level, many of these piles are swept away, down come the houses, bringing their occupants with them, who are carried away in the current. Whatever becomes of the remains of these unfortunates, no one seems to know or to care; not one in twenty is recovered or ever seen again. Of course there is great lamentation among the survivors for the next week; crackers are let off by the thousand, small floating fires are set adrift on the stream to pacify the river god, gongs are beaten, and altogether the priests have a busy time.

So little value do the Chinese set upon human life in disasters of this description, which are of yearly occurrence in one part of the Empire or another, that the whole thing is soon forgotten, a fresh crowd occupies the places of the former crowd, piles are re-driven, shanties re-built, and so the new lot live their careless, contented lives till, history repeating itself, these people follow the lead of their predecessors.

In the early summer of 1887, the *Bothwell Castle*, a large ocean-going steamer of three thousand tons, was lying at anchor opposite Hankow, waiting for a cargo of tea. She had already been there two or three weeks, and was likely to remain two or three more; the weather being very bad, she made her holding secure with two anchors and a great length of cable. Before receiving her full cargo, one of these sudden floods occurred, and a week or two later I received from Captain Tod the following account of the disaster. He said:

'There had been a good deal of rain for the previous week, and we had heard that the melting snow from the eastern slopes of the mountains of Thibet was coming down the river. The river Han, which has its source in the mountains to the north of Szechuen, and runs for about eight or nine hundred miles through the provinces of Shensi and Hupeh, was also very much swollen and increasing in bulk, from the heavy rains that had lately fallen to the north-west of Hankow.

'One morning, shortly after breakfast, we heard a rumbling noise far away up the stream, and not long after an immense rush of water, like a large wave, came rolling down the river, carrying with it numbers of junks, boats, houses, trees, cattle, and I should be afraid to say how many human beings, all mixed up in the most inextricable confusion. We heard that the river Han had somewhere received an enormous and sudden flood of water, which, added to its already swollen state, had for many miles flooded the country, and was washing all before it into the Yangtze. Across our anchor-chains eight or ten junks had drifted, and were washed and piled up one over the other. It was impossible to reach them to set them adrift, and I was very much afraid the extra strain on the cables would be too much for them. Fortunately they held, thanks to the best of iron, without a flaw in any of the links.

'Numbers of junks came sweeping down with the flood, all unmanageable, many coming broad-side on across our bows, which went through them like a knife, the two parts of the junk floating past on either side of our ship. It was quite impossible to launch a boat, she would have been rolled over and swamped the moment she touched the water. With great difficulty and with much risk, we managed to save the lives of three or four dozen people; but, strange to say, some of them were very much displeased at being fished up out of the water. The Chinese said it was 'joss pidgeon', their fate, and, as the river joss had taken away their all, he had much better take themselves also. Three or four afterwards tried to jump overboard.

We put them ashore as soon as we could, and so relieved ourselves of any further responsibility.

'Our most successful haul consisted of a wooden house, nearly complete, that appeared to have been carried bodily away without breaking up. We succeeded in getting a grapnel fixed in among the timber, and so floated the house round to the stern of the steamer, where it was much protected from the current. From the house we rescued the entire family, father, mother, three children, and a couple of cats. They all recovered. Two days after, when the water went down a little, we towed the house ashore. Among others that we picked up was a woman with a small baby clinging to her. They were both apparently dead when brought on board, but were recovered by the doctor. Houses floated past with people clinging to them, some hanging on to branches of trees, while scores of corpses and the bodies of cattle seemed all over the river. Everything not drowned, everything living, both human and animal, were yelling, roaring, and screeching. All this, combined with the grating and crashing of houses, the sullen rush of water, the howling of the wind, and the swish, swish of the blinding rain, made such a pandemonium that I hope never to see again.'

If a Chinaman, or a European, on a calm and quiet day accidentally falls into deep and perfectly still water, cannot swim, and is in danger of drowning, and if a Chinaman happens to be near him in a boat, and could, without the slightest risk, and with the most infinitesimal amount of trouble to himself, save the unfortunate drowning man, he will never even attempt to do so, but will immediately paddle his boat away as quickly as he possibly can. This I have known several times to occur in the Shanghai river. Not very long ago the Spanish Consul fell into the water when stepping from his boat to the pontoon. The boatman could have saved him by simply leaning over the side of the boat and stretching out his hand. But no; instead of doing this very simple and natural thing, he paddled his boat a short distance higher up the river, and went ashore to the consul's house, more than a mile away, to tell his wife that her husband was drowned. The poor man's body was found three days afterwards within a dozen yards of the place where he fell in. Such is the value a Celestial sets upon human life.

But supposing a European accidentally kills a Chinaman, then we get quite another view of the matter. The Celestials in such a case appear to find it difficult to set a high enough estimate on the life of the most miserable coolie. The *Taotai* [chief official in the district] is appealed to; consuls, judges, and lawyers are solicited for their assistance; the whole machinery of the criminal law is brought into active operation; the unfortunate man is arrested, indicted, tried, sentenced, and finally locked up for so many years that a very big slice is cut out of his three-score years and ten. . . .

Some years ago, I was driving a skittish horse through the Hongkew quarter of Shanghai, when the natives, seeing its restless disposition, would insist upon running across the road, just under his nose—a common trick of theirs, as they consider the nearer they can escape being run down by a horse the better luck will follow them for the remainder of the day. The boatmen and junkmen have much the same idea, and frequently run their boats across the bows of a passing streamer, occasionally getting sunk. When this does happen,—which the Celestials generally manage shall happen with an old and rotten junk,—off rush the owners to one of the members of the legal profession; the value of the lost junk is doubled, her cargo trebled, several lives are stated to have been lost—generally quite fictitiously—but a high value is placed on each man's life, and a very high sum-total is demanded from the unfortunate steamer. The matter ends in a long, costly, and vexatious law-suit, the steamer in some way or other being always found to be in fault, and in five cases out of six, ultimately appealing to the judicial committee of the Privy Council for redress at a great expense.

18

BEACON FIRE

CHEN SHIXU

Chen Shixu was born in 1948 in Nanchang, the capital of Jiangxi Province. After graduating from junior middle school in 1964, he was sent to work in the Yangtze port of Jiujiang, a busy centre for shipping goods from all around nearby Poyang Lake. One of the worst Yangtze floods of this century was in 1983; this story was written not long afterwards, and portrays a community who are certainly not resigned to whatever the river may bring, but who fight back with all their might.

A young village girl, Qiuxia, is dazzled by the handsome city boy, Li Xin, who has been sent to the countryside to help with flood prevention. Entranced, not only by his diving skills and good looks, but also by the idea of moving to the city, Qiuxia does her best to win him. Although the ambitious Li Xin is flattered, he has no intention of marrying a country girl and does not commit himself. But ultimately his behaviour in a crisis disillusions Qiuxia, and the story ends with her setting off to see Chunfu, the local boy to whom her parents have betrothed her.

Typical of much post-1949 literature, this story has a clear moral, contrasting the simple, upright peasant with the talented but morally dishonest city dweller.

The water level was higher than in 1954. Sand and stone were being carried day and night to Yangqiao Dyke, which had already collapsed in a few places. Chunfu and his boat had been sent here to help while all available labour power reinforced the dyke and old men and women patrolled it, watching out for new dangers. Li was put in charge of the patrol.

It continued to pour and the murky waters of the river were less than a metre from the top of the dyke. The wind effortlessly whipped the water into waves, occasionally splashing across the dyke onto the other side. It was like walking on deck in a stormy sea and the thought that the water could crush you like a hand closing round an eggshell terrified everyone. . . .

The willow trees by the dyke where they used to wade were now almost completely submerged. The flood peak had interrupted their life, calm and rhythmic so far. Qiuxia often didn't see Li for days. They were unable to spend time together anymore.

When Qiuxia came off patrol at midnight, she ran into Li making the rounds with his torch. 'I'll go with you.' She waded in with a splash.

The torch could hardly pierce the dense night. Rain poured down while the river lapping at the dyke kept splashing on them. The ferocity of nature had increased several fold in the night. 'I'm terrified.' Qiuxia leaned closer, huddling against him.

Li took her arm. He was grateful for her company in this dark night. He didn't want to patrol the dangerous dyke all by himself.

They stopped at an empty watchhouse. There was no one out on the dyke. 'Damn it,' Li cursed. It often happened this way. The first shift had already left and the second shift was late.

'What's that?' Qiuxia cried, as Li shone his torch. She grabbed his hand and steadied the light on the suspicious spot.

About ten metres from the dyke a 50 cm column of water was gushing out of the ground. Then they saw water bubbling up in several places in a ten-metre area.

'That looks like it's going to go.'

Li's head throbbed. 'Give the signal, quick.'

But they found nothing in the watchhouse. No gongs, drums or guns.

Just then came the sound of a mud slide. A section of the dyke nearest the water columns collapsed and water rushed in though the breach.

'Gracious!' Qiuxia exclaimed, covering her eyes in horror.

'Light a bonfire, quick,' Li took her hand and ran towards a pile of firewood behind them. Each dangerous section of the dyke had wood, so a fire could be lit as a warning if necessary.

The matches went out one by one. Once or twice the straw caught fire but before the wood could catch the wind blew it out. 'Damn it,' Li swore. He was trembling.

'Wait for me.' Holding the flashlight Qiuxia suddenly remembered that there was a pumping station nearby where there was some diesel oil. She scrambled down the dyke.

Li stood alone in the darkness. The rumbling water pouring through the continuously widening breach carried across to his frightened ears. He remembered the stories he'd heard: The water could make pits a dozen metres deep as it poured in. If you fell into it there would be nothing left of you. He felt limp, as if the dyke was giving way beneath him.

When Qiuxia returned with a bucket of diesel oil, Li was not there. Panic-stricken, she shouted his name.

Li replied from a long distance. 'Come quickly, Qiuxia, we haven't got time to light the fire, it's too dangerous.'

Qiuxia suddenly seemed to hear nothing, as though the world had fallen silent.

'Go, you go as quickly as you can,' she said quietly. She felt a tenderness she'd never felt before, like a mother blessing her son.

Unhurried, she turned around, poured oil on to the wood and, standing with her back to the wind, struck a match. She waited to make sure that the fire was big enough to be seen in the very far distance before she ran off.

At daybreak, the flooded Yangqiao Dyke was very calm. The storm, which had been abusing its power for so many days, had stopped as if in response to a powerful order. It had seemed as if its sole aim had been to demolish this insignificant village.

Li was wounded. He had courageously thrown himself into

evacuating the villagers when he ran back, moving grain and property until a brick from a falling wall had hit him on the head. Now he was lying calmly in the watchhouse which he and his group had built when they arrived. He was waiting to be taken to the county hospital and his friends were gathered around him.

The fact was that the two local men on patrol had discovered the impending breaches. Having forgotten to bring their gongs and drums they had tried to fire a gun but discovered that the firing pin was broken. Seeing that the situation was hopeless, they had raced back home to salvage their own belongings. They would be severely punished. In comparison Li was particularly brave. Everyone showed great respect and gratitude towards this outstanding young man.

'We'll report what you have done so you'll get an award,' said his colleagues from the county, exhausted and haggard. 'That was a fine thing, young man, we're proud of you.' They smiled with cracked lips. This time they were sincere, there wasn't an ounce of sarcasm.

Suddenly, an anxious Qiuxia appeared. She dashed over to Li and squatted down beside him.

'Where were you hurt? Is it bad?' Disregarding the people around him, she leaned over Li's bandaged head.

'No,' he said softly, and turned away in embarrassment. His colleagues tactfully retreated.

After they had left, Li took her hand in his and asked, 'How are you?'

'Fine,' Qiuxia sobbed, her head lowered.

'I've been thinking about you. I was so afraid that something might happen to you.' Li reached out and smoothed her hair.

Qiuxia trembled.

'I'll be taken away soon, I want to say something to you before I leave.'

She nodded.

'You've been wanting to go to the city, haven't you? I can help you.'

Her face burned. 'Don't talk about that now. Everything will be fine provided you get well,' she said, hoping that he would go on talking.

'But you must promise me something,' Li rubbed her hand.

'Tell me what you want, I'll promise anything.'

'Really?'

'Have I ever lied to you?'

'Fine, it's something quite simple. Everyone thinks I was the one who lit the signal fire. I hope . . . you'll say the same. Will you do that as a witness?'

'What?' Her eyes opened wide and she turned pale. She pulled her hand away and put in on her knee. 'Was that what you wanted to tell me?'

'You won't do that for me?' Li's mouth twitched pitifully. 'Please, Qiuxia. . . . You know I'm still on probation in the Party. Besides, besides . . . I like you.'

'I promise.' She said slowly and quietly, and let Li take her hand again.

Li secretly heaved a sigh of relief. At the same time he felt sad, as if he had lost something. 'She's really infatuated with me, it'll be hard to refuse her now. What bad luck. Damn the flood and damn this rotten village,' he swore to himself.

As Li was boarding the boat after breakfast, he was surprised that Qiuxia had not come to see him off.

She had boarded another boat at another place. She was on her way to Qili Dyke to see Chunfu.

19

DRUNK SONG

LU YU (1125–1209)

For Chinese poets, travelling along the Yangtze often brings sad thoughts, both of 'history's ups and downs' and of personal setbacks. Wine enhances the melancholy mood. Here is Lu Yu again, further upriver on the same voyage in 1170. This was written while he passed through Hubei, once part of the kingdom of Chu (Ch'u) during the Warring States period in the third century BC. Lu Yu is reminded of how the kingdom was conquered by the first man to unify all of China, Emperor Qin Shi Huangdi.

The sorrows of Chu would have been well known to any Chinese reader. Qu Yuan (Ch'u Yuan), one of China's greatest poets and a minister of Chu, advocated uniting with another state to fight against Qin Shi Huangdi, but his advice was ignored and he was banished from the capital. In 278 BC, on hearing of the fall of Chu, he drowned himself in the Miluo River near Dongting Lake. Memories of Qu Yuan are inextricably linked with the Yangtze. He was born near the riverside town of Zigui above Yichang, and there is a shrine to his memory there.

Old boatman unsteps the mast, brakes it against green rocks;
drops of water pock the sandy shore, foot after foot of stains.
Autumn's gone but here by the Yangtze no foliage
withers or falls;
oak leaves are thick and shiny, maple leaves red.
Men of Ch'u from times past have had many sorrows;
even now, songs they sing walking the road bring a twinge of
    pain.
Wild flowers blue and purple—gather them by the fistful;
valley fruit green and red—now just right for picking.
On the way I found some wine, watery but still not bad;
at river's edge, getting drunk as I please, no regret in the world.
A thousand years of history's ups and downs here before my eyes;
this great bustling border, the river soaked in evening hues.

A hungry swan, wings drooping, skims over the boat;
in its heart too, it must feel the same sadness as I.
Three times I thump the gunwale, can't shake this depression
  off!
The moon brightens—now it shines on my crooked crow-black
  hat.

20

THE TRIALS OF TRAVEL

AUGUSTUS R. MARGARY

In August 1874, young Augustus Margary, a British Consular officer, set out from Shanghai on a perilous journey. His task was to travel to the Burmese border to meet a British mission there and to conduct them through China back to Shanghai. Margary's attendant, 'the invaluable Leila', was probably an Indian Sikh.

At Hankou Margary left his comfortable steamer for a small boat, and was, as he describes it, 'plunged into darkness for six months'. He describes in his journal the first leg of his journey beyond Hankou in early September; the rest is taken from a letter to his parents written on 11 September 1874 when he was 130 miles (209 kilometres) beyond Hankou.

My preparations were completed for starting on the 3rd, but unfortunately an attack of illness obliged me to put off the departure till next day. The boat was one of those commonly called a mandarin boat, long and narrow, and divided into five or six compartments which ran the whole length of the craft, the centre being occupied with a somewhat wider and neater space, fitted with chairs and tables, and suited for the reception of guests. Each compartment contained a couple of low berths, one on each side of the passage running down the middle. But as a Chinaman's average stature falls far short of an Englishman's proportions, I found it necessary to lengthen the bedside of my compartment by removing the dividing panel. A similar precaution had to be taken with regard to the floor, whereof the boards were lowered fully six inches, to save my head from the pains and penalties of trying to unroof the not too substantial top.

Letter to his parents: I have been a whole week away from my fellow kind, for I cannot look upon the Chinese always in the light of brothers, yet my journey is not fairly commenced. For on the second night of my sojourn in this boat, a messenger from the Consulate overtook me with important covers enclosing a telegram from Calcutta which stops my farther progress. As there are neither railways nor telegraph to Pekin, at least a fortnight must elapse before Mr. Wade's decision can reach me. I cannot describe the discomfort and annoyance this delay causes me. My boat is not large, and the thermometer has frequently been over 90. I have as few comforts as possible, and the plainest fare. Movement alone can make up for my miseries, and I am obliged to 'slow down'. I had no direct orders, so the strong current decided me to push on to the Tungting Lake and there await instructions. If I am to go back, the rapid current will carry me down in a brace of shakes; and if I am to go on, I shall have saved time by surmounting so much of the Yangtsze as forms part of my course. In order to eke out the time, we have gone very short stages, and hope to have as few days of actual halt as possible. Our last stage afforded me the delicious surprise of a clear stream running down from the hills, so I remained there all yesterday and bathed morning and evening. The sensation of a free swim after being pent up in the boat was something transcendent. The people in this part of the country have seen very little of foreigners, and I have frequently to bear the annoyance of mobbing and the impertinent cries of children, when at a safe distance.

The clouds have been gracious today and staved off the power of the sun, and the thermometer only reached 85. I catch cold now at 83. The other day a sudden thunderstorm sent the temperature down from 92 to 82 in a quarter of an hour. I was delighted, but caught cold of course on the spot; but in spite of this and a grand mass of clouds which seemed to cover the ends of the earth, I was soon being broiled again at 98. It is an incomprehensible sky. . . .

18th.—Here I have been six days, this is the seventh, waiting orders. I wish I had scattered the telegram to the winds and gone on; they could not have stopped me. However, I can easily make up my six or seven days, as I have chosen a shorter route than we were aware of, and saved both time and expense. Stopping here all this time would have been intolerable but for two or three circumstances. First of all there is a most delicious stretch of scrubby downs extending some distance, and as I have my boat anchored right under them I am able to go out very often and have a shot at the pheasants and grouse which I occasionally find in this excellent cover. Secondly, a thunderstorm and rain, which confined me to the boat for three days out of the six, although I managed twice between showers, reduced the temperature from 97 to 85, which was a boon in spite of its severity. Thirdly, I am jolly strong and regaining health rapidly. I think I told you how much I had been pulled down by the Shanghae summer. I lost sixteen pounds in a month, and I believe if I had not been moved I should have drifted into a typhoid. When I left Hankow I was scarcely well enough to undertake such a journey, but a course of tonic has rapidly restored me.

The people here are new to the sight of a foreigner, and my first experiences were uncomfortable, to say the least. It so happened that a convoy of recruits for the war with Japan were on leave ashore, and these young braves with the rollicking devilry that characterises Chinese soldiers stirred up a hubbub which became mighty annoying to me. Along the whole route of about half-a-mile from my boat to the mandarin's wretched abode, my chair was preceded, surrounded, and followed by a screaming, shouting demoniacal mob, crying 'Ha! ha! here's a foreign devil; beat the foreign devil'. I began to feel sorry I had left my thick stick behind. They got more troublesome, and seized the poles of my chair, the rudest vehicle of the kind I ever saw, to have a better look, thereby causing it to oscillate on the shoulders of the two bearers. I was meditating with a smile on my face whether or not I should spoil the countenances of one or two of them, when a kick delivered by my attendant, the invaluable Leila, right in a fellow's chest, sent him reeling among the crowd and made me laugh outright; the rest soon cleared off.

We reached the official house, and the rabble, as usual with Chinese, burst in, and were spectators of my interview with the mandarin, who proved to be a quiet, agreeable man. We got on very well. He sent two of his lictors to conduct me back safely, and they certainly fulfilled their office well in licking the common herd. On arriving at the boat I harangued them on their want of politeness. They listened in silence, and most of them went quietly away. I have not been insulted since, but walk about and shoot and chat with all I meet in the most amicable spirit, and they are as civil to me as possible. It is the nature of Chinamen to give in to anything which asserts its superiority. A kick and a few words in his own tongue telling him he is an ignorant boor will make a common Chinaman worship you. Singly or in small groups, they are the pink of civility, but a mob is rather dangerous. I shall probably have to pass through many similar scenes on my long journey.

Alas for poor Margary. There is a tragic post-script to this letter, as in the end, sang-froid was not enough to save his life. Although he reached the Burmese border and successfully met the delegation, he was murdered soon afterwards in the wilds of Yunnan, when he went ahead on reconnaissance for the group. Admiral Tolley's account of Margary's death in his book Yangtze Patrol, *is probably myth, but is too good a story to omit. Apparently Margary had left his sedan chair and was walking some distance behind it in order to get some exercise. Meanwhile, he had put his dog in his place, to save the pet's feet. According to Tolley, 'On entering the domain of a rather important magistrate, the procession was greeted by this dignitary, who, assuming that the impressive chair with four bearers and drawn curtains contained the august personage of the expedition's leader, bowed low as it passed. When the magistrate saw Margary afoot and learned that he had just made obeisances to a dog, there were clearly only two options; either take an overdose of opium and join his ancestors, or see that—the least objectionable from his viewpoint—Margary joined his.'*

21

THE RED CLIFF

SU DONGPO (1037–1101)

*During his time in Huangzhou, where he was sent in disgrace to serve
as a lowly assistant commissioner, Su Dongpo often visited a nearby
cliff overlooking the Yangtze. He mistakenly identified it as the site of
the famous battle of the Red Cliff in AD 208, during the Three Kingdoms
period.*

*Cao Meng-de (Ts'ao Meng-te), author of the verse quoted by Su's guest
in the first part of the following essay, is usually known as Cao Cao
(Ts'ao Ts'ao), leader of one of the three rival kingdoms. He and his officers
were feasting on board ship, when he heard a raven cawing in the night
as it flew. He was told that because the moon was shining so brightly
the bird believed it was day and had left its perch. In high spirits, Cao
Cao immediately composed a song, which included this verse about the
raven. But one of his followers remarked that these words were ominous
and unlucky. Enraged, Cao Cao killed him on the spot for his audacity. The
next day, however, falling into Zhou's (Chou Lang's) trap, all of Cao
Cao's ships and men went up in flames at the battle of the Red Cliff.*

*Today the place is known as Dongpo's Red Cliff to distinguish it from
the actual battle site.*

PART ONE
In the autumn of the year Jên Hsü [AD 1082], when the seventh moon was just on the wane, I, the son of Su, was drifting
with a friend in a boat below the Red Cliff. A fresh breeze was gently passing, the surface of the water was becalmed. Raising my
winecup, I asked my friend to recite a poem to the bright moon,
singing the verses of the Chaste Maiden.

After a little while the moon rose over the eastern hills, roaming
amidst the stars. Like dewdrops glistening over the river, her
beams merged water into sky. We let our boat float along, sailing
over the vast expanse, fascinated by the sensation that we were
riding on air, with the wind as our chariot, bound we knew not

whither. Light and airy, it seemed that we had forsaken the world, and were flying unfettered through the air like the Immortals. And so we drank our wine with much rejoicing, and, beating time on the side of the boat, we sang as follows:

'With cinnamon boat and orchid oars,
We pierce the moonbeams,
ascending the stream of light.
Impenetrable are my inmost thoughts—
Illustrious Men of Old, in what corner
of the heavens do ye dwell?'

My guest accompanied the song on his flute. The notes poured forth like sobs of regret or longing, querulous and plaintive, far-floating as an endless thread. They would arouse the dragons lurking in their dark caverns. And the boatwoman, who was a widow, wept.

Overcome with a feeling of sorrow, I drew my coat around me, and, sitting up, asked my guest for an interpretation of his song. He replied:

'The moon is bright, the stars are few,
The raven flies towards the south.'

Is not this the poem of Ts'ao Mêng-tê? To the west we see Hsia-K'ou, to the east Wu-Ch'ang, where mountain and river, covered with dense jungle, intermingle. Was it not there that Mêng-tê suffered at the hands of Chou Lang?

'When about to vanquish Chingchow at Chiang-Ling, he went downstream towards the east. His fleet from stem to stern covered a thousand *li*; his pennons and banners filled the sky. As he approached Chiang-Ling he poured out wine, and with his lance lying across his saddle, composed this poem. He was undoubtedly a hero in his day, but where is he now?

'You and I have fished and gathered fuel on the river islets. We have consorted with the crayfish, we have befriended the deer. Together we have sailed our skiff, frail as a leaf; in close companionship we have drunk wine from the gourd. We pass through this world like two gnats in a husk of millet on a boundless ocean!

I grieve that life is but a moment in time, and envy the endless current of the Great River. Would that I might clasp to me some flying sprite and forever wander with him! Would that I might embrace the lightsome moon for all eternity! But I realise that this is no sudden attainment, and so commit these dying notes to the sad breezes.'

'But do you understand,' I asked him, 'the water and the moon? The former passes by, but has never gone. The latter waxes and wanes but does not really increase or diminish. For, if we regard this question from the viewpoint of impermanence, then the universe cannot last for a twinkling of an eye. If, on the other hand, we consider it from the aspect of permanence, then you and I, together with all matter, are imperishable. Why then this yearning?

'Moreover, everything in this world has its owner. If it does not belong to me, not one single atom of it can I take. But, the fresh breeze over the river, the silvery moon amongst the hills—things which become music to the ear and colour to the eye—these we may take without hindrance, enjoy without cessation. They are the creations of the Deity—neither finite nor hidden away. And so you and I are delighting in them together.'

My guest laughed as he washed his cup and refilled it with wine. And when our repast was finished, with cups and plates lying about in disorder, we laid ourselves down in the boat. For we had not noticed that dawn was already appearing in the eastern sky.

PART TWO

In the same year, when the tenth moon was full, I left the Hall of Snow with the intention of returning to Lin Kao. Accompanied by two friends, I passed over the hill slope of yellow mud already covered by frost and dew. With the trees stripped of their leaves, our shadows fell upon the ground. Above we could see the bright moon. In sheer delight, we sang in chorus as we walked along. Then, with a sigh I said, 'Here we have guests and no wine. Should we have wine, there would be no viands. A gleaming moon and a fresh breeze, what should we not do on a wonderful night like this?'

One of my friends replied, 'This very evening I pulled in my net and caught a fish, large-mouthed and small-scaled, in appearance like the carp of the Sung River. But where are we to get wine?'

Accordingly, we went back to devise some plan with his wife. 'Oh!' said the good woman, 'I have a peck of wine long stored away in case you wanted it.' And so, carrying wine and fish, we set out once more towards the Red Cliff.

The stream rushed roaring by through riven cliffs that towered a thousand feet. Lofty hills dwarfed the moon, while through the falling waters there jutted rocks. How many days and months had passed, and yet I could scarcely recognise again the river and the hills!

Gathering up my gown I climbed the precipitous crag. I thrust through the thick undergrowth, and crouched upon the Tiger and Leopard Rock. I scaled the Horned Dragon, reaching up to the hawk's perilous eyrie, and looked down upon the dim temple of Fêng I far below. Now, my two friends had been unable to follow.

Suddenly there arose a deafening roar, long-drawn, so that trees and bushes trembled, hills thundered and valleys echoed, and the wind whipped the waters into a raging torrent. Utterly disconsolate and awestruck, I became too depressed to remain. So I returned and got into the boat which we let loose into mid-stream, allowing it to go where it would, while we rested.

It was nearly midnight; and on every side was profound silence. It chanced that a solitary crane flew across the river from the east, its wings like chariot wheels, feathers like fine white silk. With a long piercing scream it overtook our boat, and passed over towards the west.

After a little while, my guests departed and I slept. And I dreamed that a Taoist priest, with feathery robe fluttering like an Immortal, passed by Lin Kao. Bowing low to me, he said, 'Has your visit to the Red Cliff been pleasant?' I asked him his name but he lowered his head without replying. 'Alas!' I cried. 'Now I understand. Did you not last night fly over me and scream?' The Taoist priest looked at me and smiled. Waking up in alarm, I opened the door and looked out. But I could see no one.

Battle Strategies

Although over 1,500 years apart, the heroes of the next two extracts faced a similar problem: lack of equipment. One lacked arrows, the other boats. Against all odds, both invented ingenious tactics to overcome their difficulties.

22

K'UNG MING BORROWS SOME ARROWS

LUO GUANZHONG

No anthology on the Yangtze would be complete without an extract from the fourteenth-century novel Romance of the Three Kingdoms *by Luo Guanzhong (Lo Kuan-chung). This epic, a mixture of fact and legend, is based on the true story of the struggle for power lasting from AD 220 to 265 after the fall of the Han dynasty. The Han empire had broken down into three main rival kingdoms: Wei, the area of north China, ruled by the villain of the novel, the Machiavellian and ruthless Cao Cao (Ts'ao Ts'ao); Shu, which is now Sichuan, was led by Liu Bei (Liu Pei), the novel's hero and a claimant to the Han throne; and Wu, the lower Yangtze region, was controlled by Sun Quan (Sun Ch'uan), who switched from one side to the other. Zhou Yu (Chou Yü) is one of Liu Bei's generals, and Kong Ming (K'ung Ming), one of his best strategists.*

Just before this extract begins, Kong Ming has proved himself so uncannily clever that his superior officer Zhou Yu feels jealous and threatened. 'We absolutely cannot allow this man to stay. I am determined to kill him,' he says in alarm. Zhou's subordinate Lu Su objects that if Zhou murders such a brilliant asset to his own army, he will be a laughing stock in Cao Cao's eyes. But Zhou replies, 'No, I can do it openly and legitimately. Wait and see.'

The next day in the assembly of generals, Chou Yü asked K'ung-ming: 'When we engage Ts'ao Ts'ao in battle, crossing arms on the river routes, what weapon should be our first choice?'
K'ung-ming: 'On the Yangtze, the bow and arrow.'
Chou Yü: 'Precisely. But we happen to be short of arrows. Dare I trouble you, master, to take responsibility for the production of one hundred thousand shafts? This is a public service which you would favor me by not declining.'
K'ung-ming: 'Whatever you assign I will strive to achieve. Dare I ask by what time you will require them?'

Chou Yü: 'Can you finish in ten days?'

K'ung-ming: 'Ts'ao's army will arrive any moment. If we wait ten days, it will spoil everything.'

Chou Yü: 'How many days do you estimate you need, master?'

K'ung-ming: 'It will take only three before I can respectfully deliver the arrows.'

Chou Yü: 'There is no room for levity in the army.'

K'ung-ming: 'Dare I trifle with the chief commander? I beg to submit my oath in writing. Then if I fail to finish in three days, I deserve the maximum punishment.'

This elated Chou Yü, who accepted the document.

K'ung-ming: 'On the third day from tomorrow, send five hundred small craft to the river to transport the arrows.'

After K'ung-ming left, Chou Yü said to Lu Su: 'I will have the artisans delay things intentionally, just to be sure that he misses the appointed time. But go to him and bring me back information.'

Lu Su went to K'ung-ming, who said: 'I *did* tell you not to speak of this to Chou Yü. He is determined to kill me. I never dreamed you would refuse to cover for me. And now today he actually pulled this thing on me! How am I supposed to produce one hundred thousand arrows in three days? You're the only one who can save me.'

Lu Su: 'You brought this on yourself. How could I save you?'

K'ung-ming: 'I need you to lend me twenty vessels, with a crew of thirty for each. On the boats I want curtains of black cloth to conceal at least a thousand bales of straw that should be lined up on both sides. But you must not let Chou Yü know about it this time, or my plan will fail.' And Lu Su obliged him, and even held his tongue.

The boats were ready, but neither on the first day nor on the second did K'ung-ming make any move. On the third day he secretly sent for Lu Su: 'I called you especially to go with me to get the arrows.' And linking the vessels with long ropes, they set out for the north shore and Ts'ao Ts'ao's fleet.

That night tremendous fogs rolled over the heavens, and the river mists were impenetrable. People could not see their companions who were directly in front of them. K'ung-ming urged his boats on.

From the ode 'Great Mists Overhanging the Yangtze':

Everywhere the fog, stock still:
Not even a cartload can be spotted.
All-obscuring grey vastness,
Massive, without horizon.
Whales hurtle over waves, and
Dragons plunge and spew up mist.
East they lose the shore at Chai Sang,
South the mountains of Hsia K'ou.
Are we returning to the state without form—
To undivided Heaven and Earth?

At the fifth watch the boats were already nearing Ts'ao Ts'ao's river stations. K'ung-ming had the vessels lined up in single file, their prows pointed west. Then the crews began to volley with their drums and roar with their voices.

Lu Su was alarmed: 'What do you propose if Ts'ao's men make a coordinated sally?'

K'ung-ming smiled: 'I would be very surprised if Ts'ao Ts'ao dared plunge into this heavy a fog. Let us attend to the wine and take our pleasure. When the fog breaks we will return.'

In his encampment, Ts'ao Ts'ao listened to the drumming and shouting. His new naval advisers rushed back and forth with bulletins. Ts'ao sent down an order: 'The fog is so heavy it obscures the river. Enemy forces have arrived from nowhere. There must be an ambush. Our men must make absolutely no reckless movements. But let the archers fire upon the enemy at random.'

The naval advisers, fearing that the forces of the Southland were about to breach the camp, ordered the firing to commence. Soon over ten thousand men were concentrating their fire toward the center of the river, and the arrows came down like rain. K'ung-ming ordered the boats to reverse direction and press closer to the shore to take the arrows, while the crews continued their drumming and shouting.

When the sun rose high, dispersing the fog, K'ung-ming ordered the boats to rush homeward. The grass bales in gunny-sacks bristled with arrow shafts. And K'ung-ming had each crew shout its thanks to the Chancellor for the arrows as it passed. By the time the reports reached Ts'ao Ts'ao, the light craft borne on swift currents were beyond overtaking, and Ts'ao Ts'ao was left with the agony of having played the fool.

K'ung-ming said to Lu Su: 'Each boat has some five or six thousand arrows. So without costing the Southland the slightest effort, we have gained over one hundred thousand arrows, which tomorrow we can return to Ts'ao's troops—to their decided discomfort.'

Lu Su: 'You are supernatural! How did you know there would be such a fog today?'

K'ung-ming: 'A military commander must be versed in the patterns of the Heavens, must recognize the advantages of the terrain, must appreciate the odd chance, must understand the changes of the weather, must examine the maps of the formations, must be clear about the disposition of the troops—otherwise he is a mediocrity! Three days ago I calculated today's fog. That's why I took a chance on the three-day limit. Chou Yü gave me ten days, but neither materials nor workmen, and plainly meant for my flagrant offense to kill me. But my fate is linked to Heaven. How could Chou Yü succeed?' When Chou Yü received Lu Su's report, he was amazed and resigned. 'I cannot begin to approach his uncanny machinations and subtle calculations!'

23

CROSSING THE YANGTZE

NOEL BARBER

One of the famous incidents of the Long March, the Communists' epic trek across China pursued by the Nationalists, was how the Red Army slipped across the river in its wild upper reaches in 1935, thwarting attempts to keep them bottled up south of the Yangtze.

Fourteen years later in 1949, the Communists were to cross the lower Yangtze in triumph. This time it was they who were on the attack, facing a corrupt and demoralized army. Yet although the Communists outnumbered Chiang Kai-Shek's forces, strategically Chiang had the advantage. He had modern gunboats and aircraft ready to defend the river, while the Communists had no boats at all, and had never fought a battle on water before.

Journalist Noel Barber describes how Mao and his generals won over and trained the local river people to help carry out one of the most daring and cleverly planned attacks of the civil war. It was a sort of Dunkirk in reverse, as Mao's armies crossed the river in a flotilla of every imaginable kind of craft, from large junks and bamboo rafts, especially built to carry tanks, down to tiny sampans and fishing boats.

M ao Tse-tung was now poised in force on the north banks of the Yangtze, yet one problem remained to be solved before he could attack the enemy. Throughout the years he had fought them on land. Now he had to mount his first waterborne assault against the Nationalist forces which included naval units he could never hope to match. He needed an armada of boats of all kinds—and the men to sail them.

Always a man of broad vision, Mao Tse-tung in his planning had scorned the first tentative advice of his commanders to make just two or three powerful thrusts opposite Nanking, Chinkiang and Kiangyin which lay between the capital and Shanghai. Instead he decided to attack simultaneously along a 400-mile front using four field armies—more than a million battle-trained troops. Two armies would attack on the 200-mile front between Nanking and Shanghai, where the Yangtze flowed from west to east until it reached the sea. It was along the south bank in this area that the Nationalists had built their strongest defences. The Yangtze, however, does not run from west to east along its entire course. From the city of Kiukiang, hundreds of miles to the south of Nanking, the river pursues a north-easterly course, turning right, so to speak, when it reaches Nanking: thus these two stretches of the river form an obtuse angle.

Mao had decided that he would, in the months of preparation, bluff the Nationalists into expecting a major offensive across the river between Nanking and Shanghai, but in fact he concentrated huge armies around Angking, South of Nanking, where he planned to cross the river and land on what was in that area the east bank. He could then race eastwards, well south of the Nationalists on the south bank between Nanking and Shanghai, and cut them off. At the same time he could march in a north-easterly direction to positions south of Shanghai where his forces would link up with troops which had crossed the Yangtze near the capital.

Strategically it was brilliant, but even if Mao could find enough boats, the Yangtze was rarely less than a mile wide, and where were the sailors versed in the vexing local currents and shifting shoals that had always made the river so dangerous to cross? To allow a soldier to manœuvre a frail sampan through currents of which he was ignorant was unthinkable—or was it? General Chen Yi had once boasted that given good instructors he could train a peasant to be a soldier in six weeks. Now he suggested that, given the help of skilled local river-dwellers, he could turn a soldier into a sailor in two weeks.

First the local peasants who lived along the north bank of the Yangtze had to be recruited. It was not difficult. Until a few weeks previously the peasants and fishermen had been caught up in the Chiang regime, in which landowners had kept them under the lash. Because of transport difficulties, the peasants south of Nanking might be starving while those on the north bank of the Yangtze were producing, in a good harvest, more than they needed. It was always the long-suffering peasants who paid, while the wealthy manipulators of agricultural produce increased their fortunes.

Yet this northern bank was peopled by sturdy men and women who asked only to be allowed to carry on living as they had done for centuries. The Communists, most of whom had come from the far north, discovered a life of luxury and richness they had never seen before. There was fish for all—caught by the teams of cormorants perched on the gunwales of the fishermen's boats, who darted for their prey but were never allowed to swallow it because of the rings fastened round their necks. Old forts dotted the river banks, giving better shelter than makeshift tents. Every possible inch of the marshy land, laced with inlets and dikes, was cultivated by women, their black hair coiled and shining with oil. Behind the swamp bamboo groves provided perfect camouflage for guns. Fir, cinnamon and camphor trees shielded many of the inland villages; others were surrounded by groves of mulberry trees carefully protected to feed the silkworms. To the men from the north, it seemed to be a magical country, with ducks and squealing pigs in every village, with lush crops of wheat and beans grown in one season and rice and tea in the hot summer.

The first thing the Communists did was to expel the landlords and give every peasant an acre and a half of land. Local political commissars made certain that it was distributed fairly. This was the first time any of the villagers in the area had achieved even a simple form of security in their farm holdings; but even more important, in a way—since man always dreams of escaping his bonds—it was the first time any of them had been influenced by that most magical of words, 'progress'. The commissars instituted the first 'schools'. At this stage they did not bother with the children so much as with the adults. Using a method that had been successful elsewhere, the Communists chose men who knew, perhaps, 500 basic Chinese characters, and made them teach their fellows 5 characters a night. Their pupils would then pass on their knowledge to their children.

From every swirling creek, from every hidden inlet along hundreds of miles of this north bank of the river, a motley flotilla of river boats slowly emerged. Many had been holed by the retreating Nationalists the previous autumn. Almost all had been hidden in the reeds and swamps and the scrub where water and land met.

The vessels ranged from junks that could hold a hundred men, or sampans that might take a dozen, to narrow fishing boats in which there was barely room for three or four to crouch. Every one was pressed into service and repaired. At the same time local peasants started constructing bamboo rafts big enough to transport tanks, while long snakes of landing craft which could hold small vehicles made their way slowly from Tsinan, hundreds of miles to the north. These vehicles had originally been captured from the Japanese, and were now transported on China's famous Grand Canal which ran all the way to the north shore of the Yangtze.

Along the river bank there was the intense activity and training that precede a great offensive. One Communist general, Liu Chen, remembered later how 'every road leading to the Yangtze was alive with a continuous movement of guns, armoured cars, cavalry "like a gust of wind", while behind them thousands of peasants arrived with masts, ropes, sails, anchors, which they had hidden from the Nationalists. Some pushed wheelbarrows, some carried stretchers, others used their buffalo to pull carts towards the river and its forest of masts.' Liu had made his headquarters in the small village of San Chiang Ying, on the banks of a typical Yangtze creek known locally as the Sim Ni Mu Ho. Behind the creek lay dozens of boats, all hidden in reeds or fingers of water shaded by trees. But they had been immobilised by peasant farmers and fishermen who had dammed the waterways to provide irrigation channels, so that General Liu found many of the craft landlocked. There were thirty-seven of them, mostly in good condition: he had to get them to the river somehow.

There was only one way: 5,000 troops stripped to the waist, armed only with spades and hoes, worked for 13 days and nights, in shifts, to break down the dams and then dig a connecting channel 50 yards long. Women carried the earth away in wicker baskets, while men shored up the banks with huge squares of criss-crossed bamboo plastered with stones or earth. When the canal was finished the boats were towed to hiding places under trees near the river.

East of Nanking, a retired railway engineer called Fein Rui-lai invented a remarkable contraption. Using laths of thin wood, he constructed a kind of miniature water wheel powered by a hand crank. When this was fastened to a boat, even those unversed in the art of handling a sampan could turn the handle and increase speed noticeably. Soon every village was making water wheels, and hundreds were ready by the middle of April—not only to increase the boats' speed, but to ensure that they could be propelled even if there was no wind.

While this was going on, every soldier who could not swim was given a daily lesson. As a precaution, specially selected men were trained in rudimentary 'navigation'; for though the boats would, in theory, be taken across the river by their owners, there was always the chance that a boatman would be killed. Gun emplacements were hidden in trees behind the river. Shells— more than a hundred to each gun—were brought south along the roads or the Grand Canal, the convoys always facing the danger of air strikes by Chiang, though these rarely materialised.

Across the river, the armies of Chiang Kai-shek waited, 300,000 men at key defence points on the south bank. They had thrown up artillery emplacements, concrete block houses, machine-gun posts, and dug trenches. Another 300,000 troops were stationed further south. A dozen Nationalist gunboats could patrol the river. The Air Force had half a dozen landing fields which could put fighters over any battlefield within ten minutes. So, though the Communists had by now a numerical advantage, the Nationalists, fighting from entrenched positions, with an air force and naval units, should in theory have been able to repulse any crossing easily.

By 18 April, with barely forty-eight hours to go, all was ready for the Communist gunners to tear off their camouflage and prepare to lay a massive barrage across the river to protect the crossings. Every unit held its 'ceremony of dedication', with triumphal arches in the village square and red pennants fastened to every tree, building, even to the rocks, with a huge portrait of Mao behind every arch under large red flags. Junior officers distributed small red flags to the 'shock regiments' which would lead the crossings. The flags were to be planted on the south bank. There were martial bands, pep talks, even free cigarettes, for this was to be the greatest river crossing in the history of Chinese warfare. . . .

When the moment came to strike, Mao Tse-tung had concentrated two Army Groups under General Chen Yi, conqueror of Hsuchow, between Nanking and Shanghai; and two more Army Groups were poised south of Nanking under General Lin Piao,

hero of Mukden and Peking. Their combined forces now numbered more than a million, and they had almost two million—
some put the figure higher—civilian auxiliaries, recruited willingly from the surrounding countryside.

Though the attack was by river and not on land, it was in many
respects almost a carbon copy of the classic German *Blitzkrieg* used
against the Low Countries in 1940, in which fanatical shock-troops,
utterly dedicated to their cause, attacked unrelentingly and with
astonishing mobility a dazed and doubtful enemy. In place of
German dive-bombers, the Chinese employed tremendous
firepower, mostly from 75 mm and 105 mm guns.

The New China News Agency report broadcast by Peking Radio
summed up what happened more or less accurately:

> On the night of 21 April [24 hours late?] there was some anxi-
> ety because of a westerly wind but it veered at dusk and boatmen
> said Chairman Mao had 'borrowed the east wind' for the cross-
> ing. Officers synchronised their watches and troops armed with
> American-made automatic weapons took up positions covering
> the opposite bank. Forward units near the river were in com-
> munication with headquarters by field telephone. Suddenly
> heavy guns opened up from behind infantry lines and a signal
> flare was the sign for the boats to set sail across the river. Shock-
> troops jumped into the shallow water thirty-five metres off the
> south bank and waded ashore. More signal flares showed that
> Nationalist troops had either been driven off or mown down by
> automatic fire.

In most cases, the attack did open with a ferocious barrage,
sometimes lasting for four hours, and aimed at softening up the
enemy defences. . . . South of Nanking, near Angking, General
Bao remembered: 'We started at 5.05 p.m., and through binoculars I could see the enemy forts crumbling. By 6 p.m. the time to
attack had arrived. The band played 'The March of the
Guerrillas'. The artillery cover intensified and the artillerymen
were so hot they had to take off their tunics.' He added graphical-
ly, 'Even Heaven was alarmed' as the first boats set off. At that
moment he had a more down-to-earth thought: 'Oh, for some out-
board motors!'

On the north bank opposite Rose Island (but with his troops spread out eastwards towards a point opposite Kiangyin) General Liu had much the same experience. 'I stood there proudly as my helmeted shock-troops, each man knowing just what to do, passed through a hero's arch while the civilians tried to stop up their ears to shut out the roar of our guns. There were pillars of black smoke from fires on the opposite bank as our first boats prepared to leave at nine o'clock.'

The boats poured out in some sort of ragged formation from all the creeks that laced the bank; hundreds of boats of all kinds, each with its complement of armed troops. The landing craft followed, and against virtually no opposition, certainly not in the Kiangyin sector, most boats made the crossing in a matter of minutes. On the north bank General Liu was waiting for a signal. When two green flares lit up the sky, proof that the first wave of his shock-troops had landed, 'I jumped on the next boat, standing in the bow. The wind smelt of gunpowder.' General Liu was not afraid— and there was no reason why he should be, for though Kiangyin boasted a heavily defended fortress on the promontory at a narrow part of the river, the defending guns had been silenced by bribes long before the Communists started to cross the river.

General Tai, the Nationalist commander of the fort, had taken good care to earn the Communist bribe that was being held for him by a neutral banker. At the first sign of any instinctive reaction by his colleagues, he turned the guns under his command on loyal artillerymen and silenced them. He also shelled two small Nationalist gunboats anchored at Kiangyin when they suggested moving into the river to attack the Communists' boats. Of the Air Force there was no sign. In the end one full Nationalist division and an artillery regiment defected, many of the men turning their guns on 'loyal' colleagues who were retreating. So Kiangyin had the doubtful honour of being the first city on the south bank to fall to the Communists.

When Liu crossed with the victors and landed, he was, he said, horrified to find thousands of Chinese refugees in rags, with no shoes, straggling from the scene. 'Enemy documents were scattered everywhere. So was ammunition, supplies, clothes, blankets, cooking utensils.' But Liu was really intrigued to find among the debris, 'pictures of women, items of ladies' under-clothes, women's shoes, even rouge'—proof that the Nationalist officers, even in the front line, were still provided with that most welcome of all camp comforts. Comforts of a nature denied to members of Mao's austere regime.

While General Liu was inspecting the fortress of Kiangyin, hundreds of barges and boats were pouring towards the larger ancient walled city of Chinkiang, which nestled in a semicircle of hills behind the river. Once a British treaty port, it had long since run to seed—except as a sector headquarters of the Nationalist Navy. Half a dozen gunboats were stationed there to help to protect Nanking fifty miles or so up river. The Nationalists had built pillboxes, erected gun emplacements and barbed-wire fences, and dug foxholes. They poured in enough men and equipment to enable the city to hold out for a long time while the Navy blasted any approaching vessels out of the water; this should have been an easy task, since at Chinkiang the Yangtze was considerably wider than in other parts of the area.

Without a shot being fired on either side, the mixed fleet of Communist vessels drew abreast the Nationalist warships stationed at the edge of the city. 'Nobody made a belligerent move, the men looked at each other and understood,' according to one eyewitness. The Communists were well aware that Commodore Lin Tsun, head of the squadron at Nanking, had been bribed and had, as part of his treachery, previously visited Chinkiang during the peace talks. There he had called all hands to a mass meeting and, warning them that the Communists were bound to win, had suggested that it would be wiser to defect. A vote was taken, the motion was carried.

When the attack on Chinkiang started—and when it was obvious that the Navy was not going to fight—the loyal head of the Nationalist Navy, Chief Admiral Kewi Yung-chun, who was in Shanghai, radioed Commodore Lin, begging him to order the naval units to flee to Shanghai, from where they could go to Taiwan. Lin refused. Then Admiral Kewi managed to get through on the telephone. This time he offered to promote Lin to the rank of Vice-Admiral, 'stationed safely in Taiwan'; he suggested a bribe, and finally offered Lin 'all the medals you care to choose'. Lin refused apologetically. He had already accepted a huge bribe, and he could not go back on his word—whether because of a twisted sense of honesty, or whether because he feared that the Communists would ferret him out if he double-crossed them, nobody knows. Within twenty-four hours the red flag was flying above the roofs of Chinkiang.

South of Nanking the armies of General Lin Piao also met virtually no opposition, largely because Communist strategy had given the Nationalists the impression that the main thrust would be launched between Nanking and Shanghai, and that only a secondary attack would be made below Nanking. Thus the Nationalist south of Nanking were almost unprepared for the ferocity of the attack. 'The men had a pleasant junket. The attack was unopposed, the crossing uneventful, the weather fine,' wrote one of the officers. Entire divisions moved easily in a north-easterly direction across undefended country to cut off the retreating Nationalist troops and effect a link-up with General Chen Yi's army which was quickly advancing south of Chinkiang and Kiangyin, taking in thousands of square miles of paddy-fields in the Changchow and Wusih area, a rice 'granary' which fed most of Shanghai's six million people. Worse: by executing a turning movement the attackers from the south were able to cut vital railways and trap the Nationalists' eastern flank. . . .

In the event there was no bloodshed at Nanking. Indeed, nothing illustrates the ease of the Communists' advance more clearly than the manner in which Nanking fell. Hardly any of the million inhabitants of Chiang's capital knew what had happened until they woke on the morning of 24 April, for the Communist troops entered the city at 2.30 a.m. marching behind a jeep crowded with several Communist officials and three Nanking politicians. With the dawn, students chanting patriotic songs walked out to meet troops marching in from the north-west gate and down North Chung Shan Road, past the imposing executive Yuan Building, until so recently the office of the Nationalist Prime Minister.

By early morning crowds of Chinese gathered along the line of march. Some were manifestly pleased, but without doubt the dominant emotion was one of curiosity. The troops were armed with a motley assortment of weapons—some Japanese-made rifles, but more often American-made sub-machine-guns. Many carried baskets of vegetables dangling from bending bamboo poles across their shoulders. It was in no way a staged 'triumphal' entry arranged with ceremonial pomp. Soldiers just marched to their new barracks as quickly as they could or, if not, those on immediate duty sat in neat rows all over the city singing in unison or listening to talks by their officers.

Dreams of the Past, Visions of the Future

For many, such as Su Dongpo, the sight of the Yangtze was humbling, encouraging reflections on the sweep of history and the transience of life and glory. Mao's grandiose dreams were quite different. He aspired to changing both the course of history and the course of the river itself.

24

MEDITATION AT RED CLIFF

SU DONGPO (1037–1101)

Here is Su Dongpo again, musing on the famous battle at Red Cliff, which took place 800 years earlier in AD 208, part of the struggle of the Three Kingdoms.

The protagonists were the heroic young general Zhou (Chou), also referred to in this poem as Kung-ch'in, and his enemy Cao Cao (Ts'ao Ts'ao). Although Cao Cao had been tricked into providing Zhou with ammunition ('K'ung Ming Borrows Some Arrows'), he was still fighting against impossible odds. Cao Cao had over 800,000 men while Zhou had only 30,000. Plainly, another ruse was necessary. So Zhou sent Pang Tung, a well-known military strategist, to Cao Cao, pretending to defect. Many of Cao Cao's troops were ill, and Pang Tung advised that it was because they were not used to the roll of the river. He suggested tying the boats together so that they would be more stable; also it would then be easy for horses and men to cross from ship to ship. Cao Cao did so, thus walking straight into a trap.

Pang Tung returned to Zhou's army under the pretext of arranging for more defections. Soon Cao Cao received a letter from another of Zhou's generals, saying that he was coming and bringing grain boats with him. However, the boats were filled not with grain, but with dry reeds and sulphur. As they approached they were set alight, and the blaze of these huge floating torches ignited Cao Cao's ships, which were so conveniently tied together. All the men and horses on board were burnt to death. The flames burnt so high and fiercely that they left permanent scorch marks on the cliff above, which was renamed Red Cliff in commemoration of the victory. To this day, every Chinese is familiar with this story.

Eastward runs the Great River
Whose waves have washed away
All the talented and courteous men in history.
West of the old fort, they say, there lies Red Cliff,
Where Chou, the young general in the time of the Three
Kingdoms,
Defeated the enemy.
Broken rocks pierce the clouds,
Thundering billows dash on the shore,
Rolling up thousands of flakes of snow.
What a picture of rivers and mountains!
How many heroes there were at that time!

I cannot help thinking of the day
When Kung-ch'in first married Hsiao Ch'iao,
And with a bright warlike air,
A feather fan in his hand, a blue turban on his head,
Annihilated in the midst of his talk and laughter
The strong enemy who vanished like smoke and dust.
Travelling through this ancient kingdom in my imagination,
I should be laughed at for such sentiments,
Turning my hair gray so early.
Life is a dream. Therefore to the river and the moon,
I sprinkle this bottle of wine!

25

SWIMMING

MAO ZEDONG

Chairman Mao loved swimming, and in his later years he made several much-publicized swims across the Yangtze at Wuhan, a distance of fifteen to twenty kilometres (nine to twelve miles), to prove his good health. This poem was written in June 1956, following his first swim, and apparently immediately after his discussion with the Yangtze Valley Planning Office about building a huge dam across the river. As with many of his poems, it is full of classical references and extravagant plans for the future.

Changsha has long been famous for its water and Wuchang for its fish. 'Chu' is the name of one of the kingdoms of the Warring States period (471–221 BC), while 'the master' is Confucius. 'Tortoise' and 'snake' are the names of mountains facing each other across this part of the river. When Mao wrote this, a bridge linking the two was already underway. He christened it 'Iron and Steel Rainbow' when it opened a few months later. But the controversial 'walls of stone', the dam across the Three Gorges, did not rise in his lifetime. They are being built now. The mountain goddess he refers to is the famous goddess peak, a deity turned to stone, who towers over Wu Gorge.

have just drunk the waters of Changsha
And come to eat the fish of Wuchang,
Now I am swimming across the great Yangtse,
Looking afar to the open sky of Chu.
Let the wind blow and the waves beat,
Better far than idly strolling in a courtyard.
Today I am at ease.
'It was by a stream that the Master said—
Thus do things flow away!'

Sails move with the wind.
Tortoise and snake are still.
Great plans are afoot;

A bridge will fly to span the north and south,
Turning a deep chasm into a thoroughfare;
Walls of stone will stand upstream to the west
To hold back Wushan's clouds and rain
Till a smooth lake rises in the narrow gorges.
The mountain goddess if she is still there
Will marvel at a world so changed.

THE UPPER REACHES:
YICHANG TO CHONGQING

It is easier to climb to Heaven
Than take the Sichuan road....

Peak follows peak, each but a hand's breath from the sky;
Dead pine trees hang head down into the chasms,
Torrents and waterfalls outroar each other,
Pounding the cliffs and boiling over rocks,
Booming like thunder through a thousand caverns.
What takes you, traveller, this long weary way
So filled with danger?

Li Bai (701–62), 'The Sichuan Road'.

Li Bai did not exaggerate. Whether by land or water, any journey through Sichuan used to be perilous indeed. Aptly enough, boats travelling upstream cross the border from Hubei to Sichuan while in Witches Gorge, one of the dramatic and beautiful gorges between Yichang and Baidicheng. Without doubt the gorges are the most awe-inspiring part of the journey to Chongqing, and for most people they are the most unforgettable stretch of the entire Yangtze.

Today, the most dangerous obstacles, such as Yanyu Rock mentioned by Bo Juyi ('Alarm at entering the Yangtze Gorges') have been dynamited, and the rapids tamed, so that cargo and cruise ships sail serenely through. Yet until only a few decades ago, to brave the Three Gorges was to take your life in your hands. Generations of writers have described these bleak cliffs and frothing waters hurtling through chasms as narrow as 150 metres (500 feet). It is a wild landscape, formerly the domain of the Ba (Pa) people, a once large ethnic group that mysteriously died out sometime in the seventeenth century. Little remains of them besides their eerie wooden coffins, many of them 2,000 years old, suspended high above the Gorges, either on beams jutting out from the cliff faces or hidden in caves. Nobody knows how the Ba managed to place the coffins there.

The Three Gorges are the Xiling, the Wu (or Witches Gorge), and the Qutang—each with its own store of legends, its fancifully named peaks and its dark record of those who lost their lives there. The Xiling Gorge, longest and originally the most dangerous, is

124

made up of seven smaller gorges. Wu Gorge is watched over by the most famous legend of all, a benevolent deity turned to stone, known as Goddess Peak. The story goes that in the twenty-first century BC, Emperor Yu, known as Yu the Great, founder of Chinese agriculture and the first to organize flood control projects, was battling a huge flood near Wushan (Wu Mountain), which overlooks Wu Gorge. He asked Goddess Yao Ji for help and with her magic powers, she assisted Yu in building a tunnel through the mountain so that the flood waters flowed into the Yangtze. Yao Ji found the sombre scenery of Wu Gorge so beautiful that she and her maidservants couldn't tear themselves away. Every day she would stand on a cliff gazing at the boats going through the gorges, and using her magic to help out when necessary. But she stood there too long and she and her eleven attendants were gradually turned into stone peaks.

THE THREE GORGES DAM

According to legend then, men and women have struggled to subdue the river for the last 4,000 years. But the most ambitious attempt yet is the Three Gorges Dam, said to be the largest of its kind in the world. It will generate a much-needed 84 billion kilowatt-hours of electricity annually, at the cost of flooding 570,000 acres of farmland and the homes of between 1.2 million and 1.3 million people. The dam is being built inside Xiling, the first of the Three Gorges and its vast reservoir will stretch for 600 kilometres (370 miles) through the Gorges and beyond, all the way to Chongqing.

Despite the official confidence expressed by the government, many experts both within China and abroad believe that the dam will be an environmental disaster. Some predict that it will be impossible to solve the problem of siltage, and that within eighty years the reservoir behind the dam could become a morass of mud, bringing shipping to a halt. In addition, since most floods in recent years have come from waters originating below the dam site, it may not alleviate flooding as much as is commonly claimed. It might actually increase it, as the river, leaving much of its silt in the dam's reservoir could flow down with even more force than before through the middle and lower reaches.

Naturally such a huge project will affect what little wildlife is left along the river. Certain creatures downriver from the dam, such as the 'baiji' dolphin ('The Plight of the Baiji'), the Chinese alligator, and the finless porpoise already are almost extinct. The environmental changes that the dam will bring may kill them off altogether. According to Beijing's *China Daily*, the Gorges are also home to over 3,000 kinds of plants. Thirty-six of these grow only in the Three Gorges area, while an additional eleven kinds, although not unique to the Gorges, are in danger of extinction. The Chinese Academy of Scientists has set up a group of botanists who are working on transplanting these rare species to a nearby, almost barren mountainside, the best land they can afford.

Not only will over a million people have to leave their homes and the land they have tilled for generations, but also countless ancient relics will be lost. In 1995, archaeologists estimated that at least 1,200 ancient sites will be submerged. Their findings in the area, many of which are almost 7,000 years old, confirm that the Yangtze area can claim to be one of the earliest cradles of Chinese culture. When accepting an environment award, journalist Dai Qing, who has courageously spoken out time and again against the dam, quoted a Chinese philosopher: 'It is more dangerous to silence the people than to dam a river'. In any case, work on the dam is going ahead and only time will tell whether the good effects will outweigh the bad. But the landscape the travellers describe here will be changed forever, as 'a smooth lake rises in the narrow gorges', as Mao envisaged in his poem 'Swimming'.

The Three Gorges

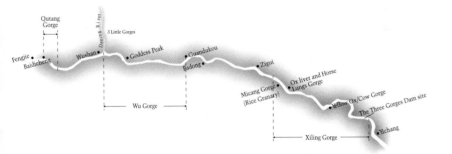

Qutang
Gorge

3 Little Gorges

Fengjie
Baidicheng

Wushan

Goddess Peak

Guandukou

Badong

Zigui

Ox liver and Horse
Lungs Gorge

Micang Gorge
(Rice Granary)

Yellow Ox/Cow Gorge

The Three Gorges Dam site

Yichang

Wu Gorge

Xiling Gorge

Danng River

STRUGGLING UP THE THREE GORGES

LI BAI

In these two poems, Li Bai (701–762) describes the terrible journey upstream through the Gorges, battling all the way, and then the same trip going downstream, coasting quickly and effortlessly. The contrast reflects his mood. In the first poem, written in 759, Li is on his way into exile for life. Later that same year Li benefited from an amnesty, and was allowed to return home. The second poem, probably the one the most often quoted about the river, describes his exultant return trip.

This stretch of the river was called the Ba (Pa), since it ran through the Kingdom of the Ba people. Dramatically situated high above the mouth of Qutang Gorge, White Emperor City (Baidicheng, also translated as 'White King City') dates back to the first century AD, when soldier Gong Sunshu made it his headquarters, and declared himself the White Emperor. Two hundred years later Liu Bei, hero of the Three Kingdoms, died here.

Miserably the Wu Mountains squeeze the slender blue sky,
Making the Pa River rush down through the tortuous Yangtze Gorges.
The Pa Waters might pass and turn suddenly away,
But the slender blue sky would remain there forever!

For three mornings my boat struggled up by the Yellow Cow Peak,
And another three evenings—too slowly had I been proceeding.
Gazing still at that high peak for three weary mornings and evenings.
Unwittingly my hair turned into white threads!

LEAVING WHITE EMPEROR CITY AT DAWN

LI BAI

At dawn amid coloured clouds I left White Emperor City:
A thousand miles to Chiang-ling—I was there in a day!
Chattering monkeys on the cliffs, no end to their bawling.
So the light boat slipped past the ten thousand mountains.

SETTING OUT IN A HOUSEBOAT

ISABELLA BIRD

Numerous writers have described the preparations and delays in setting off through the gorges, but Isabella Bird's 1890s account, together with her description of the scenery, still stands as one of the best.

I was very impatient to be off on my western journey, but after the boat was engaged, the tracking ropes examined by experts at the customs, and my few stores—tea, curry powder, and rice —had been bought, I had four days of 'hanging on'. The boatmen made various excuses for delay. One day it was that the *lao-pan*, or master, had not advanced them money wherewith to buy stores; another was a feast day; a third must be spent in paying debts or they would be detained; and on the fourth they said they must visit certain temples and make offerings for the success of the voyage! The weather was raw, grim, and sunless. I had had a fire day and night in my room at the customs, and a fireless, draughty boat was a shivery prospect, but things usually turn out far better than either prophecies or expectations, and this voyage was no exception.

I was fortunate in being able to take as far as Wan Hsien Mr. Owen Stevenson, of the China Inland Mission, who had had ten years' experience in Yunnan, accompanied by Mr. Hicks, a new arrival; and they engaged the boat for the next stage to Chung-king, which gave Mr. S. some little hold on the *lao-pan*, who was a mean and shifty person, coerced into evil ways by a terrible wife, a virago, whose loud tongue was rarely silent, who had beaten her eldest boy to death a few months before, and of whom the remaining boy—a child of eight—lived in piteous terror, lest he should share the same fate. This family of five lived in the high stern cabin, but were apt to run over into parts of the boat which should have been *tabu*. The crew consisted of a pilot who is responsible for the navigation, a steersman, a cook, and sixteen trackers and rowers.

The boat itself was a small house-boat of about twenty tons, flat bottomed, with one tall mast and big sail, a projecting rudder and a steering sweep on the bow. Her 'passenger accommodation' consisted of a cabin the width of the boat, with a removable front, opening on the bow deck, where the sixteen boatmen rowed, smoked, ate, and slept round a central well in which a preternaturally industrious cook washed bowls, prepared food, cooked it, and apportioned it all day long, using a briquette fire. At night uprights and a mat roof were put up, and the toilers, after enjoying their supper, and their opium pipes at the stern, rolled themselves in wadded quilts and slept till daybreak. Passengers usually furnish this cabin, and put up curtains and photographs, and eat and sit there; but I had no superfluities, and my 'furniture' consisted only of a carrying-chair, in which it was very delightful to sit and watch the grandeurs and surprises of the river. But gradually the trackers and the skipper's family came to overrun this cabin, and I constantly found the virago with her unwelcome baby girl, or a dirty, half-naked tracker in my chair, and the eight-year-old boy spent much of his time crouching in a corner out of reach of his mother's tongue and fist.

Abaft this were three small cabins, with windows 'glazed' with paper, and a passage down the port side from the stern to the bow, on which I cannot say they 'opened', for they were open(!), and a partial privacy was only obtained by making a partition with a curtain. Abaft these was the steersman's place, which was also a kitchen and opium den, where my servant cooked, and where the pilot and most of the crew were to be seen every night lying on the floor beside their opium lamps, passing into felicity. Abaft again, at a greater height, the skipper and his family lived. On the roof there were hen coops and great coils of bamboo rope for towing.

It was an old boat, and the owner was not a man of substance. The paper on the windows was torn away; the window-frame of the cabin in which I slept, ate, and carried on my various occupations, had fallen out, the cracks in the partitions were half an inch wide; and as for many days the sun seldom shone and the mercury hung between 38° and 43°, and hugging a charcoal brazier was the only method of getting warm, and that a dubious one, the earliest weeks were a chilly period.

On the afternoon of January 30th I embarked from the customs pontoon much exhilarated by the prospect before me but we only crossed the river and lay all night in a tremendous noise among a number of big junks, the yells of the skipper's baby being heard above the din. This man excused this last delay in starting by sending word from the shore that he was waiting for the mandarin's permit, and would be ready to leave on the following daybreak.

I was up at daybreak not to lose anything, but hour after hour passed, and no *lao-pan* appeared, and at ten we started without him to meet him on the bank a few miles higher, when there was a tremendous row between him and the men. We were then in what looked like a mountain lake. No outlet was visible; mountains rose clear and grim against a dull grey sky. Snow-flakes fell sparsely and gently in a perfectly still atmosphere. We cast off from the shore; the oars were plied to a wild chorus; what looked like a cleft in the rock appeared, and making an abrupt turn round a high rocky point in all the thrill of novelty and expectation, we were in the Ichang Gorge*, the first and one of the grandest of those gigantic clefts through which the Great River, at times a mile in breadth, there compressed into a limit of from 400 to 150 yards, has carved a passage through the mountains.

The change from a lake-like stretch, with its light and movement, to a dark and narrow gorge black with the shadows of nearly perpendicular limestone cliffs broken up into buttresses and fantastic towers of curiously splintered and weathered rock, culminating in the 'Pillar of Heaven,' a limestone pinnacle rising sheer from the water to a height of 1,800 feet, is so rapid as to bewilder the senses. The expression '*lost* in admiration' is a literally correct one. At once I saw the reason why the best descriptions, which are those of Captain Blakiston and Mr. A. Little, have a certain amount of 'fuzziness', and fail to convey a definite picture.

With a strong, fair wind our sail was set; the creak and swish of the oars was exchanged for the low music of the river as it parted under our prow; and the deep water (from fifty to a hundred feet), of a striking bottle-green colour, was unbroken by a swirl or ripple, and slid past in a grand, full volume. The stillness was profound, enlivened only as some big junk with lowered mast glided past us at great speed, the fifty or sixty men at the sweeps raising a wild

---

* Ichang Gorge is the first section of Xiling Gorge.

chant in keeping with the scene. Scuds of snow, wild, white clouds whirling round pinnacles, and desolate snow-clothed mountains, apparently blocking further progress, added to the enchantment. Crevices in the rocks were full of maidenhair fern, and on many a narrow ledge clustered in profusion a delicate mauve primula, unabashed by the grandeur and the gloom. Streams tumbled over ledges at heights of 1,000 feet. There are cliffs of extraordinary honeycombed rock, possibly the remains of the 'potholes' of ages since, rock carved by the action of water and weather into shrines with pillared fronts, grottoes with quaint embellishments—gigantic old women gossiping together in big hats—colossal abutments, huge rock needles after the manner of Quiraing, while groups of stalactites constantly occur as straight and thick as small pines, supporting rock canopies festooned with maidenhair. Higher yet, surmounting rock ramparts 2000 feet high, are irregular battlemented walls of rock, perhaps twenty feet thick, and everywhere above and around are lofty summits sprinkled with pines, on which the snow lay in powder only, and 'the snow clouds rolling dun' added to the sublimity of the scenery.

133

It was always changing, too. If it were possible to be surfeited with turrets, battlements, and cathedral spires, and to weary of rock phantasies, the work of water, of solitudes and silences, and of the majestic dark green flow of the Great River, there were besides lateral clefts, each with its wall-sided torrent, with an occasional platform green with wheat, on which a brown-roofed village nestled among fruit trees, or a mountain, bisected by a chasm, looking ready to fall into the river, as some have already done, breaking up into piles of huge angular boulders, over which even the goat-footed trackers cannot climb. Then, wherever the cliffs are less absolutely perpendicular, there are minute platforms partially sustaining houses with their backs burrowing into the rock, and their fronts extended on beams fixed in the cliff, accessible only by bolts driven into the rock, where the small children are tied to posts to prevent them from falling over, and above, below, and around these dwellings are patches of careful culture, some of them *not larger than a bath towel*, to which the cultivators lower themselves with ropes, and there are small openings occasionally, where deep-eaved houses cluster on the flat tops of rocky spurs among the exquisite plumage of groves of the golden and green bamboo, among oranges and pommeloes with their shining greenery, and straight-stemmed palms with their great fan-like leaves. Already in these sheltered places mauve primulas were blooming amidst a profusion of maidenhair, and withered clusters and tresses showed what the glory of the spring had been and was yet to be when the skirts of these spurs would be aflame with azaleas, and clematis, and great white and yellow roses, and all the wealth of flowers and trailers of which these were only the vestiges.

Another feature was boats large and small, and junks, some laboriously tracked or rowed like my own, when the wind failed, against the powerful stream, or descending, keeping the necessary steerage headway by crowds of standing men on the low deck, facing forwards, vigorously working great sweeps or *yulows*, five or ten at each, the gorge echoing all along its length to the rise and fall of the wild chants to which the rowers keep time and which are only endurable when softened by distance. After some hours of this region of magic and mystery, near sunset we emerged into open water, with broken picturesque shores, and at dusk tied up in a pebbly bay with glorious views of mountain and woodland, not

far from the beautiful village of Nan-to, and the 'needle' or 'pillar' of heaven, well known to the dwellers in Ichang. The Ichang gorge is about twelve miles long; the Niu-kan, grander yet, about three; the Mitan about three and a half; the Wushan about twenty; and the Feng-hsiang, or 'Wind Box,' the last of the great gorges, about four*. These are the great gorges. . . .

I have found that many of the deterrent perils which are arrayed before the eyes of travellers about to begin a journey are greatly exaggerated, and often vanish altogether. Not so the perils of the Yangtze. They fully warrant the worst descriptions which have been given of them. The risks are many and serious, and cannot be provided against by any forethought. The slightest error in judging of distance on the part of the pilot, any hampering of the bow-sweep, a tow-rope breaking, a submerged boulder changing its place, and many other possibilities, and life and property are at the mercy of a raging flood, tearing downwards at the rate of from seven to eleven miles an hour. I have no personal perils to narrate. A rock twice knocked a hole in the bottom which took a day to repair, and in a collision our bow-sweep was fractured, which led to a severe quarrel lasting half a day; this was all. I never became used to the rapids, and always felt nervous at the foot of each, and preferred the risk of fracturing my limbs

---

* Niu-kan, now spelt Niugan (Ox Liver), and Mitan, now spelt Micang (Rice Granary), are also part of Xiling Gorge. Wushan (Wu Mountain) must be Wu Gorge, while Feng-hsiang is now known as Qutang Gorge.

among the great boulders and shining rock faces of the shores to spending hours in a turmoil, watching the fraying of the tow-ropes.

Although Isabella Bird's boat passes through the rapids safely, she is delayed at Kwei Fu (Fengjie), since the Chinese Lunar New Year is approaching, and the captain has decided that he wants to spend it there. Here she describes how she occupied her time. Reading of how she matter-of-factly leaned over the ship's gunwale to bathe her negatives in the Yangtze, it is hard to believe that this was a sixty-four-year-old Victorian widow, suffering from 'fatty degeneration of the heart', gout, and a bad back.

On two days, owing to the crowds on the shore, I did not leave the boat. In the bright sunshine, 'light without heat,' the view was always delightful, as it changed from hour to hour, and disappeared at sunset in a blaze of colour—distant snow peaks burning red after the lower ranges had passed into ashy grey. The picturesque grey city, the magnificent opening of the Feng Hsiang, or 'Wind-Box' gorge, the hill slopes in the vividness of their spring greens and yellows, the rapid, with its exciting risks and the life on the water, made a picture of which one could never weary.

Yet five days of crouching and shivering in a six-foot square room, really a *stall*, with three sides only and no window, taxed both patience and resources, especially as the virago and the boat baby were more aggravating than usual, and the trackers ignored the existence of passengers. The *lao-pan* gave himself up to the opium pipe, and was consequently obliterated. Be-dien, my servant, whose temper and pride were unslumbering, made himself unpleasant all round. It would require some very old-fashioned Anglo-Saxon words to describe the smell of the cooking of the New Year viands. Yet somehow I did not feel the least inclined to grumble, and my slender resources held out till the end.

I had Baber's incomparable papers on Far Western China to study and enjoy, a journal to 'write up', much mending and even making to accomplish, and, above all, there were photographic negatives to develop and print, and prints to tone, and the difficulties enhanced the zest of these processes and made me think, with a feeling of complacent superiority, of the amateurs who need 'dark rooms', sinks, water 'laid on', tables, and other luxuries. Night supplied me with a dark room; the majestic Yangtze was 'laid on'; a box served for a table: all else can be dispensed with.

I lined my 'stall' with muslin curtains and newspapers, and finding that the light of the opium lamps still came in through the chinks, I tacked up my blankets and slept in my clothes and fur coat. With 'water, water everywhere', water was the great difficulty. The Yangtze holds any amount of fine mud in suspension, which for drinking purposes is usually precipitated with alum, and unless filtered, deposits a fine, even veil on the negative. I had only a pocket filter, which produced about three quarts of water a day, of which Be-dien invariably abstracted some for making tea, leaving me with only enough for a final wash, not always quite effectual, as the critic will see from some of the illustrations.

I found that the most successful method of washing out 'hypo' was to lean over the gunwale and hold the negative in the wash of the Great River, rapid even at the mooring place, and give it some final washes in the filtered water. This chilly arrangement was only possible when the trackers were ashore or smoking opium at the stern. Printing was a great difficulty, and I only overcame it by hanging the printing-frames over the side. When all these rough arrangements were successful, each print was a joy and a triumph, nor was there disgrace in failure.

The day before the New Year was thoroughly unquiet. The population of the boat was excited by wine and pork money, and was fearfully noisy, shouting, yelling, quarrelling, stamping overhead, stamping along the passage outside my cambric curtain, stamping over the roof, sawing, hammering, and pounding rice. A mandarin's boat tied up close to my window had engaged a 'sing-song' boat, and I had all the noise from both, and many glimpses of the mandarin, a good-looking young man, in fur-lined brocaded silk. Like all others that I have seen of the higher official class, he looked immeasurably removed from the common people. The assumed passionlessness of his face expressed nothing but aloofness and scorn. One of the servants died in his boat after a few hours' illness, during which the beating of drums and gongs, and the letting off of crackers to frighten away the demon which was causing the trouble, were incessant and tremendous. We sailed in company, and shortly after leaving Kuei Fu one of the mandarin's trackers, in a very minor rapid, was pulled into the river and drowned.

I had an opportunity of taking an instantaneous photograph of my trackers at dinner. Their meals, which consist of inferior rice mixed with cabbage or other vegetables fried in oil, with a bit of fish or pork occasionally added, are worth watching. Each man takes a rough glazed earthenware bowl and fills it from the great pot on the fire. All squat round the well, and balancing their bowls on the tips of the fingers of the left hand close under the chin, the mouths are opened as wide as possible, and the food is shovelled in with the chopsticks as rapidly as though they were eating for a wager. When the mouth is apparently full they pack its contents into the cheeks with the chopsticks and begin again, packing any solid lumps into the cheeks neatly at once. When mastication and swallowing took place I never quite made out, but in an incredibly short time both bowls and cheeks were empty, and the eaters were smoking their pipes with an aspect of content. The boats, unless sailing, tie up for meals. The Chinese never, if they can help it, drink unboiled water, which saves them from many diseases, and these men drank the water in which the rice was cooked.

On three such meals the poor fellows haul with all their strength for twelve hours daily, never shirking their work. They are rough, truly, but as the voyage went on their honest work, pluck, endurance, hardihood, sobriety, and good-nature won my sympathy and in some sort my admiration. They might be better clothed and fed if they were not opium smokers, but then where would be their nightly Elysium?

THROUGH THE GORGES IN A WUBAN

EDWIN J. DINGLE

In February 1909, Edwin J. Dingle and friend, whom he refers to as The Other Man, set out to walk across China. Describing himself as a newspaperman on holiday, it had been his hope for many years to see Interior China "ere modernity had robbed her and her wonderful people of their isolation and antedeluvianism'. Not all of the journey was on foot however. Here he describes their journey through the Gorges. While Isabella Bird travelled in a larger style of boat, a kuaizi ('kwaidse' or 'kwadze'), Dingle chose the smaller wuban ('wu-pan') for maximum speed. Wuban literally means 'five planks'. Even smaller is the 'sanban' (more usually spelt 'sampan'), literally 'three planks'.

Our wu-pan was to get through the Gorges in as short a time as was possible, and for that reason we travelled in the discomfort of the smallest boat used to face the rapids.

People entertaining the smallest idea of doing things travel in nothing short of a *kwadze*, the orthodox houseboat, with several rooms and ordinary conveniences. Ours was a *wu-pan*—literally five boards. We had no conveniences whatever, and the second morning out we were left without even a wash-basin. As I was standing in the stern, I saw it swirling away from us, and inquiring through a peep-hole, heard the perplexing explanation of my boy. Gesticulating violently, he told us how, with the wash-basin in his hand, he had been pushed by one of the crew, and how, loosened from his grasp, my toilet ware had been gripped by the river—and now appeared far down the stream like a large bead. The Other Man was alarmed at the boy's discomfiture, ejaculated something about the loss being quite irreparable, and with a loud laugh and quite natural hilarity proceeded quietly to use a saucepan as a combined shaving-pot and wash-basin. It did quite well for this in the morning, and during the day resumed its duty as seat for me at the typewriter.

Our boy, apart from this small misfortune, comported himself pretty well. His English was understandable, and he could cook anything. He dished us up excellent soup in enamelled cups and, as we had no ingredients on board so far as we knew to make soup, and as The Other Man had that day lost an old Spanish tam-o'-shanter, we naturally concluded that he had used the old hat for the making of the soup, and at once christened it as 'consommé à la maotsi' [Hat]—and we can recommend it. After we had grown somewhat tired of the eternal curry and rice, we asked him quietly if he could not make us something else, fearing a rebuff. He stood hesitatingly before us, gazing into nothingness. His face was pallid, his lips hard set, and his stooping figure looking curiously stiff and lifeless on that frozen morning—the temperature was 36 degrees below freezing point, and our noses were red too!

'God bless the man, you no savee! I wantchee good chow. Why in the name of goodness can't you give us something decent! What on earth did you come for?'

'Alas!' he shouted, for we were at a rapid, 'my savee makee good chow. No have got nothing!'

'No have got nothing! No have got nothing!' Mysterious words, what could they mean? Where, then, was our picul of rice, and our curry, and our sugar?

'The fellow's a swindler!' cried The Other Man in an angry semitone. But that's all very well. 'No have got nothing!' Ah, there lay the secret. Presently The Other Man, head of the general commissariat, spoke again with touching eloquence. He gave the boy to understand that we were powerless to alter or soften the conditions of the larder, that we were victims of a horrible destiny, that we entertained no stinging malice towards him personally—but . . . *could he do it*? Either a great wrath or a great sorrow overcame the boy; he skulked past, asked us to lie down on our shelves, where we had our beds, to give him room, and then set to work.

In twenty-five minutes we had a three-course meal (all out of the same pot, but no matter), and onwards to our destination we fed royally. In parting with the men after our safe arrival at Chungking, we left with them about seven-eighths of the picul—and were not at all regretful.

I should not like to assert—because I am telling the truth here—that our boat was bewilderingly roomy. As a matter of fact, its length was some forty feet, its width seven feet, its depth much less, and it drew eight inches of water. Yet in it we had our bed-rooms, our dressing-rooms, our dining-rooms, our library, our occasional medicine-room, our cooking-room—and all else. If we stood bolt upright in the saloon amidships we bumped our heads on the bamboo matting which formed an arched roof. On the nose of the boat slept seven men—you may question it, reader, but they did; in the stern, on either side of a great rudder, slept our boy and a friend of his; and between them and us, laid out flat on the top of a cellar (used by the ship's cook for the storing of rice, cabbage, and other uneatables, and the breeding-cage of hun-dreds of rats, which swarm all around one) were the captain and commodore—a fat, fresh-complexioned, jocose creature, strenu-ous at opium smoking. Through the holes in the curtain—a piece of sacking, but one would not wish this to be known—dividing them from us, we could see him preparing his globules to smoke before turning in for the night, and despite our frequent raving objections, our words ringing with vibrating abuse, it continued all the way to Chung-king: he certainly gazed in disguised wonder-ment, but we could not get him to say anything bearing upon the matter. Temperature during the day stood at about 50 degrees, and at night went down to about 30 degrees below freezing point. Rains were frequent. Journalistic labours, seated upon the upturned saucepan aforesaid, without a cushion went hard. At night the Chinese candle, much wick and little wax, stuck in the centre of an empty 'Three Castles' tin, which the boy had used for some days as a pudding dish, gave us light. We generally slept in our overcoats, and as many others as we happened to have. Rats crawled over our uncurtained bodies, and woke us a dozen times each night by either nibbling our ears or falling bodily from the roof on to our faces. Our joys came not to us—they were made on board.

30

ALARM AT FIRST ENTERING
THE YANGTZE GORGES

BAI JUYI (772–846)

Bai Juyi (Po Chu-i) began his career as an official at court, but soon made himself unpopular. He wrote memorials criticizing a campaign being waged against a minor Tartar tribe, and his poems not only sympathized with the sufferings of China's poor, but made fun of greedy officials. In AD 814 Bai's enemies contrived to have him banished to Jiujiang on the Yangtze's middle reaches (then called Hsunyang) to take the post of sub-prefect. After three years there, he was given the governorship of remote Zhongzhou (Chungchou, known today as Zhongxian), far upriver above the Gorges. As for Li Bai almost sixty years before him, to be sent up to the wilds of Sichuan was a bitter punishment. The first poem here, written in 818, describes his journey to Zhongzhou. The second describes his feelings of despair and isolation once he got there. Ba (Pa) was the name of an ancient kingdom of the region. The Ba people were not Han Chinese, but a minority nationality, now extinct. Man and Mo were other 'barbarian' kingdoms.

Above, a mountain ten thousand feet high:
Below, a river a thousand fathoms deep.
A strip of sky, walled by cliffs of stone:
Wide enough for the passage of a single reed.
At Chu-t'ang a straight cleft yawns:
At Yen-yu islands block the stream.
Long before night the walls are black with dusk;
Without wind white waves rise.
The big rocks are like a flat sword:
The little rocks resemble ivory tusks.

We are stuck fast and cannot move a step.
How much less, three hundred miles?

Frail and slender, the twisted-bamboo rope:
Weak, the dangerous hold of the towers' feet.
A single slip—the whole convoy lost:
And *my* life hangs on *this* thread!
I have heard a saying 'He that has an upright heart
Shall walk scatheless through the lands of Man and Mo'.
How can I believe that since the world began
In every shipwreck none have drowned but rogues?
And how can I, born in evil days
And fresh from failure, ask a kindness of Fate?
Often I fear that these un-talented limbs
Will be laid at last in an un-named grave!

ON BEING REMOVED FROM HSUN-YANG AND SENT TO CHUNG-CHOU

BAI JUYI

Before this, when I was stationed at Hsun-yang,
Already I regretted the fewness of friends and guests.
Suddenly, suddenly—bearing a stricken heart,
I left the gates with nothing to comfort me.
Henceforward,—relegated to deep seclusion
In a bottomless gorge, flanked by precipitous mountains,
Five months on end the passage of boats is stopped
By the piled billows that toss and leap like colts.
The inhabitants of Pa resemble wild apes;
Fierce and lusty, they fill the mountains and prairies.
Among such as these I cannot hope for friends
And am pleased with anyone who is even remotely human.

THROUGH CH'ING-TAN RAPID AND OTHER STORIES OF THE GORGES

WILLIAM GILL

Before the most dangerous rocks in the Gorges were dynamited in the 1950s, one of the worst rapids was the Xin Tan (Hsin-tan, Ch'in or Ch'ing Tan). The name means new rapids: new by Yangtze standards, they date to a landslide in the sixteenth century. Said Isabella Bird, 'No description can convey any idea of the noise and turmoil of the Hsin-tan. I realized it best by my hearing being affected for some days afterwards.'

Here, another of those intrepid late nineteenth-century English explorers, Captain Gill, recounts how his boat breasted this terrible stretch of water. His companion Edward Baber was on his way to set up a British Consulate in Chongqing. Gill's journal continues with his visit to Kuizhou (Kuei-Chou, now called Fengjie) a description of the trackers at work and the story of the thrice-married woman who owns the ship. Unlike in the West, there was no taboo against women on board ship and boat owners often brought their wives and children along. But it was rare for a woman to own a boat.

March 13.—When we looked out in the morning, the steep slope of the water was so apparent that it seemed as if it were impossible any boat could ascend it. Rocks cropped up in most unpleasant places, a broad sheet of white foam extended right across, and the very fish were jumping and leaping in their efforts to ascend.

Our accompanying official, Sun, sent to say that he had no intention of risking his valuable life in any boat up that awful torrent; and that we had better follow his example, and not only walk up ourselves, but send our valuables also by land.

We, however, came to the conclusion that all our goods were equally valuable, and that unless we regularly unloaded the ship, we could do little good; and as for ourselves, we determined that the excitement of going up was worth any risk there might be. We thought, too, that if we remained on board the people might be more careful than if we went ashore.

There was a long time to wait before our turn came, and we watched a small junk make several attempts to ascend before finally succeeding; whilst a crowd of people gradually collected who had come to see the unwonted sight of two foreigners going up the rapid.

The shore was strewn with gigantic boulders, amongst which knots of Chinamen in their blue cotton clothes sat and stood in every conceivable attitude; some were perched on the tops of the rocks, others at the edge of the water were catching fish about the size of sprats, and little ragged and dirty boys had arranged themselves in artistic groups that Murillo alone could have painted.

A steep bank rose up thirty feet, on which the town was built, but the level ground was so scarce that the houses were obliged to seek extraneous aid, and support themselves on crooked and rickety-looking piles.

Beyond towered the giant mountains above an almost perpendicular wall of rock that rose many hundreds of feet straight up from the river.

The ship was now lightened as much as possible by the removal of some of the heavy cargo; and all the morning was occupied in laying out warps. One, 400 yards long, led straight up the rapid; and two other safety ropes were made fast ashore, so that if the first and most important should have parted, we should have merely glided back whence we came, always provided that we did not strike one of the vicious-looking rocks whose wicked heads rose above the foam.

Just at this time a little sampan with two rowers and a helmsman came down, and it was really a fine sight. As they entered the broken water the boat disappeared altogether from view, and the fearless yet anxious look of the steerer was quite a study. A couple of seconds, and they were through, and floating in the smooth water below.

Presently a most important functionary came on board, a serious-looking man, with a yellow flag, on which was written, 'Powers of the water!! a happy star for the whole journey.'

This individual must stand in the bows and wave his flag in regular time; and if he is not careful to perform this duty properly, the powers of the water are sure to be avenged somehow. Another method of softening the stony hearts of these ferocious deities is to sprinkle rice on the stream all through the rapid; this is a rite that should never be omitted.

At this rapid it is necessary to take a pilot, and at three o'clock the chief pilot and his mate came on board. They were gentlemanly-looking men, dressed in light grey coats, and they gave their orders in a very quiet but decided manner. The pilot's mate was certainly the most quiet and phlegmatic Chinaman I ever met; but these men have to keep their heads uncommonly cool. Directly they came on board our crew became very silent, with the exception of one hungry-looking coolie with a pair of breeches so baggy that he looked as if he could carry about all his worldly goods in them; but the severe looks thrown at him by the rest soon silenced him, and he seemed to subside into his capacious nether garments.

Just as all was ready a most ill-mannered junk put its head into my bedroom window, smashed it in, and threatened to do the same to the whole side of the deck-house. She was, however, staved clear, and eventually all damage was rectified with some paper and the never-failing pot of paste.

At half-past four our bows entered the foam. Everything creaked, groaned, and strained; the water boiled around us as we passed within a couple of feet of a black and pointed rock. The old ship took one dive into a wave, and water came on board at a rate that very soon would have swamped her; the drum was beaten and the flag waved; ashore the coolies (nearly one hundred of them) strained the rope, and their shouts could be heard above the roar of the foaming torrent; one line parted, and gave the vessel a jerk that made her shiver from stem to stern; but in ten minutes we were through, and anchored safely in smooth water.

Our small junk followed without much difficulty; the boat of our protector Sun received no more damage than the loss of her rudder; and our gunboat, a handy affair, making very light of it, we all at last found ourselves together above the dreaded spot.

Ropes were then to be coiled down, and our junk made shipshape, before starting afresh and sailing through the Mi-Tsang gorge.

This is one of the most striking of all the gorges in the Yang-Tzu. Huge walls of rock rise up perpendicularly many hundreds of feet on either hand; the banks are strewn with débris; and where a gully or ravine opens up nothing is seen but savage cliffs, where not a tree, and scarcely a blade of grass, can grow, and where the stream, which is rather heard than seen, seems to be fretting in vain efforts to escape from its dark and gloomy prison. A fair breeze took us through the gorge, and we anchored for the night at the upper end.

March 14.—The next morning the commander of our gunboat fired his starting gun at six o'clock; and passing another insignificant rapid we arrived opposite the walled town of Kuei-Chou, whose officials came to visit Baber, bringing presents of fowls, ducks, and mutton, as a leg of goat, with a large bone and not much meat, was facetiously called.

The town of Kuei-Chou is a small place, but enclosed by a wall that runs up the side of a steep hill, and contains a considerable extent of open ground at the back, where, as is often the case in China, the people seem to like the idea of freedom, and build the greater part of their houses outside the wall. How the citizens of this flourishing place find a living it is difficult to say. There was very little cultivation around it, there were no junks stopping at it when we were there, and all the traffic passed by contemptuously on the other side. There were no fishing-boats belonging to it, and when there is neither commerce, agriculture, nor fishing, there are not many sources of wealth remaining. Baber said that it must live like a gentleman,—on its own private fortune!

In a report made by the delegates of the Shanghai Chamber of Commerce, they observe that many of the towns on the banks of the river thrive without agriculture, commerce, or other apparent means of livelihood. These delegates say that the people subsist upon piracy, and that when a junk is wrecked (as happens almost every day, when the river is in a flood), the coolies run away, and the inhabitants come down and appropriate the cargo.

This statement, however, should be received with caution, for it is not likely that piracy to such an extent would be permitted on the great highway of China. On this journey we ourselves passed several wrecks; in every case the cargo was safe ashore under the care of the coolies, who, in one instance, had built themselves temporary sheds of matting on the bank, and were living in a little encampment of their own, while the junk was being repaired.

I took a walk opposite Kuei-Chou, where the tracking path was cut out of the rock, and where in the steepest parts regular steps had been made. In many places the tracking line had cut deep grooves in the faces of the cliffs, and at one point, where a nasty projecting rock runs out into the river, rollers had been fastened for the ropes to work on. I came back just in time to see Sun and his boat swept down the stream. The tracking line had parted, an eddy spun the junk round, and the current carried her a mile, before the men on board could shoot her into the calm water close inshore.

During the day we went through two rapids, but in the low state of the water they were trifling, and the extra number of coolies employed was small.

The coolies fasten themselves to the tracking line in a very ingenious manner. They wear a sort of cross-belt of cotton over one shoulder, the two ends are brought together behind the back, and joined to a line about two yards long. At the end of this line there is a sort of button or toggle, with which one half-hitch is taken round the tracking rope. As long as the strain is kept up, it holds; but if the coolie attempts to shirk his work, and slackens his line, the toggle comes unhitched, and his laziness becomes apparent to his comrades, and to the overseer or ganger who superintends the work.

This ganger is armed with a stick, and it is his duty, by shouting or gesticulating, to excite and encourage the men. He rushes about from one to another; sometimes he raises his stick high in the air over one of them, as if he were going to give him a sound thrashing, but bringing it down he gently taps his shoulders as a sign rather of approbation than of wrath.

When all the coolies are harnessed, they walk forward swaying their bodies and arms from side to side, and shouting a monotonous cry to keep the time. Sometimes the path where they can track is only twenty or thirty yards long, then as soon as a coolie arrives at the end he casts himself off, runs back to the other end, fastens himself on again, and begins pulling afresh.

During the day we entered the coal districts. The people here do little more than scratch the surface, and the coal they obtain is not of a very first-rate quality.

Whilst we sat at breakfast Baber's headman Hwu-Fu, who was waiting on us, was in an exceedingly merry frame of mind, so much so that even in the august presence of his master he was unable to contain his mirth. Baber wishing that we should enjoy a share of the laughter, asked him what was the matter, and although he found his story so amusing that it was with difficulty he could tell it, yet Baber managed to extract from him some interesting episodes in the life of the old lady, the owner of our vessel.

She had been married some years previously, and was apparently able to exist in the society of her husband, until the river gods decided to wreck their vessel in a rapid.

The appalling spectacle so terrified the unfortunate man, that although he received no corporal injury, he died of fright.

The old lady shed a parting tear, and would have wiped the corner of her eye with her pocket-handkerchief, if she had had one; but soon after, finding the care of a big ship and a little child too much for her unaided self, she, whilst vowing to the shades of her departed spouse that it was an act of paramount necessity, and that no disrespect to him was meant, decided to take another help-meet. Not being altogether destitute of this world's goods she found no difficulty, and at I-Ch'ang recommenced a married life. But whilst yet in the honeymoon at Hankow a slight difference of opinion ended in the husband falling down a well, calumny going so far as to say that she pushed him down; but, be that how it may, the lady returned home quietly, and would have been quite prepared for a widow's lot, if some meddlesome folk passing by had not pulled the man out, and sent him back not much the worse. The pair, however, thought that after this accident married life would possibly not be unmixed bliss; so giving him her blessing, or her curses, and endowing him with a small sum of money, the woman sent him to his home.

Again surrounded by a flattering crowd of admirers, she selected a husband for the third time, and they went back together to I-Ch'ang; but here evil-minded people told such wicked stories, that the husband ran away, and returned to Hankow by the first opportunity. Since that time she had been unable to get another spouse, and remained a widow.

A YANGTSZE DRAGON

WILLIAM FERDINAND TYLER

This is the true tale of a young British Deputy Coast Inspector who was sent up the Yangtze in 1897. His destination: Xinlong tan (Hsin-lung-tan or New Dragon Rapid). His mission: to tame a dragon. A huge landslide had fallen into the river the previous year, forming a whirlpool which had wrecked over a hundred large junks, drowning at least 1,000 people. It was clear that a dragon was at work, and the Chinese government appealed to the British for help.

B ut here at last was the Hsin-lung-tan. There was the scar where a young mountain-top had tobogganed down a greasy film that lay between two sloping limestone strata; and thus formed a groyne of monstrous blocks of stone that reached two-thirds across the river. In a portion of the gap lay the smooth tongue of convex water, like a bent fan with the point down-stream where the water boiled. The law of gravity seemed to be suspended; the water did not find its level; it was humped up higher in the middle—irregularly like a piece of warped veneer. On the left bank for several hundred yards the water ran up-river with a speed of several knots—four or five; and between that upward current and the tongue—caused by the two—there lay the gruesome whirlpool.

The summer previous a concave curve of shore with peaceful flow of water had lain where now stood that agglomeration of fallen boulders, and there was a farm or two and cultivation on the hillside, for here there was no gorge and at high river its width was half a mile or so. It was later that I learnt from levels that that summer rise had reached 170 feet, an exceptional amount of water being held up by the narrow gorge some distance down. Probably the saturation of the bottom of the greasy film between the strata had been the trigger that had launched the slide.

But now a young town had sprung up on that filled-up bay. A town of mat-sheds; streets of them with a population of many thousands. The trackers alone ran into thousands, for a single junk would occupy four hundred to haul it up between the whirlpool and the groyne. There were shops, theatres, brothels, opium dens, hotels of sorts, a Prefect's *yamen*, and police—a little town, in fact. But like all these trackers' towns it was a thing of annual birth and growth and death, for at high river the site was submerged a hundred feet or more.

Hsin-lung-tan means New Dragon Rapid, and the Prefect, when he called, explained at once the reason for that name. In the story of the rapid's origin which followed, he professed his disbelief; it was that of the ignorant, superstitious junkmen steeped in the fables of the past; yet to ignore the opinion of the river population would be, he said, unwise. And so he told the story.

For untold ages there had been a dragon in the river whose only food was human corpses, and he had caused the various rapids as a means to get his sustenance. But of late years, greater care in navigation, and particularly the lifeboat service, had robbed him of his rightful meals. So in the deep water of the gorges on moonlight nights was heard the dragon's wail:—

I have no food, what shall I do?
Hi yeh! Hi yah!
Those things I eat are now too few.
Hi yah! Mei yu fan-chih. [Nothing to eat.]
What shall I do? I'll tell you what.
Hi yeh! Hi yah!
I'll drop a mountain in the pot.
Hi yah! Hao to fan-chih. [Plenty to eat.]

That wail was nothing new—for untold years these have been the words of a junkmen's shanty, and now the thing had come to pass. Thus the grounds for their belief; but the junkmen further say, and this is the important point, that with the thousand bodies he has eaten in the year, the dragon has grown a fiercer beast than ever; so much so that it will ill-brook interference. This rapid is bad enough. Who knows it better than the men who risk their lives in it? But they say they would rather have it as it is than risk a worse one made by the dragon if his food is stopped.

That, in effect, was the story I was told; but with far more fantasy of detail than I can now remember. The Prefect, I am sure, believed in it himself, though in deference to a foreigner's opinion he said it was based on the ignorant superstition of the junkmen.

So through the Prefect I sent a message to the people which was posted as a Proclamation. I would give the dragon all consideration; I could not, even if I would, obliterate the rapid; my orders were to examine and report, though I had authority to do what might prove possible to render navigation safer. As to dynamite, it would be used mainly to break the boulders on the groyne. I would remove that groyne to low-river level, so that at next high-river the current would get a chance to scour away some more. On the right-hand bank, opposite the groyne, I would cut a channel through the rock that would even out the slope of water and enable upward junks to track with safety. For downward junks I could provide no improvement of conditions until next season, when nature would have added its assistance. Further, I would do no heavy blasting in the pool below, where the dragon dwelt, and thus the beast would have no cause for grievance.

The people gathered round the Prefect's Proclamation and discussed it. But an old junk *laodah* [captain] uttered 'Hau,' which indicated acquiescence and so tipped the scale in active favour of the work. A few days later the village caught on fire, and several hundred houses were destroyed, and people rendered homeless and in distress. This gave an opportunity for a substantial gift of money, which added to the favourable auspices for beginning operations.

Then began recruiting; and in a week or so we had two thousand men, and later more. Mostly they were for mere coolie-work—carrying stone; the rest were masons and these were taught rock-drilling. Our blacksmith made the drills and was kept busy with re-shaping and re-sharpening them; there were foremen of the coolies, and gangers of the stone-cutters, each with his distinctive coloured badge—a turban or an armlet, so that they could be recognized; there were food contractors for this crowd, and, of course, they tried to cheat the men, until the Prefect had a culprit publicly bambooed.

Szechuen is a very wealthy province but it produced great quantities of opium—the white and pink and purple of the poppy fields was a striking feature of the country—so the coolie class was opium-ridden, and consequently poor and underfed, and ophthalmic and scrofulous and lousy; yet they were a cheery goodnatured lot, amenable, industrious and appreciative of decent treatment. Their life must have been one long and weary itch; but it may be that they thought it worth it for the pleasure scratching gave them. Where with western navvies one would give at intervals ten minutes for a smoke, our routine board showed ten minutes for a scratch. When the gong beat for that interval, the spread crowd coalesced in squatting strings like monkeys, each man scratching another's back; and there was great contentment on their faces.

We lived in our house-boats tied up to the left bank above the rapid. The Scotsman—a cruiser engineer—was in charge of rock removal from the groyne. The diver—from whom diving work was not required—had charge of the making of the channel on the other shore for upward junks. This merely meant the cutting of an even slope for a foot or two below low-river level, so that when the water rose some feet, junks could pass up in safety where they had never passed before. Near the centre of the river on the edge of the fall and bordering one side of the sloping tongue of water was exposed a rock. In size it was about thirty feet square with a height of some six feet above low river. I proposed to shatter it as thoroughly as my means permitted and trust to scour to remove the debris; thus the downward channel would be widened. This work I made my special task. I was told that no one had ever landed on the rock, and that work there would be quite impossible owing to the danger of access to it; but that was because they did not understand the purpose of an anchor. It is curious that an anchor is an article unknown among that Upper Yangtsze traffic; and I blessed my foresight in providing one. With some difficulty a boatman was persuaded to meet my needs; we drifted down towards the rock, dropped my heavy anchor some fifty feet above it—and the fall—in six fathoms; then another boat, powerfully manned, brought a bamboo rope, one end of which was fastened to the shore. To drop down to the rock in a third boat and fix thereto another rope was now an easy matter; so there we were on that hitherto untrodden rock on the edge of what seemed like a waterfall.

We scaled it down to a foot or so above low-water level and built a rampart round it to prevent fluctuations of the level interfering with the work, and then we drilled holes six feet deep and five apart, which took several weeks to do. We filled those holes with dynamite—about five hundred pounds in all—and fitted electric fuses and then wired up, a single cable leading to the shore, for I used an earth return as in naval mining. Now there are ways of knowing all about an electric circuit of this kind; what its resistance is and the amount of current needed, and lastly a means of testing whether all is right, so that when the key is pressed one knows for certain the result. I had this knowledge and the means, but when I made my tests I found a phenomenal resistance which my current could not overcome. I racked my brain to find the cause but failed.

A feature of the situation was that great preparations had been made. Within a circuit of five hundred yards all had been warned to shelter and the junks had been evacuated; the local gentry for miles around had come to see the show; my little world was looking on in expectation, and now I was confronted with this miserable fiasco.

The unexplained resistance was plainly that due to the return current by the water, and had there been another length of cable a double circuit would have met the case; but there was not. A length of bare wire would have served, but I had not got that either. So the only way to avoid the great fiasco was to double the cable between the rock and the boat, and to press the button in the latter. It happened that there were some planks available, and with them a small pent-house on the boat was rapidly arranged to give some shelter.

To fire that charge of five hundred pounds at a distance of a hundred feet may appear to have been folly. There was risk, of course, but not as much as most would think. I had already had an experience, when breaking up a boulder, of a premature explosion caused by a defective time fuse; I was within a few feet of it at the time and was not touched. There is a sort of safety zone within the immediate neighbourhood; the stones fly up and outwards, but not sideways as a rule. And I judged my boat would be within that safety zone. . . .

Facing the rock I lay beneath that little pent-house with the key in front of me. I knew that what I was doing was exceptional, that few would risk the confidence in estimated chances to do this thing for such a reason—to avoid a loss of face—and the thought exhilarated me. I enjoyed the situation and lingered to get its savour to the full. I have known what fear is, as I have told before; but here there was no fear, only the pleasurable excitement as of cross-country riding, when one takes an unknown jump.

Let me tell too of a curious matter connected with this affair. Doubtless many know but I have never seen it said, that in certain experiences duration moves with extraordinary slowness. I have seen some heads cut off by Chinese executioners, and to me the movement of the sword and its passage through the neck has been just like a slow-motion picture on a cinematograph. And so, when I pressed the button, the minute fraction of a second that passed before the rock hove up was most curiously elongated in duration, and the heave itself and the movement of the flying fragments was a slow-motion picture.

My judgment proved correct; and doubtless there was also luck, for though small fragments rattled on my shelter the heavy pieces curved over and beyond me. One of them killed an old lady in a junk five hundred yards away, who had refused to leave her cabin.

So that was that; and shortly afterwards I realized my error. Obsessed by the practice of an earth return in naval mining, I had overlooked the fact that while sea water is a good conductor fresh water is a bad one.

It has been said that all my little world was looking on in expectation, and that what I did was to avoid a loss of face; but this was much more than a mere personal affair. A failure, even a temporary one, might have meant a serious loss of confidence. I had been most uncomfortably embarrassed by the wondrous powers which rumour gave me. It was said I had tame ducks trained to dive and place dynamite where directed, and that I had an instrument which, pointed at a rock, would pulverize it; so to fail in a simple matter might have been seriously unfortunate.

The work went on successfully. The channel on the right bank was cut and used before we left. On the groyne over two thousand men were working like a lot of ants, and they cut it down to near low-water level.

In the meantime the dragon put in an appearance. I was working on the central rock and saw that there was great excitement on the groyne. When we met—the three of us—at lunch time the Scotsman said: 'You won't believe what I am going to tell you, but I have seen that bally dragon'. He had only seen its head—a monstrous snout some six feet long with a tubular mouth like a fire-engine suction pipe. Then my 'boy' appeared and with great excitement told how he had also seen the beast—and he had seen its tail. I knew the fish from their description; I had seen them in the market at Ichang, six feet and more in length. It was said that they were sturgeon, though they differ from the Amur fish.

I never saw the creature; I watched for hours in vain; but it appeared occasionally round about the whirlpool for a period of some weeks. The Chinese swore it was the body-eating dragon that had caused the rapid; and undoubtedly it must have been a monster fish. The conclusion that I came to was that it was not less than thirty feet in length; and sturgeon of that size are recorded as existing in the Amur river. . . .

It was said that the dragon never came again and that the sacrifice had been successful; but there may have been another explanation. The rising river stopped our season's work. Of our stock of dynamite there remained four hundred pounds; there were objections to either storing it or shipping it, so I used it for a purpose which, while it might be useful, would have spectacular effect. I made a mine and buoyed it and let it drift until it caught below a rocky ledge immediately above the rapid; then fired it. The great column of water impressed the people vastly, and the shock of the explosion impressed, no doubt, the dragon. The explosion being above the rapid and sheltered by the ledge, the shock would not be transmitted to the whirlpool with sufficient strength to stun the monster, though many fish five feet or so in length floated on the surface.

I had been strongly tempted to fire that mine below the fall and so kill or stun the beast if it was there. But I had promised when the work began that I would not do so; and I had also to think of its continuance next season.

34

THE SADNESS OF THE GORGES

MENG JIAO (751–814)

Despite repeated attempts, Meng Jiao failed to pass the civil service exams until he was about fifty years old, after which he finally received a minor government post. Most of his life was spent wandering in poverty, which probably accounts for the rather bitter, sinister quality of many of his poems.

The 'rotted coffins' still hang high above the gorges today, suspended there some 2,000 years ago by the ancient people of Ba. Li Bai (701–762) and Bai Juyi (772–846) also mention the Ba, Bai Juyi comparing them to wild apes ('On Being Removed from Hsun-Yang and Sent to Chung-Chou'). When the three poets passed this way, the Ba people still lived here, but they have long since disappeared.

Above the gorges, one thread of sky:
Cascades in the gorges twine a thousand cords.
High up, the slant of splintered sunlight, moonlight:
Beneath, curbs to the wild heave of the waves.
The shock of a gleam, and then another,
In depths of shadow frozen for centuries;
The rays between the gorges do not halt at noon;
Where the straits are perilous, more hungry spittle.
Trees lock their roots in rotted coffins
And the twisted skeletons hang tilted upright:
Branches weep as the frost perches
Mournful cadences, remote and clear.
A spurned exile's shrivelled guts
Scald and seethe in the water and fire he walks through.
A lifetime's like a fine-spun thread,
The road goes up by the rope at the edge.
When he pours his libation of tears to the ghosts in the stream
The ghosts gather, a shimmer on the waves.

Bitter Strength

All those travelling through the Gorges remarked on the tow-men known as trackers, those who hauled the boats over the rapids. A large cargo junk would need to hire anything from one hundred to four hundred men to drag it upstream, step by groaning step. The word 'coolie' was used for trackers and all those who carried and dragged loads. It literally means 'bitter strength'.

Today there are few trackers on the river as most boats are mechanized, although men can still be seen dragging boats along the tributaries. Yet in most Yangtze towns coolies still wait for work by the steep flights of steps linking the river to the town, squatting patiently beside their bamboo carrying poles and ropes, the tools of their trade.

35

THE TRACKERS

MARION H. DUNCAN

Missionary Marion Duncan describes the trackers' conditions in the 1920s. He and his new bride were travelling upriver to take up a posting in Batang, on the border between Sichuan and Tibet. Fengdu (Fengtu), 'city of ghosts', is described in detail in 'Entrance to Hades'.

The life and labors of the trackers is fearfully hard and monotonous. They receive two Chinese dollars (less than one in American money) and their food for this trip, which going up and down will take ten days. For ten to fourteen hours they must pull like horses on the bobbing cable. When pulling upstream they eat five times a day, a meal that usually consists of rice and cabbage made palatable with oils and peppers. Occasionally they have horse-beans, cucumbers or greens. Pork may come once a week depending upon the generosity of the boat-renter. We give them three pork feeds during the six days, one for each of the major rapids, and also extra tips at the end of the journey. Going downstream the pulling of the oars to keep the boat in the current requires less strength so the trackers eat but three times a day. Upstream they get no rest from the everlasting tracking except when they must pile quickly into the boat and row to the opposite shore to avoid bluffs or to seek the least dangerous channel of a rapid. Tracking upstream they wear only a loin cloth or short pants but when moving sedately downstream their white turbans, blue jeans and naked brown chests are a colorful contrast as they chant while rocking backward and forward on their oars.

Junkmen have their own deity. This patron saint is Chen Chiang Wang Yeh or River-guarding King, a deified pirate, who roamed over Tungting Lake south of Hankow in the twelfth century. He was born about 1127 and during a short life of some 35 years defied all forces sent against him, boasting that he could only be captured by air. He is reputed to have invented the paddle wheel. Finally defeated by General Yo Fei, he committed suicide by jumping into Tungting Lake. When junkmen die a letter is sent, by a ritual of burning the missive with fire, to the Lord of the Dead who lives at the temple of Tientseshan at Fengtu which is on the Yangtze above Wanhsien. It is said that some courses of rivers are so dangerous that providing a coffin is part of the contract in the hiring of trackers.

36

OLD PEBBLE, HEAD TRACKER

JOHN HERSEY

Voyagers may have pitied the trackers, marvelled at their endurance, and sometimes cursed them as rascals, but few tried to get to know them well. John Hersey's novel, A Single Pebble, *is one of the most evocative and empathetic pieces ever written about these men. The narrator is a young engineer on a reconnaissance trip up the river, to determine whether his company should try and persuade the Chinese government to build a huge dam across the gorges. This was in the 1920s, when the dream of a dam was new. It was to haunt the river until this day. There are more dramatic passages in the book, but the studies of Old Pebble, the head tracker, are particularly striking.*

The poem that the narrator recalls hearing Old Pebble sing, about skimming a thousand years in a day, is Li Bai's famous 'Leaving White Emperor City at Dawn'. Su-ling is the junk-owner's young wife, but is secretly in love with Old Pebble. The narrator mentions that Old Pebble punishes one of the boys for turning over a fish: Chinese sailors believe that to turn over a fish when eating is very bad luck and will lead to the turning over of the boat.

I t was here at the mouth of Yellow Cat Gorge that I first saw the trackers at work, as we had too little wind to sail against the constricted current; and it was here, therefore, that I first noticed the head tracker. As the lugsail was taken in and the junk was rowed toward the left bank by a squad of trackers. I noticed that one of them, a lumpy, broad-faced fellow with a shaven head, who was dressed in new blue cotton pants and a drab ragged jacket, took the lead in all that was done. From his powerful larynx to his square feet, this man, whom the owner addressed with a nickname, Old Pebble, seemed to be one whole, rhythm-bound muscle. Everything he did had rhythm. As he gave orders on board the junk, he kicked his feet on the slapping unbolted planks of the deck; he punctuated what he said with tongue-clicks; his hands moved in rope-pulling gestures, all in time with his cadenced speech. His head was spherical, and he had the crow's feet of cheerfulness all the way from his narrow eyes back to his ears. I have never been able to tell with certainty how old a Chinese is; I would guess that this one was in his mid-thirties. At any rate, the 'Old' of his nickname was surely an affectionate term; he seemed young and strong. I saw that he wore a silver ring, and although his hands had no more grace than monkey-wrenches, he had let his fingernails grow rather long, in the old style, evidently to show that he was of the boatmen's nobility.

That evening, after we had made perhaps ten miles between amazing limestone battlements, turrets, and buttresses, towed every inch of the way by the chanting trackers, with the one called Old Pebble out in front, singing weird rhythmic melodies—that evening, when we were securely moored in a little eddying cove at the head of Yellow Cat Gorge, I spoke to the head tracker. He received me openly and without deference.

I began to question him about his life.

'I pull the towline,' he said, and stopped, as if to say: What more is there? What more could there be?

But, I asked, what of the future?

'I have very little,' he said, and he spoke as if having little were the greatest fortune, and the greatest buffer against the future, that a man could wish.

Again I tried to ask him what his goal was.

'In my spare time ashore I drink wine,' he said. 'I never fight when I get drunk. I just talk when I'm drunk and lean against a wall and go to sleep. I hate fighting, and really no one wants to fight me. I am an "old good". I don't save money, I spend it on my friends. I buy them wine. I buy friendship. I save friendship. But some of the men on the river are no good. If they know you have money, they want you to gamble with jumping sticks or cards. If you refuse, they form a circle around you and threaten you.'

He cleared his throat and spat over the side into the Great River, and he seemed very pleased with himself.

'What do you want?' I asked.

'I have no home; my body is my home,' he said. 'But I am an old good. I shall stay on boats, and there will always be someone to

hire me, and when I am old, all my brothers in the boatmen's guild and all the captains on the riverside who know me will give me a few coppers in payment for the friendship I have hoarded for them. I will have plenty. I will have a fine funeral.'

This was the way he spoke. At the time I wanted to believe him, and mostly did, though I thought him full of guile; in my Occidental complacency I then considered all Chinese liars, anyhow. I guess I wanted to believe that he was a simple, good man, but I was troubled by his obvious inner enjoyment of his account of himself; from time to time he had pursed his lips, so that his face had looked shrewd, as if he had been saying to himself, 'I am the grandest liar in the world, and see how I have this stupid foreign boy on my towline!' I thought he might be dramatizing himself as a poor, pure-hearted wanderer, one of Heaven's minstrels, to me, a foreigner who asked questions. I could not imagine that a young, vigorous, and cheerful man could live without distant goals: wealth, family, and a good name widely known. . . .

The head tracker seemed to have been nowhere so much at home as he was in Witches' Mountain Gorge, the longest, most beautiful, and most mysterious of all the chasms of the river. This gorge, I remember, was fully twenty miles long, and at places it was no more than a hundred and fifty yards wide, and as it afforded the river's most awesome sights to this point, so also it presented some of its most arduous problems for the trackers, and these difficulties seemed to raise Old Pebble's spirits, so that for three days he sang and flew about like a wild strong bird.

The river, which in that fantastic stretch seemed not great but actually puny, had somehow during the ages cut its narrow brown way straight through vast rock mountains, which rose vertically from the water for hundreds of feet, then, falling back at knee-, hip-, and shoulder-terraces, rose again, and again, and again, all but perpendicular, until, seen through sudden clefts, they reached craggy pinnacles, like those of the Tetons, far up in the springtime sky. Sometimes the sky was cloud-streaked, and more than once we saw, back in the tallest ranges, a needle of rock piercing the under-side of a layer of mist, and then, higher up, its point, visible and dry and gray in clear air above the thin plate of vapor. The rocks were limestone with overlying sandstone, and at the riverfront, where the softer rock had been washed away leaving the limestone sheer and upright, there were enormous up-and-down potholes in the faces of the cliffs, giving them weird, fluted surfaces. Caves could be seen high on the cliffs. Here and there villages clung to ledges, and sometimes these blue-gray hamlets straddled, with lovely high-arching bridges, little foaming bourns—one of which, I recall, poured out of the mouth of a cavern far up the side of a peak.

Going through Witches' Mountain Gorge gave me the feeling, as in the song Old Pebble had sung in the rapids of Hsintan, of skimming a thousand years in a day.

The water of the river itself was mostly deep and relatively quiet, but here and there, where jagged cliffs jutted boldly forward, or where heaps of detritus had been thrown out from streams on the banks, or where piles of enormous, square-cornered, house-sized blocks of sooty rock, which looked as if they had been blackened in a mountain-builder's furnace, had tumbled from the crags down into the sides of the channel—in such places there were eddies and cross-sets and whirlpools of unexpected violence. What a setting for a dam!

For the trackers, and particularly for Old Pebble, the gorge was an ever-changing challenge. The ingenuity of the head tracker was tested every hour, and he met each test with fiery joy. Here he led his towing gang over a mass of fallen boulders; next he put them aboard in a swarm, and they took up oars in erect ranks on the foredeck, sometimes pushing and sometimes pulling at the long oars, and they chanted and stamped in unison and beat up a brown froth with the wooden blades, in order that the junk might ride a cross-current to the opposite bank and there have the benefit of an upstream eddy; then for a while, shouting hoarse commands unlike any other cries of his, he would supervise his men as they stood on deck and literally clawed the junk with lizards and poles and bare hands along some sheer wetted palisades; later he would lead them on their harnesses high along a little-known ledge, or over a shoulder of rock, or across a steep scree—scrambling, singing, hurrying with elated whoops from one piece of horrible work to another. Often the head tracker was in the sampan, sculling madly from the shore out to the junk to consult with the bow steersman, or standing up in the skittish boat pulling it back ashore hand over hand on the towing hawser and roaring directions to his trackers, who had only one guttural voice to answer his shouts: 'Ayah! . . . Ayah! . . .'

Yes, this variable work was obviously a delight to the head tracker. Yet I saw him, more than once, in those days, after a meal or in the early evening, altogether composed, huddled up like a great-grandmother, with a pensive face and a hint of easy-paced melancholy in his eyes. I found him one evening before dark lying on his stomach on the deck lining up a dozen peach pits, which he had been drying for the sake of their almond-like meat, in a row, and with a single chopstick flipping one over the others along the row, in a kind of tiddly-winks, and he seemed satisfied quite alone with this game for more than an hour. Yet I found that he was amazingly cultured, for he owned somewhat the same rather disturbing fund of folklore and history and myth as Su-ling; I suppose what made me persist in thinking him simple in spite of this education was the fact that his learning had all been acquired orally. I guess I thought book-learning the only true enlightenment. I remember sitting by one evening while Su-ling taught him some lines by a poet of the T'ang dynasty, Tu Fu, entitled *Unable to Visit Judge Wang Owing to Rain*. Taught him? She recited the poem once, then he perfectly repeated it, and some time later, asking her if he still had it right, pronounced it again to her without a single mistake. His mildness was deceptive. It made him seem nerveless and phlegmatic—until various crises arose, such as that when, doubling as pilot, he had tended toward the wrong sluice at New Rapids, or such as an incident which occurred a few days later in Witches' Mountain Gorge, when the young farmer boy slipped and got his foot caught between two boulders; during these crises the head tracker gave way to explosions of swiftness and violent motion, which then seemed to me mere animal reflexes, but which I now regard as having been examples of almost perfect concord between perception and action. What could be more civilized than that harmony? I remember now that he was a hypochondriac, with many a quaintly expressed anxiety about decaying muscles and shriveling tendons, but then I saw him only as a package of wonderful rhythmic power. He had a strange, halting grace, and I loved to watch him fill, tamp, light, and smoke his pipe, with its tiny brass bowl and a stem nearly three feet long—of such a length, he once said, that he could take a light from a passing junk.

Most of the time Old Pebble seemed kind, considerate, open, and warm. His moments of wrath, such as the one I had seen at the end of the gambling game that night, or when he had punished the farmer boy for turning over his fish, were rare, and they appeared to go against his nature. In those days, his goodness seemed to me innate, built-in, almost organic in him, like muscle tissue. It seemed not to be a matter of conscience and effort and struggling feeble heart. Only now on reflection, as I remember the signs of helplessness that lurked now and then momentarily in his eyes, do I see how hard he must have striven for virtue, and what a triumph of hard-working philosophy his simple goodness was. His life was a towpath; he was hauling himself wearily along it; his head and his heart were his stubborn trackers. He must have been trying his best, I now realize, to free himself from delusion, to struggle to rise above existence and pain, to speak truth, to be pure, to hurt no living thing, to have self-control, to have a wakeful mind, and rapturously to contemplate his short and awful life.

WHERE APES HOWL ENDLESSLY

CAPTAIN ZHANG

This 1980s interview is with the captain of a motorboat who hauled boats by hand until 1971, when he was in his forties. He gives a lively account of his life and of the changes he has seen.

A clear tributary at the mouth of Wu Gorge is marked on the map as the River Daning. Having sheer cliffs on both sides, it is known locally as the Small Gorges. A motor-boat chugs upstream through the narrow gorges. He is standing in the prow watching out for rapids. The crew call him Captain Zhang.

'Where do you expect to find towmen? Ha, comrade, we're all towmen. We've been towing boats all our lives here, like our fathers and their fathers before us. In '71 we switched to a motor-boat. In tricky stretches we still have to punt. In places like this with sheer, slippery cliffs you couldn't tow the boat, had to stick close to the cliff and punt it along. See all those little holes chiselled in the rock? They were for the old plank towpath along the precipice dating back to the Three Kingdoms [Third century AD]. How was it made? Stone masons were roped round the middle and lowered from the top of the cliff to chisel those holes. All the way to Wuxi, wherever there are sheer cliffs you'll find a plank towpath. And from Wuxi all the way to Shennongjia. A motor-boat takes half a day to reach Wuxi, for towmen it used to take five days upstream. Sit tight! If you don't want to get wet sit in the cabin. There are several rapids like this; it's not the worst. In one place there was a big rock in midstream which disappeared when the river was in spate. A boat knocking into it would be smashed to pieces. Each time a man with a rope had to swim to that rock and haul the boat along, while the crew used

poles to ward it off the rock—if it got sucked over you'd had it! Now that rock's been blasted away.

At four or five I played about on a boat; at eleven or twelve I started towing; at eighteen I became a 'skipper' in charge of a boat. My dad didn't have to teach me, it's not hard to manage a boat if you know the river and have guts. Helps if you drink and eat meat.

This river used to be busy, not any more. There's a highway now on the other side of that hill to Wushan County, used by trucks and motor-coaches. In the past all goods had to be shipped in or out. By Wuxi there are mountains, very wild, getting wilder the farther you go. They produce rare herbs as well as local products, and some strange people too—some live just on grass. What's sent in from outside is mostly coal. In the past not many people travelled by boat, only merchants and KMT troops. Not many people lived here, but lots of troops were stationed here: KMT troops, local troops and other units. We dreaded soldiers using our boats to ship guns and ammunition. They made us carry it ashore, beat us if we weren't quick enough for them, and paid us with mouldy rice. Today it's a different world. Isn't that right?' [He questions one of the passengers behind us, one of the district propaganda committee who looks something of a scholar. 'Yes, indeed. Wu Gorge is the longest of East Sichuan's three gorges. Apes gibber above it.'] 'Those were the days with boats plying to and fro when the river was really busy. We all grabbed at business, buying goods one trip for the next. For a skipper, knowing the river wasn't hard; the tricky thing was grabbing business. One trip you might make several dozen strings of cash, enough for a bushel of good rice. At Wushan waiting for a cargo you had your fling. Of course there were prostitutes, that was in the old days. Wushan County town was lively then. The dockyard bosses, those devils, stung you for each day you moored, and the damn shipping bureau taxed you too, whether you'd made money or not. Where I lived there was a swine. When KMT troops came he collected taxes; and when the power changed hands and other troops came he went right on collecting taxes! After Liberation he was still in charge but I paid no attention to him. In the 'cultural revolution' they gunned for him, such a piddling little official! I felt sorry for him and said a few words to him, but now that he's in the clear again I ignore him. The prostitutes weren't so bad, everyone has to eat; the worst people are those who throw their weight about no matter who's in power.

In those days, yes of course, we were superstitious, sacrificed on the boat to the Dragon King, and burned incense and let off firecrackers when we landed. When we'd eat meat we first offered a bowl to the Dragon King. Boatmen had a special jargon, special names handed down from the past. We never liked women passengers, had all kinds of taboos. If they broke one we fined them red cloth or fire-crackers; oh yes we were strict about it, because we didn't want the boat to capsize. No one believes that stuff any more, we've got rid of superstition. It's odd how many strange things used to happen on the river, but rarely nowadays. We say the Communist Party has driven away most ghosts—maybe the Dragon King's fled?

My home's in Dazhang, the first big town after the Gorges. I've four sons, lucky aren't I? Ha! This woman back here bore me three, and brought one with her. My first wife was no good, I divorced her. At first I thought nothing of it when my mother quarrelled with her daughter-in-law. That's the way women are. When I went home I gave them a talking-to. Then I discovered that my wife wasn't treating my mother right. That was during the hard years, and if the old lady ate an extra bite she'd curse: Drown yourself, drat you, when you cross the river! My mother lived on the bank opposite Dazhang. I told her off for cursing the old lady, told her off time after time and beat her up, then lost patience and divorced her. We had a daughter, she took off with her. I hear she's since married someone in the hills. My present wife's first husband was a skipper too, drowned in an accident. When she was introduced to me I liked the look of her, so I took her and her son. We've never had a row, and she's good to my mother. Actually my mother, how should I describe her? After my dad died she remarried, then she died, and my step-father took another wife, then he died.[*] But she's an old lady, isn't she? We have to show her respect. If there's anything good to eat, she gets helped first. We have to set an example for the young ones. Put yourself in her place, how do you want to be treated when you're old? Do as you would be done by.

See that wooden boat being towed there? Now the policy's changed, private citizens can own boats. In a stretch like this boats can only be towed where there's a beach on the bank. You could do it yourself if you were strong enough. You strip to the skin, just wearing shoes, otherwise your feet would be burned by the sun on the pebbles, no matter how thick your soles are. When the going's hard you get down on your hands and knees.

Bah, this doesn't count as a chanty. You don't need to sing rousingly on a motor-boat. When you reach a rapid, a couple of shouts, all punting together, and you're over it. . . . In our town we've a fine singer, a big strapping fellow. When he bellows out a chanty it re-echoes through the gorges! Want to hear one! Next rapid we come to, I'll get the crew to sing at the top of their voices.

Just before Liberation I managed to get myself a wooden boat. I'd saved up seven strings of cash after several trips, and half-way home found a man in a hurry to get his old boat off his hands, so I bought it and shipped a load of stuff to Wuxi, delivered my cargo and sold the boat then built myself a new one to take home. My mother couldn't believe it! When I joined the co-op they reckoned its cost but never paid me the money, gave me some grain later on. In '71 we switched to motor-boats. I was still in the three-in-one group.' [A combination of old, middle-aged and young in the 'cultural revolution'] 'We didn't get up the rapids till the fifth go—the horsepower wasn't enough.

---

[*] In other words, the woman he refers to as his mother is not his birth-mother, but the woman his step-father married after his real mother's death.

Look back, stand up. See those coffins hanging in that cave up on the cliff?

We have a contract now, four men to a boat, each month we pay our collective one thousand yuan, and each of us can make over a hundred. A lot? It's not easily earned. Nowadays we take passengers. People going into the hills on business, but mostly tourists, especially in summer, not in winter. Last year a lot of foreigners from different countries came, to help open up tourism in Sichuan they said. They went back this way and all opted for this place to invest in. We helped ship those foreigners. It pays when they book a boat. So much per boat, not so much per head. Last time we had retired Red Army veterans and old workers. We stopped whenever we came to something worth seeing and let them have a good look, sometimes helped them ashore. Our country owes them so much.

There's another company in Wuxi which competes with us for passengers, seeing who can give the best service, whose boats are smartest and most comfortable. After this trip we'll overhaul the boat, not that I want to, but it belongs to our company and what they say goes. With the boat in dry dock we can't earn a cent. During this overhauling we've decided to fix up a removable awning that can be rolled up on both sides, so that passengers in the cabin will be able to see the top of the cliffs and the clouds above the gorges.

Do I think it a lovely landscape? Ha, after all these years on the river I'm used to it. Anyway these gorges are natural, not man-made. In April the hillsides are a mass of flowers, red, yellow and the water's really clear then, clearer than now. If you watch it from the bank you can make out distinct currents of brown and green. It's a fine sight, even after all these years.

I'm fifty-eight, we boatmen retire at sixty. I've two sons at home waiting for jobs, waiting to take over from me. Oh, young fellows in a small town have nothing to do when they leave school but kick their heels. What jobs are there for them? They've no land to farm. My elder son doesn't want to be a boatman, my second boy's dead keen. Not unless I retired early, but I'm still strong. I can't spend a single day idle at home. Each trip missed out on would mean so much less money. Taking passengers you can't count on a steady income, so our company's thinking of buying a big boat to ship goods along the Yangtse. I shall stick to this stretch of river though. My Number Two ought to make out all right. All my life? I've just plied this stretch from Wu Gorge to Wuxi, where boats can't pass. I've never sailed right down the Yangtse.

Monkeys? Yes. Sometimes troops of them come down to drink. It's said there used to be black monkeys on this cliff and brown monkeys on the other side. They never crossed the river but gibbered at each other across it every day, scaring people with their row. When boats passed they all chucked down stones. There aren't many left now. Henanese like performing monkeys. They used to come up through Shennongjia to trap them here, but later they weren't allowed to. If they were caught they'd be fined. Monkeys are really smart. See that bare cliff going sheer up? They can swarm up it. Once one of them slipped and fell, fell into the river. We punted over and picked it up, but it died before we got home.

Can you see them now? Yes, with any luck you can.

The Steam Age

By the late 1860s, American and British steamers were busily plying the river between Shanghai and Wuhan. But because of
Chinese opposition and the dangers of the river above Wuhan, it
took another twenty years before steamers were sailing to Yichang,
and about ten more for a small steamer to reach Chongqing for
the first time in 1898. When they got to Wuhan, passengers would
transfer to smaller steamers to continue upriver. Even so, the boats
often had to resort to trackers to drag them over the worst rapids.

Naturally, once the boats were established, they took business
away from the junks. Despite the dangers, during the 1920s, the
glory days of steam, there were over sixty steamers on the river.

THE ADVANTAGES OF STEAM

ARCHIBALD J. LITTLE

The Chefoo Convention of 1876, signed as a result of British outrage over Augustus Margary's murder, opened up Wuhu and Yichang to foreign trade. More importantly, Chongqing (Chungking), far upriver beyond the Gorges, was also declared open, though with the stipulation that the city must be reached by steamer, as the Chinese were confident that this was impossible. But they reckoned without Archibald Little. Travelling up the Yangtze by junk as far as Chongqing in 1883, Little was convinced that steamers could do it and that this would be beneficial both to foreigners and Chinese. In his preface to an account of his trip, he argues his case.

With the exception of the ubiquitous missionary, the travellers who have ascended the 'Great (and sole) Highway' of China to its highest navigable point may be counted on the fingers of one hand. So tedious are the antiquated modes of travel, that of the thousands of European residents at the treaty ports, few have the leisure or inclination to journey outside of the routes covered by our 'barbarian' steamers. Of the voyage up to Chung-king, up the Yang-tse river, a distance of 1500 miles, 1000 miles are traversed by steamers to Ichang in a week's time. The remaining 500 miles occupy from five to six weeks, a longer time than it takes to go from London to Shanghai. Since the execution of the celebrated 'Chefoo Convention' in 1876, the placing of steamers on this upper route has been under discussion, but Chinese obstructiveness has thus far succeeded in staving off the evil day, and nothing but strong pressure on the part of the foreign ministers accredited to the Court of Pekin will bring about this much-needed innovation, an innovation as much desired by the native merchants and traders as it is dreaded by the official and literary classes. Apart from the laudable fear of injury to the livelihood of the existing junk-men, anything that leads to further ~~contact between foreigners and the people at large is deprecated~~ as lessening the influence of the profoundly ignorant ruling class; and thus, notwithstanding the heavy losses in life and property that the present system of navigation entails, this further contemplated invasion of the inner waters of the Empire is strenuously resisted.

In reading this journal, in which I have depicted the existing difficulties of the route, it must be borne in mind that the Yang-tse is not only the main, but the sole road of intercommunication between the east and west of this vast Empire. Roads, properly so called, do not exist in China; narrow footpaths alone connect one town and village with another, and, except by the waterways, nothing can be transported from place to place but on men's backs. In the far north, it is true, cart-tracks exist, and clumsy two-wheeled springless carts are there in use, but in Central and Southern China, land travel is absolutely to paths, so narrow that two pedestrians have often a difficulty in passing each other. Traces of magnificent paved roads, of the ancient dynasties, still exist in nearly every province; but they have been destroyed by neglect, and have been disused for centuries past. Since the date of the Mongol invasion [1279], every incentive to progress has come from without, and every foreign well-wisher of the Empire, especially if resident, is impelled to do his utmost to carry on this progress.

Archibald Little built his first steamer, the Kuling *(175 foot, 500 tons) in 1889, but it never got further than Yichang. This was not owing to any defect in the ship, but simply because the Chinese were determined to prevent her. They came up with all sorts of objections, such as that monkeys would throw stones at it, and refused to let the ship proceed. Eventually the Chinese government bought it and sold it to a private Chinese shipping line, who ran it very profitably from Yichang to Hankou for the next twenty years. But Little refused to give up. He built the much smaller launch, the* Leechuan, *(fifty foot, seven tons), too tiny to be regarded as a threat to the junkmen's livelihood. The* Leechuan *reached Chongqing in March 1898.*

39

PERILS OF THE YANGTSZE

H. G. W. WOODHEAD

In this passage, written in 1931, Shanghai journalist and editor of the China Yearbook, H. G. W. Woodhead, describes the difficulties of sailing the Yangtze during the 1920s. The natural dangers of the upper river were only a part of the problem. Although after the fall of the Manchus in 1911 the country was supposedly a Republic, in reality power was divided between rival warlords, each with his own domain. The warlords had to be bribed or conciliated and there were also bandits to be avoided.

In mid-1926, Chiang Kai-shek, (at that time in a short-lived alliance with the Communists) set out from his base in Guangzhou to subdue the Northern warlords one by one. His troops marched up the Yangtze, seizing cities as far upriver as Wuhan, and looting and killing as they came. Many of those Westerners and Japanese who did not evacuate to Shanghai in time were murdered.

Through all the turmoil, foreigners continued to run the Customs and to act as River Inspectors. Captain Cornell Plant was an important figure in the river's history. Originally a pilot along the Tigris and Euphrates rivers, he played a major role in designing the first commercial steamers, and spent the rest of his life along the Yangtze, holding the position of River Inspector for many years. Upon his retirement, the Chinese government built a bungalow for him overlooking the dreaded Xintan Rapid. Steamers would sound their horns in salute as they passed, to be rewarded by the cheery wave of a white handkerchief.

Anyone who travels up the Upper Yangtsze at low or medium level will gain some idea of the perils of navigation. For reefs of rocks, extending far out into the channel, are being encountered frequently—obstacles which can be avoided when they can be seen, but become a serious danger when they are submerged. A rapid is defined by the late Captain Plant as generally consisting of a head, a tongue and an approach.

The head is the banked up belt of smooth water 'which occupies the whole breadth of the channel immediately above the actual rapid and triangular smooth and cambered slope of water which forms the axis or tongue, and which carries on through a mass of whirlpools and eddies extending for some distance down stream, called the approach.'

No two rapids are the same, and the technique employed for ascending them has to be varied in each case. (Four different directions are given on the charts for ascending the Fu T'an at varying water levels). But the aim is always to get the steamer, as nearly as possible, end on to the tongue of the down-rushing current, 'to avoid being shot off at a tangent broadside athwart the stream'. In descending, the centre of the tongue is steered for, and the axis then followed down the approach.

Besides the rapids there are other dangers to the navigator, including whirlpools, stationary and running, what is described as a 'boil' of the water, quicksands, and the current, which varies from $1\frac{1}{2}$ to 11 miles an hour.

At certain periods of low water not even the most powerful steamer can ascend some of the rapids, particularly the Hsin T'an and the Hsin Lung T'an, without recourse to haulage.

The Captain of the *I Ping*, on which I travelled, recalls an experience in the *Chi Ping* in March, 1929, when he had no fewer than eight wires out, with some 400 coolies hauling, at the Hsin T'an, and, after struggling for four hours and 20 minutes, his windlass was torn out, and with great difficulty he backed downstream and got out.

At the Hsin T'an in the winter the trackers charge $180 for getting a large steamer over. At other rapids the price is usually lower—$60 to $80.

The aids to navigation on the Upper Yangtsze consist mainly of watermarks painted on rocks and cliffs, in white paint on a tarred background. These are quite numerous. At bad bends and approaches to the rapids there are signal stations, which hoist signals showing when up- or down- bound steamers or junks are in the channel. A steamer is not expected to enter a bad rapid, if it can be avoided, when junks are signalled in the channel. For the wash created by them often renders the channel unsafe for junks for an hour or more afterwards. As a general rule the down-bound steamer has the right of way when up- and down-bound vessels are approaching the same rapid, but this right has to be waived if the up-bound craft is already in a rapid.

A few beacons, consisting only of tarred poles, are placed on the top of dangerous rocks on the Wanhsien–Chungking section and these are also flag-marks, trees in rocks and a few mark-boats.

The best charts available are those compiled by the Hydrographic Department of the French Navy. The set of 38 sheets was originally engraved from surveys made by members of Lt. Commander Hourst's Mission in 1902, supplemented by surveys by Lt. Commander Dupuy Dutemps and Lieuts. Lartigne and Fay in 1910–13, and Lt. Commander Robbe in 1921. Every experienced Captain annotates these charts and endeavours to keep them up to date with his own observations, and data furnished by the Maritime Customs.

Piloting is entirely in the hands of the Chinese. The pilots serve an apprenticeship of six or seven years and usually have had considerable practical experience as helmsmen of junks. They have no theoretical knowledge of navigation, never look at a compass, and could not take a cross bearing. But they are able to read underwater conditions from the appearance of the surface with almost uncanny accuracy. The standard wages according to Customs Regulations, are: No. 1, $300; No. 2, $200; No. 3, $75 per month. Some exceptionally good Pilots, however, earn as much as $450 per month.

The pilot usually brings his own quartermaster, who fully understands his mysterious signals. He seldom gives verbal orders, which it would, in any case, be difficult to hear above the noise of the swirl, but issues his instructions by lifting one or more fingers, or by gesture of the hand. The quartermasters themselves are usually experienced men, who know the river, and intend in due course to qualify as pilots, also.

Most of the pilots are Hupeh men. The *I Ping*'s No. One Pilot on this trip was one of the best known of the Upper River pilots. His name is Hsu Ta-hai, he comes from Hupeh and he has never had an accident on any steamer when he has been on the bridge. Although a fragile, youthful looking man, he told me that he had started at as ordinary member of a river junk's crew at the age of 15. After four years' service in this capacity he was promoted to the position of junk pilot, and wielded the bow sweep, serving 10 years at this task. There followed eight years as a junk master, whereafter he was employed by the late Captain Plant to assist him, in his surveys. Finally he passed through the stages of apprentice, No. 3, No. 2 and No. 1 pilot.

There appears to be a good deal of jealousy between the Hupeh and the Szechwan pilots.

On the vessels that employ Chinese engineers the pilots have to be carefully watched on the up-river trip, as they frequently will conspire to slow down in order to ensure a night anchorage at a point at which they can pick up opium, to dispose of down river on the return voyage.

There are now no foreign pilots on the Upper River, though several of the foreign captains are quite competent to take their ships, unaided, up and down. Captains Turner and Pitcairn took the ship *Hsia Kiang* on the round trip between Ichang and Wanhsien, during some trouble with the pilots in the early 'twenties.

During the general evacuation of the foreign community from Chungking in March 1927, it was very doubtful whether the water level would permit H.M.S. *Mantis* to make the trip downriver, the danger point being a tortuous channel known as the Taipantzu. The advisability of sinking or blowing her up was being discussed seriously by the British Naval authorities, when the master of one of the Yangtsze Rapid boats, Captain Tornroth, an American citizen, suggested that she might just as well be wrecked as intentionally destroyed, and volunteered to attempt to pilot her down. He got her safely through the Taipantzu and down to Ichang, a magnificent feat of pilotage, for which he received the special thanks of the British Admiralty.

In 1930, presumably as part of an organized attempt to run foreign vessels off the Upper River, there was a pilots' strike. It was broken mainly as a result of the jealousy between the Hupeh and Szechwan pilots. Several of the latter were smuggled on the str. *Mei Hsia* and took her up river on April 30. Other Szechwanese also returned to duty, and were put aboard river steamers secretly during the night. Some of these men still do not dare to leave their ships at Ichang. A contributory factor to the termination of the strike, also, was the action of Captain Hughes, who with the cooperation of the Master, Captain Barden, took the *Kiawo* up to Chungking without any Chinese pilot aboard.

The pilot's job is not merely to keep the vessel off the rocks, and steer it safely through the rapids and other danger spots. At certain phases of the river, say at mid-level, it might be possible for a very high-powered steamer to make the trip most of the way up in mid river. But the ordinary merchant vessels do not possess the necessary power for this purpose, and if they did, it would not be economical to use it.

The expert pilot makes use of every current., swirl and backwash to get his ship along with the minimum of resistance from the water. He is constantly taking it backwards and forwards across the channel to make the maximum of progress with the least possible effort. It would take the average river steamer of today at least twice as long to reach Chungking if she 'bucked' the river all the way up.

There is no navigation by night on the Upper Yangtsze. The insurance policies prescribe that the vessel shall only be under way between dawn and sunset. And this means that on each upward trip a river steamer has to moor or anchor for at least three nights. An anchorage cannot always be found at a convenient hour, and recourse is then had to 'spar-mooring'. The vessel thus to be moored, cautiously approaches the bank, and wire cables are taken ashore and made fast to convenient boulders, or anchored to the ground. Oaken spars are put out at each end of the steamer and made fast to tackles on board. These keep the side of the vessel off the bank, the mooring cables being tightened until the spars form a sort of wedge between steamer and shore.

It is the practice of vessels using this form of mooring to paint their names and dates at the water level, at the point at which they made fast for the night. I saw many of these, some of them 20 to 30 feet above the then water level, on my trip up to Chungking.

The captain of an Upper River steamer not only requires a knowledge of the river in its different phases, but also an iron nerve, and a practical knowledge of emergency repairs. The late Captain Plant rightly insisted upon caution as the chief quality for a master on the Ichang–Chungking run. But even with the utmost caution accidents happen. And many a steamer is now running on the river that would have been a total loss, had not the captain shown the utmost ingenuity in effecting temporary repairs.

The percentage of casualties, especially now that steamers make the round trip at all levels, remains high. I have abstracted the following figures from a graph kindly supplied to me by Captain W. G. Pitcairn upon whom the mantle of Captain Plant has descended, and the latest Customs returns. Captain Pitcairn was for several years River Inspector, but now operates a ship of his own, and acts as a consultant and salvage expert.

	No. of Steamers on River	Casualties	Total Losses	Entries & Clearances Wanhsien	Chungking
1929	67	47	3	2,018	1,010
1930	64	31	0	1,938	897

Of the Entries & Clearances at Chungking in 1930, 168 were American, 274 British, 86 French, 129 Japanese and 240 Chinese steamers. The aggregate tonnage was 347, 245.

In former years a considerable portion of every up and down-bound vessel's cargo (and passengers) was 'pidgin', that is to say packages and passengers were put aboard without any payment to the owners.* There was literally no means of stopping this, other than by the presence of an armed guard, and the foreign naval authorities were not willing to use naval units, as a general rule, for this purpose. The officers and compradores of the ships were powerless and so, too, were the Customs officials. It was as much as anyone's life was worth to interfere.

In one instance, the A.P.C. steamer *Shukwang*, when about to make the down-river trip from the Chungking installation, was found to have on board 89 tons of pidgin cargo—mostly oranges. The wharf coolies, and the crew, alike refused to take any part in

---

* 'Pidgin' comes from the word 'business' (hence 'pidgin English').

removing it, and the only alternative to carrying it down river was to hold up the vessel indefinitely at a time when the river was falling to a dangerous level. It had to be carried down.

The junkmen did not feel overly threatened by the first few primitive steamers. But by the mid-1920s an average of thirty trading steamers a week were reaching Chungking and the situation was very different.

The advent of the steamship proved disastrous for the junks. Not only did it seriously reduce their opportunities of securing cargo. The type of junk in use was not constructed to withstand the wash of a high-powered steamer. Many of the native craft were greatly overloaded, and especially when commandeered by the military, in the hands of inexperienced crews.

In many parts of the river it is unsafe for junks and steamers to overtake or pass each other; in some of the rapids it is dangerous for a junk to attempt the passage within an hour of the passing of a steamer. On the other hand, when ascending the rapids and fighting against a current like a mill-race, it is impossible for a steamer to slow up without courting disaster.

At the approaches to the rapids and dangerous bends signal stations have been erected at which warning signals are displayed with the object of preventing more than one craft from entering a danger zone at one time. These signals, however, were not always heeded by the junks, and it is I believe, a fact, that in the early days some steamers showed little consideration for the junk traffic with the result that numbers of native craft were capsized with considerable loss of life and cargo.

'It is incumbent', wrote Captain Plant, 'on the latter (i.e. the steamer) to remember the junk was "there first" and has a host of dangers to contend against over and above those brought along by the advent of the steamer.'

The resentment of the junk-men at the loss of their livelihood and the increased perils of the river, attained such proportions in 1921, that, at the instance of the Superintendant of Customs at Chungking the foreign steamship companies agreed to a time limit of not less than $3\frac{1}{2}$ days for the up river trip from Ichang and $1\frac{1}{2}$ days for the down-journey. Thereafter offending steamers were boycotted. That recklessness on the part of steamship

Captains no longer constitutes a serious grievance is indicated by the Customs Report for 1924, which stated that:

> 'Claims against shipping companies for compensation for junks sunk by the wash of their steamers have been very frequent, and though, undoubtedly, there have been cases of carelessness in this respect on the part of Masters and Pilots, the main cause of these accidents is to be found in the fact that junks are almost invariably overloaded, and with insufficient freeboard for safety.'

The junkmen have at times made a vigourous fight to retain their livelihood, notably by demanding a monopoly for the transportation of certain commodities. And although they have usually vented their wrath upon the foreigner, nearly half of the steamers operating on the Upper Yangtsze are wholly or partly Chinese owned. There was, for some years, considerable abuse of foreign flags for the purpose of securing protection of steamers from the Chinese military.

In 1921 the number of vessels under the French flag increased until it exceeded the combined totals of British and American owned vessels. And at one time numerous vessels were sailing under the French, Italian, Swedish and Portuguese flags which, it was notorious, were Chinese-owned. This scandal was ended by the action of the respective Governments in 1927.

40

DOWN THE RIVER ON THE DOLLAR LINE

TAN SHI-HUA

By the time young Tan Shi-hua sailed down river to go to university in about 1920, foreign steamers had replaced junks as the most popular way to travel. It was a chaotic and dangerous time. While China was nominally a unified Republic, in reality the country was being fought over by warlords and encroached upon by the Japanese.

This journey was Tan's first exposure to life outside his home village of Xianshi (Hsien-Shih) and the small town of De Jian (Teh Chien), where he attended high school. 'Dog's Head', whom he mentions, was the richest and most powerful person in his small world, a landowner, merchant and moneylender.

Like his father, Tan was a follower of Sun Yatsen and a fervent believer in the Nationalist Party (the Kuomintang). He looked to Russia for inspiration and, unknown to his family, instead of sailing for Shanghai to study engineering as commanded by his father, Tan left the river at Hankou. There he boarded a train to Beijing, where he went to Beijing University to study Russian and Russian literature. One of his Russian Professors there, Tretiakov, recorded his story for a book published in the 1930s.

A few of our friends saw us off. They tied a package of tanger-ines to my fingers, and asked me to write them about Peking, about the students and the anti-Japanese boycott, and to send them the university programmes as soon as possible. Our steamer was anchored in the middle of the river. A boatman took us to the gang-plank, which was already surrounded by dozens of boats. The handkerchiefs of our friends fluttered on the shore. The striped American flag, with stars gathered in one corner of it, waved to them from the mast. The steamer belonged to the American line owned by Robert Dollar. War was going on in Szechuan then, and all Chinese steamships had been either seized by the generals and used for carrying their troops and cannons, or were navigated only in the lower Yangtze.

Robert Dollar was no fool. As soon as the monopoly of passenger traffic was his, he immediately raised the price of the tickets. Formerly the price of a third-class ticket from Chungching to Ichang—a day-and-a-half trip—was ten *da yang*, going up the river, twenty *da yang*. Now it was forty instead of ten, but, as there was no alternative, I paid the forty out of my hundred. Heavy silver coins weighed my pockets down. Paper money was not convenient for travelling purposes—its value varied in different provinces. Silver *da yangs*, with the profile of Yuan Shih-kai [President of the Republic] on them, were the only money retaining the same value all over China.

Mandarins and manufacturers travelled first class. Dog's Head and his partners travelled this way. But there was a class superior to first class—on the top decks of some of the steamers were special cabins for foreigners. Even Dog's Head would not have been allowed to go there, no matter how much money he was willing to pay. These special cabins for foreigners were only on the big boats sailing down from Ichang. Our boat was a small shallow one, which travelled only over the upper Yangtze.

The third class was in the steerage. There the people were lying around in disorder, on and under their belongings. Walking across this section, you would inevitably step on someone's foot. The human skeleton was not made for the contortions which the passengers on the Dollar steamer had to perform. Heads of snoring people were hanging down over their suitcases, their mouths turned upwards. A smell of musty blankets and unwashed clothing pervaded the place. People delayed going to the lavatory until they could endure it no longer. They cleared their throats, and then took a long time looking around for a crack in the floor where they could spit.

An inspector, a foreigner, wearing the cap of an official, came down for our tickets, walking over people's blankets and bodies. He kicked away their feet and swore at the passengers, although they had not been guilty of one disrespectful word. Two clerks in white jackets followed him, and gave orders to open all baggage. With swift hands, they turned over the carefully packed bundles and bags. The fingers of one of them dug under my books. What were they looking for? Opium? Arms? In any case they were not looking for contraband—they were not customs officials.

At twilight our steamer stopped opposite the city of Wanhsien. The long city spread out along the river underneath a black mountain. We could see a large grey spot above the city, pressed from all sides by the darkness of an enormous garden. It was the training school. The masts of many barges rose like a great comb between us and the shore. The oil tanks of the Asia Oil Company and the Standard Oil Company looked like the round concrete tombs of some rich tribal cemetery. Our anchor plunged into the water opposite the Standard Oil Company. Like iron filings pulled by a magnet, rowing-boats were drawn to our steamer. Soon it was surrounded by a ring of boat lanterns and peddlers shouting furiously. They were selling beer from some boats. After a passenger had swallowed his beer, they deftly caught the glass thrown back at them.

A stuffy steam rose over charcoal stoves on which greasy meat cakes and noodles were being cooked. The hungry passengers bought eggs, sausage, and cold jellied soup. Floating restaurant boats with semicircular awnings, lighted with kerosene lamps, bumped against the side of our craft, inviting the merchants, tired from the day's journey and accustomed to a good supper, to come in. Boats with gambling-tables were loud with the shouts of winners, the click of dice, and the ring of copper coins flung from one gambler to another. The air in the steerage was hot and still. The boats outside on the river were opened to the fresh river wind.

The gambling-boats were followed by floating brothels, rocking on the water. Women with powdered faces, gold earrings, and bracelets looked over their sides. From under the awning came the barely audible sounds of *ku-ch'in* [a musical instrument]. A high falsetto sang softly. The touts shouted, praising the virtues of their women. Passengers on the steamer took a long look at the women, fingered the money in their pockets, obviously figuring out the cost. They signalled, and the floating brothel, with a strong swing of the stern oar, began pushing its way, through the crowd of other barges, towards the gangway. With careful hands on the fat bottoms of their customers the touts helped them into their boats. Those left, who were not rich enough, watched, and envied. The lucky ones! They will spend their night in the fresh air. They will

sleep with women, who, from the deck of the steamer, in the evening light, seem to be first-rate beauties.

We stayed there all night, surrounded by the lanterns of the moving boats, for we could not travel in the dark. The great rapids and the quiet shallows of the Yangtze were too dangerous.

We reached Ichang about dinner-time. There we changed our steamer for a bigger one bound for Hankow. There were many steamers at Ichang. We took a Chinese one. After one night in the steerage, we decided to have a good time. We bought second-class tickets, paying eight *da yang* for a journey of a day and a half. Now we were travelling like millionaires. The second class had its own deck on which we could sit in a Shanghai wicker-chair. We could walk along it and talk excitedly about Peking, and tease the shy daughters of merchants, who were on their way from one city to another. Book-sellers walked back and forth on the deck. They offered the bored passengers story-books and the fat Shanghai editions of novels. If a passenger looked exceedingly bored, they extracted from underneath their pile of books pornographic pictures of actresses and courtesans.

In Hankow our travel over water ended and the journey by rail began. Fifteen minutes on the docks of Hankow nearly ruined me:

the rumble of trucks and derricks; the dust from falling bags; the sad howl of the load-carriers; the terrible wagons with bloated wheels—wagons without horses, which I had never seen before except in pictures; men, harnessed to light carriages, running and ringing shrill bells; but, most of all, the terrible dust which got into the nostrils, the throat, the eyes and ears, and settled down between the fingers, drying up your skin!

Hotel agents, swinging lanterns bearing the names of their establishments, insolently grabbed us by the elbows, and shouted their invitations into our ears. In comparison with all this fury and movement the noise of the docks in Teh Chien was like the breath of a sleeping baby. And as for Hsien-Shih—it probably did not exist at all.

I was deafened by the noise of the trucks. My eyes could not endure the sight of derricks moving up and down. I was ready to rush back up the Yangtze, notwithstanding the steerage and the swearing officials, if only I might get into the quiet room of our house in Hsien-Shih and hear once more its distant gong sound in the middle of the night.

My cousin was laughing: 'Look out, Shih-hua. This is not a village.'

41

UPRIVER ON A MERCHANT SHIP

DAVID W. SWIFT

*In 1923, David W. Swift, a representative of the American company,
Standard Oil, was assigned to Wanxian, 1,400 miles up the Yangtze. As
he drily puts it, 'the advent of steamers sailing through the Gorges
brought . . . comparative comfort with questionable safety. To the hazards
of nature were added the man-made perils of banditry. With the
inauguration of foreign steamship services and consequent possibilities
of valuable plunder, bandits were attracted in increasing numbers. They
swarmed along the river's edge like flies on a honey pot. The traveller
seeking thrills would find plenty on this voyage.'*

Here is his account of his journey to Wanxian to take up his new post.

Imagine standing on a wing of the bridge of an up-bound mer-
chantship. Passengers are few and, if you are fortunate, the captain will accord you this privilege. The powerfully built, shallow
draft steamer strains to the utmost as she tackles the current at the
entrance to one of the gorges. Her stack is red hot for a foot or
more from the top. An occasional flame leaps from the roaring
furnace below. A line has been run ashore and secured to a rock
well ahead. The line is taut as the sturdy winch takes up the slack,
inch by inch. The vessel labors the angry waters, which flow in an
almost constant stream over the forecastle. They pour down onto
the deck, giving the illusion that you are about to go under.

Legs well apart, the quartermaster grasps the wheel. Two feet in
front of him stands the pilot, his eyes glued to the river, from
which they are not once withdrawn during his two-hour watch. A
native riverman, he has spent some thirty years in studying its various moods; in low water and high, in junks and—lately—in the
steamers which the foreigners have introduced. He has little faith
in their 'wheel boats', but 'foreign devils' pay well. Why not earn
from them, in a few days, more than he could otherwise make in

as many years? As for the risk, it is well known that the river god will take him when he pleases, regardless of where he may be. So the pilot stands at the open window of the bridge house and rivets his gaze on the swirling waters ahead. He will not turn, even to direct the man at the wheel, but leans with head forward and right fist raised to shoulder level. The pilot extends his little finger and the quartermaster swings her gently to starboard, watching for the raising of his forefinger, the signal for 'Steady.' A ripple appears ahead and the pilot's thumb jerks out. The vessel is nosed over to port.

The old man wears a beaded skull cap, short waisted coat, and baggy-kneed trousers bound with tape at the ankles. Behind him squats a lad in his teens. As an apprentice pilot, it is his duty and privilege to attend the master's wants during this vigil, to place in his hand now a pot of tea, now a lighted cigarette or a fan. No word passes between them yet raw indeed must be the recruit who so misjudges his master's wish as to offer the wrong article. The pilot's hand drops to rest gently on the handle of an extended tea pot. Raising this slowly, the pilot places the spout to his lips. Inhaling the hot liquid in a series of exaggerated sips, his succulent gurgling is audible above the water's roar. Not once do his eyes leave the river. Not a word is spoken. The stillness is more impressive than a dozen quick commands.

You move to the rail and look over the side, just to relieve your tensed nerves. A glance below, and your thoughts are effectively diverted. The sight of the racing foam, licking the ship's side as if loath to admit defeat, was expected, but what is this hallucination? We seem to be riding a ridge of water. It slopes away to the main level of the muddy river, some eight feet below. The effect is that of a train traveling on a raised road bed. Can this be possible? The captain relieves your bewilderment. You are not 'seeing things'. The steamer is actually riding a crest, caused by the force of the river's ejection from the narrow mouth of the gorge. It is thanks to this false depth that the ships clears some of the shoals beneath. Dwarfed by towering cliffs, whose summits are scarcely visible, the mighty 'Son of the sea' emerges, a narrow ribbon in comparison. It is up this ribbon that you are struggling, an inch at a time, under full steam and with the aid of a line ashore. Is it any wonder that, in this region, human life is held in contempt?

Your thoughts are interrupted by the captain remarking, 'We're over the worst now.' A glance at the river, the bow, the pilot, shows no appreciable change, but sighting along a stanchion to a rock on shore, you note that the ship is visibly making headway. You recall your feelings a while back when, at times, it seemed to be the rock that moved forward.

Looking shoreward as you approach the cliffs, you see what appears to be a tiny red boat riding quietly in the lee of a boulder. The number of its crew—sixteen—brings the realization that this is no small craft. It is merely dwarfed by the surrounding gigantic rocks. These 'Red boats'—something in the nature of dugouts— manned by local rivermen, are found at the lower ends of the gorges and on extra hazardous stretches of the river. They earn their living by salvaging wreckage from junks caught in the toils of the river god. While on an errand of mercy, they operate on a strictly commercial basis, saving only what is valuable and for which the luckless owner is liable to pay. On occasions their preda- tory instincts have known no limits. One cannot have lived long on the upper Yangtze without having heard various reports of their activities. There is the instance in which a foreigner, traveling with his native servant, is reported to have witnessed a rescue. The 'Red Boat,' paddled skillfully by its expert crew, shot into the edge of a whirlpool and out again, its *laodah* [captain] dragging an unfortu- nate wretch by his hair. Imagine the spectator's horror when the rescuer drew his victim partially out of the water scrutinized his face, then plunged him back under at arm's length. Scarcely believing his eyes, he turned to his 'boy,' who calmly explained, 'Suppose catchee "live" man, must makee plenty tlouble. Can pay two dollar, maybe tlee dollar. Suppose belong die, evely man too much solly. Can pay ten dollar, maybe fifteen dollar. More better little while wait. This fashion can catchee plenty money.'

A long wail, arising out of the gorge ahead, echoes and reechoes in a series of mysterious moans from the cliffs high above. Can this be the challenge of some prehistoric dragon whose slumbers have been disturbed? Certainly your surroundings justify such imaginings, but any possible apprehension is quickly laid to rest by the mate. Seizing a pair of glasses from the rack, he steps quickly to the rail remarking, 'That will be Andersen on the *Wan Liu*'. As he speaks, the white bow of a down-bound steamer noses around the cliff. An instant later the entire vessel is in view, racing down toward you. She rides an eightknot current, over which she must make sufficient speed to maintain steerage way. Her actual rate over the ground is estimated at some twelve knots and she is opposite you, almost before you realize it. Straddling her bridge rail, a Chinese quarter-master holds up a blackboard. The mate reads aloud, 'Wanhsien 102 rising. Fired on by troops east bank Ox Liver Gorge—Andersen'. Scarcely has this message been read when she is past you. The captain gives a short blast on the whistle, signifying the message has been received. An officer's white hat waves from the *Wan Liu*'s bridge in acknowledgement. In less time than it takes to tell this, she is a white speck far astern. Passing at such speed and surrounded by the noisy river, communication by megaphone is out of the question. The reference to '102' was the water mark readings, as posted by the Customs. The average low water level being taken as 0, the water is at present 102 feet above that point at Wanhsien. The usual spring rise there passes 120 feet, from which, at extreme low water, it drops to 8 feet below 0.

The last half of the *Wan Liu*'s message is not so reassuring. The officers take it for granted and do not consider it worth comment, so you keep your thoughts to yourself. Somehow the chance of encountering bandits does not seem quite so interesting now as it did when discussed over your coffee in the American Club lounge at Shanghai. You recall what your host said about the ships' being armor plated against soldier and bandit attacks. From these, neither the steamer's flag nor the Chinese Government will protect you. Your eye rests on steel shutters hinged above all windows, requiring but the slipping of a hook to drop them into position. Painted the same color as the wood work, they have hitherto escaped your attention. You study them now with personal interest, noting the slits cut to afford the pilots a view. A couple of dents and a diagonal gash give silent proof of their effectiveness. You recall the pair of rifles and the sub-machine gun in the captain's cabin, when he invited you in last night. They were there, then, for a purpose. You now realize that similar arms and armament are carried by all foreign merchantmen on this run, as a necessary part of their equipment. Without them, the steamers could not operate, in spite of the fact that their presence on the river is secured by international treaties and welcomed by China, to whom they bring millions in wages and revenue.

The very commonness of banditry has kept it from much comment. It is accepted as a matter of course. The mere fact of having been under fire is not in itself a sufficiently interesting topic of conversation, without the added attraction of at least a minor casualty. In times of so-called 'real danger', an armed guard may be put aboard for a trip or two by the foreign naval vessel patrolling that section. This cannot be made a general practice, however, without the vessels' losing their merchant classification. In such instances the first to protest this action are the Chinese officials, who have been so incapable of guaranteeing the safety of the ships in question. I recall the amusement with which the agent of my steamer related his experience with the admiral of the Yangtze Patrol. For several trips he had tried in vain to obtain an armed guard for two upper river steamers. The refusal was based on the decision of the admiral, just out from home, that 'Conditions do not warrant such action at this time'. A couple of weeks later, the admiral's wife and party booked passage for Chungking. Arrangements were immediately undertaken for the placing of an armed guard. The agent took especial delight in replying that, since banditry was no worse than usual, he felt that 'Conditions do not warrant such action at this time'.

Having weathered one of the worst reaches of the upper Yangtze, the ship struggles on, plowing its way upstream through treacherous currents, past wild scenery of gigantic cliffs and desolate shores.

There are no railroads into Szechuan Province. About two decades earlier, when all upper river traffic was by junk, one was undertaken. Because of the impregnable mountain barriers, a trail was blazed along the river's course. The great expense involved made it a questionable venture. It was abandoned with the introduction of steam boat competition. The few miles of trackage already laid, together with the Ichang station house, remained standing. Report had it that a local merchant still boasted the empty honor of being station master on a line which never owned a unit of rolling stock. On state occasions, he solemnly donned his official cap, covered with braid which once was gold, and strutted importantly through the streets, as if the express were due in at any moment. Were anyone ignorant enough, he would be glad to sell a ticket to the provincial capital of Chengtu, many miles away. Having first carefully pocketed the fare, he would doubtless oblige with the information that the train would be in 'soon', using that overworked Oriental expression whose interpretation is based on relativity.

From this side, the Yangtze is the sole means of access to the largest province of China proper, yet the only signs of human activity are an occasional water mark, painted on an outstanding boulder, or an ancient pagoda, perched high on a cliff. Startlingly out of place in this wild region, an obviously man-made column catches the eye. This stands, a lasting memorial to an intrepid pioneer who devoted his life to studying the endless phases of these vehement waters, noting their moods and charting their courses. It is thanks to the undaunted faith and fearless devotion of River Inspector Plant that steamers are now able to ply this passage. The river is too dangerous to be ventured at night, nor is it possible to anchor, excepting at certain designated points which afford the rare combination of quiet waters and a river bottom in which an anchor will hold. The less populous anchorages are avoided if possible, as subjecting the ship to a probable visit from bandits.

With the arrival of the shore boats, the steamer assumes the appearance of a fortress being stormed. Men scrambling up her sides dispute the right of way with each other and with disembarking passengers. Everyone joins in the hubbub. Orders, instructions and unsolicited advice are shouted by all and heeded by none. A farmer, about to debark, stamps his foot and curses in futile rage while two sampan men fight over his bedding roll. Each claims to have seized it first and neither pays the slightest attention to its owner's wishes. A family of three are boarding the ship from a shore side sampan. The young man and his daughter tug at the padded clothing of his toothless mother. She swings perilously over the side, while they exchange very personal and genealogical remarks with the boatman below. He retains a tenacious grip on his fare's ankle, in a final effort to extract a few cash cumshaw. By virtue of her seniority and consequent more vituperative vocabulary, the old lady should win but everyone knows the unreasonableness of boatmen. Reluctantly the son counts out ten cash (1,800 to the dollar) and tosses them down, the expression of his face reflecting his serious doubt as to the worth of his bargain.

A blast from the whistle indicates the resumption of the voyage. The din increases to a frenzy of last minute transactions. Knowing from experience that warnings are useless, the skipper gets under way without further concern. The crew go about casting off lines and disengaging boat-hooks by force. A miniature fleet still maintains a persistent hold in the hopes of being towed a way upstream. They ignore repeated warnings of danger from wash and propellers. Yet, if an accident occurs, the ship is held entirely responsible. Local officials take the view that steamers should not be on the river and that foreigners are wealthy, so let them pay, and pay well. Incidentally, settlement of claims is made through the courts, which attach a substantial portion of the cash, thus saving the payee the inconvenience of having to remember the courts' services later. The ship's position is therefore unenviable. With this in mind, and having failed to detach the human leeches, the captain orders out the fire hose and literally washes himself free of the parasites, as speed is increased on the final run for the day.

Scenes of Sichuan

Even in the nineteenth century, many Chinese from other provinces still regarded remote Sichuan as almost foreign territory. Here are some vignettes from different eras, depicting Sichuan life along the river as far west as Chongqing.

42

CROSSING INTO SICHUAN

THOMAS W. BLAKISTON

Taking advantage of the 1858 Tientsin Treaty which allowed the British to travel to all parts of the interior, Thomas Blakiston, a captain of the British Royal Artillery, set out up the Yangtze in 1861, looking for trading opportunities. Blakiston hoped to travel upriver as far as possible by boat, and then go on to Chengdu, capital of Sichuan. He got as far as Pingshan above Chongqing, the first European to get to the navigable end of the Yangtze. But at that point, the boatmen refused to go any further because of unrest in the area. Here is his description of sailing from Hubei into Sichuan. The town of Kwei is actually Zigui (Tsekwei); the village of Guandukou (Kwan-du-kow) marks the entrance to Wu Gorge.

From Kwei we stopped once before we came to Pa-tung, the last town in the province of Hoo-peh. It is a small place without a wall, situated on rather steep sloping ground on the right bank; and on the opposite side stands a joss-house, at a considerable height above the river. Above this, the hills bordering the river are for some few miles rather less steep, and two or three streams enter. We passed one rapid and then came to the mouth of a gorge where are situated the rapid and village of Kwan-du-kow. High precipitous mountains rise on either hand, which where the rock is not bare, are covered with a growth of small brushwood, and woods of small pine and cedar occur in some places; but wherever the slopes are such as to admit of cultivation, they are occupied for that purpose by the industrious country people; while below, on the river, others are employed catching fish by various devices, among which the common scoop-net, used by one person standing on a point of rock in a rapid, or anywhere that the current is swift, is so frequent, that, in the visions of gorges and rapids which occasionally haunt my recollection, the stolid Chinaman, in his bamboo hat and reed

paletot, continually dipping his net automaton-like, and as constantly bringing out nothing, is ever in the foreground of the picture.

The gorge, commencing at the village of Kwan-du-kow, is continuous as far as the city of Wu-shan, a distance of over twenty miles, and is the longest on the river. About half-way through is the boundary between the provinces of Hoo-peh and Sz'chuan. The course of the river is nearly directly east, and one might, were it not pointed out, pass the place of boundary without notice; but the voyageurs drew our attention to the fact that we were entering their native country, and the old grey-bearded skipper went off into a long disquisition on the superiority of that favoured province over the rest of China; while our Chinese servants and Mr. Schereschewsky's[*] teacher, who were Kiang-su men, and had been listening to the marvellous stories related by the boatmen, seemed to look upon it that in entering Sz'chuan they were commencing a pilgrimage in a foreign land; and from this I think commenced the growth of their disinclination towards the idea of going out of China, which though it was never openly professed, yet, from their becoming sick one after another, and chiming in so readily when any objections were raised against our further progress, was sufficiently evident to some of us; and I believe that, notwithstanding due weight being given to mandarins, rebels, and

* A missonary and the party's interpreter.

boat-skippers, the failure of our enterprise was in a great measure caused by treachery in our own camp.

On the south side the boundary was marked by a narrow glen running into the mountains, on the Sz'chuan or western side of which were a few houses that, in this wild and desolate region, did duty for a village. On the northern bank the boundary is half a mile lower down, and is marked by a mountain stream or creek coming down a narrow ravine. We halted for the night a couple of miles or so above this point; and next morning, being favoured by a fresh breeze, we emerged from the regions of darkness and came to Wushan. This was our first sight of a Sz'chuan town, and we looked eagerly to detect if possible some change in the appearance of a Chinese city; but no—it was the same lead-coloured mass, overtopped by the curved roofs of one or two conspicuous temples, and kept together by four antiquated-looking walls, with the usual pagoda and half house-like structures over the gates and at the angles. It was of the regular pattern, and might have been punched out of the same mould with a thousand others.

43

ON WOMEN SELLING FIREWOOD

DU FU

At the end of the gorges lies the town of Kuizhou (now known as Fengjie). Du Fu was an official in this isolated spot for two years between 765 and 768 and wrote over four hundred poems during his time here, more than a quarter of his total output.

Du Fu had the misfortune to live during an era of constant war. Many of his best poems are about the anguish and poverty he saw around him, yet even as a government official, was powerless to alleviate. He also knew suffering at first-hand. When the capital fell to the rebels led by traitor An Lu-shan in 755, he was captured and held prisoner. Two years later he managed to escape, but in the meantime one of his children had died of starvation. Even when employed in government posts, Du Fu struggled just to feed himself and his family.

Not only was China ravaged by the decade-long rebellion led by An Lu-shan, but at the same time Sichuan was attacked by the Nan-chao, a minority group from Yunnan. The emperor ordered conscription, and even old men and boys were dragged off to fight, explaining why the Kuizhou women of this poem remained 'single until middle age'. Yet even when there were men around, it seems that Kuizhou women did most of the work. Salt was a government monopoly and only licence holders could sell it. As for Wang Zhaojun, she was a famous beauty of the Han Dynasty, born in a village near Kuizhou.

Kuizhou women remain single until middle age,
  Their hair already turning grey.
  In time of wars and death, marriage is more difficult;
So they sigh and regret their lives.
By custom the man sits while the woman stands;
He is master of the house; she the servant.
Most women bring firewood home to sell
While officials take the money as levies.

They age with their girlish tresses at their necks,
Wild flowers and leaves caught in a silver clasp.
Their bodies ache from the perilous climb to the fairs;
Tears smear the powder on their faces.
They risk death to sell illegal salt for profit.
Thinly clad they struggle below the narrow rocks.
If you say such women are coarse and plain,
Why was a village named after Wang Zhaojun?

44

A YANGTZE CHILDHOOD

TAN SHI-HUA

When Tan Shi-hua was a child in the 1900s, the essentials of his Yangtze world had changed little since Du Fu's time, over 1,000 years earlier. Tan writes that people were divided into four castes: the scholars at the top, followed by the peasants, then the craftsmen, and below them—the lowest and least respected—the merchants. Coolies and soldiers were beneath consideration, and had no caste at all. As the son of an official and thus a member of the scholar caste, Tan remembers an idyllic childhood even though the family fortunes were declining.

I was born in our big ancestral house in the month of January, when the magnificent Yangtze, grown shallow and blue, rushes noisily between its steep Szechuan banks. Our house—a chain of courts surrounded by rooms and terraces—spread itself on the slope of a hill. From the upper terraces, through the tops of trees, you could see the blue body of the river. The shores of the Yangtze are of stone and clay. Clay and soft stone surround the docks where the boats of fishermen and ferrymen crowd. The Yangtze at this point is five times as wide as the Moscow River near the Kremlin.

In the spring the Yangtze is magnificent. The slopes of the banks are not only green: they are red, yellow, blue with blossoms, and all these blossoms are reflected in clear, blue water. When summer nears, the Yangtze turns a rusty red, and swells with slimy, cloudy water—due to the heavy rains at its far-away sources in the wild mountains near Tibet. When the water of the Yangtze is blue, we drink it, after boiling it in our ovens. The coolies, the wandering harvesters, and the boatmen, tired out by their work and thirsty, drink it unboiled. They drink it with a bite of bitter onion, which, so they say, makes any water good.

On the slope between our house and the river there was a row of trees. Looking from the river, one could hardly distinguish our village through the black groves. Everywhere, around every wall in the village, trees were planted in orderly arrangements. The gardens were green and the air clean in Szechuan.

A large stone basin, three feet high, stood among the trees in the first big court of our house. Rainwater accumulated in it, and gold-brown and silver-violet fish swam there. The vegetation inside the court was watered from this basin. Along the wall there were nutmeg-trees. Being very expensive, they were planted under the main wall of the house to protect them from thieves. The house was built around three terrace-like courts. The uppermost terrace beyond them was used for a vegetable garden. Stairs led from court to court through the walls. Between the second and the third courts was a hall where guests were received. Behind the guest-room was the last court, and beyond this court a row of main rooms. The *li tang*, a prayer-room, was in the middle. Next to it was the room of my grandfather, the head of the family and of the house. The other side of the *li tang* was occupied by his brother. Beyond the upper wall of the house, the vegetable garden was surrounded by trees and hemmed in by a fence of live bamboo. This garden led into an orchard. There were mulberry, pomegranate, apricot, orange, peach, nut, and tangerine trees. The orchard and the garden, including the house, covered about twenty *mou*— somewhat less than four acres. This land easily supported the seventeen people of the house. The vegetable garden was as rich as a museum. Cucumbers, radishes, bitter radishes, turnips, sweet potatoes, peas, lettuce, squash, and all kinds of Szechuan cabbage— these vegetables were brought in daily from the garden to our dinner-table. Only the grown-ups might have meat every day. The rest of the family got a tiny bit of meat—and that only twice a month.

The elders lived around the family altar, in the topmost sections of the house, surrounded by store-rooms. Then came the rooms of my father, my uncles, the reception-room, and the kitchen. At the lowest end of the house were the rooms of the third generation, and also rooms for visiting guests, the janitor's room, and a big classroom where my uncle used to teach the village youngsters. The servants' rooms, no bigger than closets, were next to my father's and grandfather's quarters.

In the prayer-room, against the wall, facing the entrance, stood a big black altar. It was the *shen tang*. Its fancy wood-carving was inlaid with bone. On the black wood of its upper half there was a column of five golden hieroglyphics. They represented 'The Sky', 'The Earth', 'The Emperor', 'The Ancestor', 'The Teacher'. This column rested on a sixth hieroglyphic which read 'The Altar.' On both sides of this main column, which we call *tang-li*, hung two small strips of cypress wood, twice the length of the palm of your hand. The names of the ancestors of the three nearest generations were traced on these strips—grandfather's, great-grandfather's, and great-grandfather's father. The strips of wood with the names of more remote ancestors had been put away in the village temple.

The lower part of *shen tang* protruded and formed a shelf. In the middle of this shelf stood a porcelain incense-burner with handles. The fluffy ashes of the incense sticks accumulated in it. This lower part contained a cupboard. Incense sticks, oil for the lamp, strings of silvery coin made of tinfoil, which are burned on the day of the dead, and the family book, *Chu-pu*, were kept here. The *Chu-pu* is a book of names, of birth dates, marriage dates, deaths, days of graduation, dates of promotion, and other important events.

Every day, at morning and at night, one of the little Tans would stick three incense sticks in the ashes, and light them from a flame that burned at the spout of a small oil lamp that looked like a gravy-dish. When the family had money, this lamp used to be kept burning in the *li tang* day and night. When the Tans had no money for oil, they lit the lamp only for the night.

The incense candles would glow. Gay, blue threads of smoke rose toward the hieroglyphics, and white, cylindrically shaped ashes fell into the urn. When the urn was filled, the ashes were cast into the river under the house. 'The holy ashes into the holy water of the River Yangtze,' my grandmother used to say as she passed the heavy urn to her grandchild. . . .

Faces, words, objects, and the blue Yangtze, in a setting of blossoming mountains, emerge out of the grey, shifting twilight of childhood. When I was two (or one, as the Europeans reckon it) we removed to the village of Hsien-Shih.

The house in Hsien-Shih was much smaller than our ancestral house. It was crowded and poor inside. Father was in Japan, and we had to economise. There was one servant-girl for the house, and she came only when my mother was sick. Instead of a vegetable garden, there were only a fruit garden and a tangerine orchard.

I remember my grandmother feeding me with sun-flower-seeds which had been dried in the sun. She shelled each seed and, passing them to me one by one, she taught me to count: *i-kê, liang-kê, san-kê, sse-kê, wu-kê*—one, two, three, four, five. She also told me fairy-tales. Grandmother was the second wife of my grandfather whose portrait hung on the wall in the *li tang*. She was my father's step-mother. (Having no children of her own, she lavished all her affection on me.)

My mother either worked in the kitchen or taught little village girls to read. I was very proud of her, because in my childhood there were very few women in China who could read, to say nothing of being able to teach.

My grandmother is sewing, and I am sitting by her on a low stool. I have on a long robe, slippers embroidered with flowers, and white socks. One must not go barefoot—people would laugh at you. Only coolies go barefoot. . . . Coolies are low people: dirty, rude, ragged coachmen, boatmen, porters, wandering reapers—in a word, all those who are willing to sell their big, brown muscles, hardened by labour and fights, for copper pennies. I am a little afraid of coolies, but they are treated well in our house, especially by my younger uncle (also a teacher), who is staying with us. For that reason the well-off villagers are suspicious of him.

I am sitting by my grandmother, building houses, temples, bridges, out of wooden blocks. I imagine that I am building my favourite bridge, the one that hangs over the little river flowing into the Yangtze, near Hsien-Shih. It is a stone bridge, all sculptured. Carved dragons, six feet high, guard it. Three arches clutch the bridge with their paws. These arches are dedicated to the widows of Hsien-Shih who remained faithful to their husbands even after the latter died.

This bridge was built fifty years ago by a rich man of the village. His only son was a cripple. At the sight of a woman he would throw a fit. No descendants could be expected from this feeble-minded son. The family of the rich man was dying out and, as he had no one to leave his fortune to, he built this bridge. On its flat stones the peasants threshed their grain in hot weather. There was no better threshing-floor in the whole district.

I am arranging my blocks and mixing them all up again at my grandmother's feet, which are small and round, like ponies' hoofs. My grandmother called them roundly her 'golden lilies'. My grandmother is sewing and singing, and teaching me a song.

Fly away,
First pair of geese,
Second pair of geese,
Come back again
To find grandmother.
Grandmother does not like
Rice with pork.
Grandmother wants
A wild duck's egg.

I knew why my shrewd grandmother wanted a wild duck's egg. It was rare, and difficult to get. We ate only hen's eggs. My mother and grandmother made a mush out of clay mixed with the ashes of pea or rice straw, and smeared it over the egg. When it dried, the egg was as big as your fist. Then they buried it in the ground for twenty days. When such an egg was served at the table on holidays, its white was hard and had a brownish colour. The yolk was soft and tasted as if the egg had been freshly boiled. Sometimes there were veins in the white of the egg that looked like cypress branches. 'I had it kept in cypress ashes,' my grandmother used to explain to me.

The cool wind stirs the hot air. The blazing hearths are roaring in the kitchen and the plates are clattering in my mother's hands. Far down, at the docks of the unseen Yangtze, the fishermen are shouting loudly, and children are screaming and splashing. I want to go to the river, but I am not permitted. My mother is afraid that I may get hurt, or be insulted, or pushed into the water. 'All right,' I say. 'I'll just take a walk in the garden.' My mother looks at me suspiciously. She takes me to the classroom, dips a brush in an inkwell, puts me on her lap, and paints, with a tiny tickling paintbrush, three-petalled black flowers on the palms of my hands and on the canvas soles of my slippers. Now I may go. Should I walk over a wet place, or splash water with my hands, the flowers will be washed off and I will be discovered.

I had seen other children being spanked by their parents as a result of these tell-tale signs. I did not go to the river.

Near Hsien-Shih the river was terrifying, with its bank drooping steeply down into deep water. The children of the fishermen and boatmen swam and dived near the docks, fighting and swearing. The fish-poles bent attentively toward the water. Yellow water broke over the rocks. Shoals of fish swam by on their way to lay their eggs in the small upper streams.

45

LIFE IN WANXIAN

DAVID W. SWIFT

For David W. Swift, the representative of the American company, Standard Oil, life in a Yangtze city in 1923 was anything but an idyll. Wanxian was and is one of the more important cities along the river and was certainly imposing from a distance. Twenty-seven years earlier Isabella Bird was impressed: 'The burst of its beauty as we came round an abrupt corner into the lake-like basin on which it stands, and were confronted with a stately city piled on cliffs and heights, a wall of rock on one side crowded with refuges and temples, with the broad river disappearing among mountains which were dissolving away in a blue mist, was quite overpowering.'

But to live there year-round as one of a handful of foreigners was to see the city quite differently. Two-thirds of Wanxian will be submerged in a few years' time by the new Three Gorges Dam; judging by David Swift's comments, he would have no regrets to see it disappear.

Late in the afternoon we cast anchor in the quieter waters of the harbor opposite Wanhsien. I remember the day very well. The river was fairly low. There was a steep stone embankment with steps everywhere from the water up to the parts of the town. The so-called 'small' steps were anywhere from 25 to 30 feet wide, just one after the other. I stood there as we pulled into Wanhsien, talking to the mate. Way up, some hundred feet above us, were bolts hammered into the stone walls. The mate said, 'That's where junks tie up in high water.' I thought he was pulling my leg, but a few months later I found that he was right. There was a tremendous variation in the water level.

To the left was a small sandy beach, backed by bamboo covered hillocks. To the right the river bank rose sharply in support of a fringe of the city itself. On the waterfront stood a mass of bamboo shacks. Supported by flimsy bamboo frames and uninhabitable at

highest water, they gave a strong impression that this city of over one hundred thousand had crowded them over the brink. As the river recedes, more huts would be built at lower levels, only to be washed away on the next rise.

From out of this mass rose the two-story custom house. The curving roofs, with figures of saints and sages over the gates, bore witness to the fact that this was formerly a temple. The white-washed walls and tidy surroundings proclaimed it the residence of a foreigner. The white sun flag of the Republic of China floated from the mast in front, but the Deputy Commissioner was a Swedish-American in the Chinese Maritime Customs Service. It was largely due to such foreign supervision that the revenue reached the Customs' depositories, in spite of frequent attempts of local warlords to divert it to their own coffers.

There were only four other foreigners in the immediate area: the postal commissioner, the commissioner of customs, a French priest and—for part of the time—a representative of Gillespie and Company, dealers of tung oil.

This French father was a great lad, as most of them are, and he lived a sincere missionary life. Although his family in France were wealthy wine growers who subscribed heavily to the Roman

Catholic Church, he lived frugally, wearing native clothes and moving among his congregation as an equal. His regular meals were of cheap Chinese quality. I had him over from the native city about once a month; he was 'too busy' to come more often. We gave him a good meal and then played chess. The Father spoke no English. I spoke no French. He spoke fluent Chinese in the local dialect. I spoke only broken Mandarin. Chess does not require much conversation and, with his jolly nature, we enjoyed many a good laugh. . . .

There was no hotel at Wanhsien and the regular staff could not be expected to live in the filthy little Chinese inns, so Standard Oil had built a nicely furnished two-story house at the company's installation, several miles from town. For meals, being a bachelor, I ate whatever the 'boy' served. At this time—some 50 years later—I have no memory of what it may have been. Basic supplies were shipped up by Socony. Presumably these were garnished with whatever the Boy could find on the local market: white cabbage, an emaciated chicken, etc. I do recall that we frequently enjoyed catfish. These, though heavily sedimented with Yangtze mud, were delicious when soused in catsup; a trick learned in the Navy. Under the cognomen of 'red lead', it covers a multitude of sins: a check by one of the gunboats indicated that the water in Wanhsien was one sixth sediment. Having no ice, our 'cooler' was a dry well of some hundred feet into which perishable items were lowered in a wicker basket. Passing merchant ships were generous in selling us supplies but we could not take items from refrigerators unless for immediate consumption. I well remember one grand occasion when we got a water-buffalo calf. My mess-mate at the time had had some experience in butchering. We invited the entire white population to participate. After the slaughter we took all we could handle for immediate cooking, and gave the rest to the local staff. It was delicious!

People often speak of how lucky we were to have so many servants, but those servants were needed. I had a staff of probably twenty. The house I lived in had no such thing as running water. The only running water consisted of the coolie carrying two buckets to a little well. He lowered those five gallon buckets on a pole, carried them up to the kitchen and dumped them into some large jars. When I wanted a bath, they would heat the water and the coolies would take it upstairs and pour it in the bathtub. I could not turn on hot and cold water. There would be a pot of cold water alongside. That is the way I bathed. So I needed servants for all of those details. I had a houseboy, a cook, two coolies to clean up around the house, and a couple of gardeners to mow the lawn once in a while. None of them were too energetic, and their wages were so low it cost very little there. When the houseboy went marketing for some vegetables, eggs, or a scrawny chicken, we would send a coolie with him to carry the food, if it were more than one man could handle. There were no carts. I had a crew of six on my rowing boat and eight or ten coolies to carry my sedan chair. You had to have so many servants. Each one was necessary; it was not merely sitting back and ruling any army. . . .

The town of Wanhsien was like any other filthy Chinese city, except for the many steps up and down. The houses were crowded right together, more or less slums. It was the American's idea of what opium dens were: filthy slums and narrow alleys. The gutters were vile: since there were no sanitary facilities, people would empty their toilets and buckets in the streets. When a little dust came along, they would get the bucket they used for washing and splash it all over the street. That settled the dust for about five minutes, but then the dust, dirt and files returned. It was awful.

Wanhsien had a large population. Many of the residents were storekeepers, and out in the country they cultivated small fields of their own, mostly vegetables. They were not farmers the way you would have here. Merchants would sell whatever they had, from town to town. Chinese merchants can live and be quite happy with very little selling and buying. A good-sized store, like those operated by some of our agents, had a bit of everything, all stuck in together around their broad counters. Their staff consisted mostly of family members: sons, daughters, nephews and nieces, who would be apprenticed for at least a year. Their only pay was food and lodging. They worked all day, and turned in at night after the accounts were settled.

For accounting they used the abacus. I never could use one but they were fascinating. Every evening at dusk the merchants closed their wooden doors and locked everything up for the night. They did not have keys. When walking down the street you heard a steady hum from inside the stores. It was the settling of accounts for the day. The boss had his records. He had written down what he had sold and what he had bought. His ten or twelve apprentices are helping him. He calls out the figures and they go 'click, click, click,' on their abacuses, faster than he can talk. Click, click, click, click, click, pause, total. If one or two people have a different total the process is repeated, but ninety-nine times out of a hundred they agree. This was how they would add up and settle the accounts for the day.

Most of the time the clerks have nothing to do. They sit around in a dark, murky room and then go to bed. They are usually fed twice a day, at ten in the morning and two or three in the afternoon; the whole family dines together. They sit around the table and eat from the same dishes, and discuss the events of the day.

One of my most vivid memories of Wanhsien involved torture. I was coming home in the middle of one afternoon, riding in my sedan chair, when I heard a hideous screaming and howling, like a banshee. A man, stark naked, came racing down the street and almost knocked my bearers over. The coolies were all laughing like hell at him. I found out later, when I got back to the office, that he was a bandit or perhaps a political opponent who had been captured and thrown in jail. He and six or eight other prisoners were marched down to the river every morning with their hands tied behind their backs and forced to kneel on the river bank. An officer came along with a pistol, grabbed a prisoner by his hair and shot him. This was done to several prisoners in a row. Then, when they came to this particular one, they would skip him and continue on down the line, shooting the other prisoners kneeling beside him. That went on for two weeks. After a few days, thinking each day he was going to get it, the man went crazy. Eventually they did shoot him. The Chinese may have been cruel to foreigners at times, but they were worse to their own.

Under such conditions it is not surprising that foreigners welcomed the arrival of the river steamers. Repeated visits made the few residents familiar figures abroad, and their individual preferences for food or drink were well-known to the stewards. On the homeward voyage merchant ships paused in Wanhsien for only an hour or two. So it was their night anchorings on the upriver voyage that afforded the foreign inhabitants their only break in the monotony of their existence. Ashore, there was not so much as a club. In spite of the tropical heat, ice was an unknown luxury. Consequently the evenings spent aboard these steamers, with dinner followed by bridge or poker and a chance to talk with someone other than the five local residents, were steps back into civilization and a stimulant to their morale. They amply compensated for the midnight trip over the black, turgid river in an open sampan. To expose the lantern, carried for an emergency but screened from sight, was to invite the challenge of some doltish sentry. Failure to halt inevitably drew the fire of the coolie-warrior, ignorant of the impossibility of stopping in midstream.

In July a French gunboat anchored in the harbour for a couple of days. She was on a regular patrol, and lay over to see if all foreigners in port were 'happy'. Of course we (Socony) entertained back and forth; and welcomed the 'other ratings' to stretch their legs—and elbows—ashore. This was not a one-sided venture. When they left, our larder was replenished with a considerable stock of food, not to mention a couple of cases of beautiful wine. During her stay I learned that this was their last patrol. After calling at Chungking they would head down river, passing through Wanhsien at 1400 hours on July 14. On that day I sat at the foot of our mast with my 'crew' around me. Right on time came the warning blast of a whistle from upriver. The current was running at about four knots. To maintain steerage way the ship would be making at least six knots. As she burst into view, the No. 1 watchman dipped our colours, while two coolies held a large blackboard on which I had chalked in fractured French VIVE 14 JUILLET—AU REVOIR. In acknowledgement the gunboat dipped her colours and gave three blasts from her siren. Three white-chalked topees waved from her bridge. From her deck came a conglomerate farewell, while over her stern trailed a long white streamer. In the passing moments this could not be identified, but apparently was a roll of toilet paper. One final wail echoed as the ship entered the gorge below. As I strolled up to the Meifoo mansion, I remembered thinking that I could have made good use of the honourary streamer. In retrospect, this was the nadir of my life in China.

In the spring, when the river rose high enough, the Dollar Line sent ships all the way to Chungking, above Wanhsien. Tourists would come to Shanghai and then proceed to Hankow and up the river for the round trip. They seldom went ashore at Wanhsien.

The city was dirty and not too friendly. The trip to shore was sufficiently dangerous to discourage the tourist. Even many of the officers plying this run for years never made it. Ask any foreign resident for the most appealing aspect of this ancient city. Without hesitation he replied, 'Waving farewell from the stern of a down-bound steamer.'

46

ENTRANCE TO HADES

ARCHIBALD J. LITTLE

Archibald Little used his journal of his first trip up the Gorges in 1883 as the basis for a book, Through the Yangtse Gorges. *In this extract he describes Fengdu, known as the 'City of Ghosts'. Fengdu is one of the cities which will be submerged by the Three Gorges Dam. At present, it is a popular tourist stop along the river. Chinese visitors still burn incense and candles at the temples, some in genuine reverence and others 'just in case'.*

*T*uesday, April 3rd.—Fine warm day; light south-westerly wind still ahead. We were off at 5.30 a.m. I landed at seven at the foot of the 'T'ien tze Shan,' 'Mountain of the Son of Heaven,' which is situated on the left bank below and immediately adjoining the walled city of 'Fêng tu,' i.e. 'The Abundant Capital,' commonly called 'Fêng-tu-Chêng.' This is one of the many steep, isolated hills abounding in this level sandstone district. Being a sacred mount, it is wooded to the summit, upon which is a collection of ancient, solidly-built, but now ruinous, temples, said to date from before the Tang dynasty, at which period (eighth and ninth centuries), however, the existing buildings—with wood pillars supporting tiled roofs—were erected. This temple is dedicated to the Emperor of the 'Yin', or Dead, as the Imperial palace at Peking is to the Emperor of the 'Yang', or Living; and as that is the visible home of T'ien tze, or Son of Heaven, so this is the type of the shadowy Emperor of Hades. The only curious thing in the uncomfortably dirty range of building and courtyards, filled with grimy josses of all sizes and shapes, is the figure of a woman in an elegant modern dress, and with the usual gold or gilt face, who sits enthroned on the left hand of the image, representing the 'Yin chien T'ien tze,' which latter is a gilt figure, in no way, that I could distinguish, different from the ordinary Buddhist idol. On its right is a gilt female figure covered with dust, the god's chief wife; but

the figure on the left contains a real skeleton, to whom the women in the neighbourhood annually present a new embroidered silk dress. This second wife of the 'Infernal' Emperor was only acquired by him about fifty years ago, in the twelfth year of the reign of 'Chai-king,' in the following manner: A maiden of Ho-chow, a town situated above Chung-king, was being carried in her bridal chair to the home of her betrothed, when, half-way en route, the chair door was opened, but the bride had disappeared. The husband's family entered an action for breach of promise against the bride's family, which, after proceeding over two years, was stopped by the lady herself appearing in a dream to her parents, and informing them that on her marriage day the 'T'ien tze' had claimed her for his second wife, and carried her off from her chair; and that her body, of which only the skeleton now remains, would be found alongside her new husband's effigy on the T'ien tze Shan. Of the fact that the earthly bridegroom lost his bride, I have no doubt, nor of the ensuing action at law; of the rest of the legend, which is universally believed as I have narrated it, each barbarian sceptic must form his own explanation. Fêng-tu-Chêng is celebrated over the whole eighteen provinces, as at every death the officiating Taoist, priest indites a despatch to the T'ien tze, duly addressed to Fêng-tu-Cheng, notifying him of the newcomer. This despatch is, however, not sent through the terrestrial post, but by the celestial road, being burnt to ashes. No Chinaman will enter the precincts of the T'ien tze Shan alone, nor venture near it at all after sunset, as it is haunted by innumerable ghosts, as befits the residence of the ruler of Hades. Their presence is known, not only by their cries at night, but the priests put out every night a bundle of birch rods. Sometimes these disappear altogether; at other times they are found all in splinters, having been used to flog refractory, drunken, and other vicious spirits at the ghostly tribunals.

My Chinese companions, who are usually too lazy to leave the boat, and who do not care how long the voyage lasts as long as they can eat and sleep their fill, became genuinely excited upon arriving at Fêng-tu. They climbed up the steep hillside—about 300 feet—bought incense and candles, and performed a general Kow-tow all round. Another show-place—for cash, be it well understood—is a dry well, said to communicate with the river. We bought paper cash of the priest, which was set alight and dropped through a stone grating immediately in front of the altar, thus contributing our mite to the aid of the struggling souls in purgatory below. The burning paper soon lodged on the bottom, and hence it would appear that the ash of the billions of cash deposited in it have filled up this wonderful well to within a few feet of its mouth. We descended by a fine, broad, easy, stone path through the wood, which, interspersed with opium patches, covers this sacred mount. At each turn are small temples adorned with Buddhas; and by the roadside are inlaid stone tablets with hortatory texts engraved upon them; such as, 'The affairs of life are all vanity,' etc.; the whole arrangement of the zig-zag path reminding me of the path adorned with the stations of the Cross such as is often to be seen in Roman Catholic countries.

We passed through the city, which is a poor place with low walls and gates, and the usual crowded Chinese streets, filthy in fine, and impassable in wet weather; then to our boat across the usual long, steep sandbank, covered with a temporary bamboo town, which is moved up higher and higher as the river rises. I was followed by the customary crowd, for whose benefit I sat on the bows of the boat while delayed waiting for the relief *Ting-chai* [messenger].

We got away at nine a.m., literally threading our way through a huge reef of rocks, which extends across the river just above this city. On emerging from this labyrinth, I was not a little surprised to see on a bluff, separated from the town by a lofty, almost perpendicular, sandstone hill, the walls of another city, with the usual gates, crowned by handsome two-storied pavilions or guard-houses, its walls enclosing a large area of highly-cultivated ground and a few, possibly fifty scattered houses, the intended *yamêns* or residences of the officials. This city without inhabitants might, I at first thought, have been built for the mysterious Son of Heaven and his shadowy subjects, from whose presence Fêng-tu has acquired so great distinction. I was informed, however, that Fêng-tu-Chêng proper having been entirely washed away in the terrific flood of 1870, the then magistrate 'Ma' had built this new city at a safe height above the river, and had ordered the surviving inhabitants to remove to it. This they refused to do, preferring the risk of inundation to the inconvenience of having to carry their daily supply of water up a height of two hundred feet. They appealed to Peking; and it having been discovered that out of a total cost of £250,000 Ma had embezzled £50,000 (his real object in undertaking it, the natives say), he was incontinently degraded; but having disgorged a portion to the officials of the capital, he was permitted to retire, and the inhabitants were ordered to rebuild their houses on the old site. Meanwhile, Ma has a monument which will ensure the handing down of his name to all posterity. The walls of this uninhabited city are splendidly built of the local sandstone, and the inscriptions in the stone plaques, let in over the open and deserted gateways, I could read with my field-glass, although a mile distant.

The view of the river from the T'ien tze Shan is not unlike that of the entrance of the Niukan, or Ox-liver Gorge. The stream seemed to lose itself behind a succession of lofty points, backed by mountains of fifteen hundred to two thousand feet, each range separated from the other by the morning mist, in which the distant valleys were concealed, the rich vegetation in the foreground, and the curved temple-roofs peeping out behind the trees, adding to the beauty of the scene. On passing up we found, in fact, the banks very steep, cliff-like in many places, and strewn with huge rocks, which render the navigation dangerous in summer-time.

Making another of the usual rectangular turns, this time to the west, the river widens and flows between steep banks, every available spot being carefully cultivated with the poppy. We proceeded slowly past several small rapids, and brought up under a steep sandbank, on which poppies were growing almost to the water's edge; opposite the busy market-town of Sheng-chi Chang, the river, including a boulder-covered sandbank near the left shore, being fully three-quarters of a mile wide.

Distance run, seventy li (seventeen miles); from Ichang, 340 miles.

47

CHONGQING

THEODORE H. WHITE

During the Sino-Japanese war of the 1930s, the Japanese advanced steadily up the Yangtze. Shanghai fell at the end of 1937, followed by Nanjing, the capital of Chiang Kai-shek's government. So the Nationalists moved their capital far upriver to Chongqing. Later in 1938 the Japanese advanced to take Wuhan also. Chongqing, however, up beyond the narrow gorges, was impregnable. There is a saying that during winter in Sichuan, a glimpse of the sun is so rare that all the dogs start barking when they see it. Since Chongqing was veiled in clouds all winter, it was safe from bombing until spring. Although the Japanese bombed it regularly during clear weather, they could never succeed in capturing the city. In the spring of 1939, Theodore White went to Chongqing to take up the post of correspondent for Time magazine. At first he was full of idealism about the Nationalists, but soon became disillusioned. This is Chongqing as he found it on his arrival.

I arrived in Chungking on April 10, 1939, landing in the Yangtze River. I looked about. The runway was a sandbar paved with stone, and on both sides of the sandbar the river rushed by, yellow and muddy, carrying the silt of Inner Asia down to the ocean beyond the gorges below. The airstrip was usable only from winter through spring, when the river ran low; in summer and early fall, swollen with the melting snows of Tibet, the river flooded the airport. A footbridge now led across an eddy of the river to the foot of a gray cliff, and there, high above the cliff, ran the city wall of old Chungking.

The pilot hurried us out, reloaded the plane with waiting passengers, then roared away at once before any marauding Japanese overflight might discover his plane on the ground and destroy it.

I was at last in a country at war, in its capital fourteen hundred miles from the sea, up the Yangtze River, four hundred miles beyond the Japanese lines. Sedan-chair bearers were called to carry me up the hundreds of steps carved into the cliff wall, and I was swung aboard a hammock of bamboo slats hung between two poles, a front bearer and rear bearer yoked to the poles. It was the first time I had seen men used this way, as beasts of burden, and I remember noticing the brown calluses, thicker than leather, on the bare shoulders of the lead carrier as he sweated his way up. 'A-ya-zillah, a-ya-zillah,' he chanted in singsong at each step, and the rear bearer responded with the same 'a-ya-zillah, a-ya-zillah,' as he lurched, heaving, up one step at a time. Up the cliff, up the road, into the city wall of Chungking, and I was in another world.

The city itself for the first weeks held my attention more than my job or my ambitions.

Marco Polo had written of cities like this when he visited the province of Szechwan almost seven hundred years earlier, and by rolling back the thin veneer of the twentieth century that overlay Chungking, I might have been again in his Cathay. Let me linger over what I could see, for it was the beginning of the story of China I was to learn:

The city sat on a wedge of cliffs, squeezed together by the Chialing and Yangtze rivers, which joined flow at the tip of the wedge. The city wall, with its nine gates, had been built in the Ming dynasty, over five hundred years earlier. Much of the wall had been torn down for building material a few years before I got there, but its nine gates still stood and one of them still functioned; its huge brass-knobbed beams swung shut at sunset, opened at dawn. The gate that had opened for the imperial cart road—the T'ung-yüan Men, the 'Gate Connecting with Distant Places'—was now pierced for a motor road. This motor road, the 'old' road, was twelve years old; until 1928 Chungking had boasted no wheeled vehicles, no autos, no rickshaws, not even wheelbarrows. The 'new' motor road, circling the south rim of the wall, had been opened only the year I arrived. Sedan chairs, with their bearers, outnumbered rickshaws, with their pullers, three thousand to two thousand.

Neither road had yet significantly changed life in the city, and Chungking was still attached umbilically, as it had been forever, to the countryside. Rice paddy fields reached up to the city wall itself; down below on the fringes of the Yangtze's banks, peasants hopefully planted vegetables, gambling they could harvest before the summer floods overran their plots. As far as the eye could see, on both sides of the Yangtze, on both sides of the Chialing, the crescent paddy fields stretched to the hills, then in terraces over the hills, to the next ridge of hills, on and on to the great walled city of Ch'eng-tu, 275 miles away, and beyond that more paddy fields until the Tibetan escarpment forbade the peasants to try farther.

Inside the wall was a China I had never heard of. Flowers, for example. No one had ever told me how much the Chinese love flowers—but now, in springtime, there were more flower stalls than in my native Boston. In semitropical Szechwan, the flowers, it seemed, forgot to blossom by the season. Paper-white narcissi (*shui-hsien*) came in midwinter; plum blossoms spotted the hills and decorated the markets in March; azaleas bloomed all year round, and the stalls offered little pots of flowering shrubs, which lit the dingy, shadow-dark alleys around the calendar. Then, fruits: tiny orange cherries, sticky sweet, in baskets, as early as May; followed by peaches in June—huge yellow-skinned red-fleshed peaches, the best in all China except for those of Shantung; then the apricots and the lichee nuts of midsummer, followed by the watermelons of August and September; followed again by pears; by the red and rosy persimmons of late fall; to be overwhelmed finally by the magnificent citrus fruits of winter—pink pomelos, oranges and, at their glorious best, the tangerines of December. In a few years, I, like most Chinese in Chungking, learned to mark the rhythm of the seasons by the fruits.

Flowers and fruits gave the visual rhythm. But the real flow, the continuing beat of the city, connected it to the fields of rice where fifty million peasants in China's richest province, Szechwan, filled the granary of China at war. Rice came down from upriver in flat-bottomed scows, was shoveled into sacks, was shipped off now in wartime to the fronts instead of to the cities of the coast, where it had gone before. The richest of the rich in Chungking were the rice merchants and landlords of rice fields. Meat came from the country-side, as it always had. Pigs were carried in every morning to the city, four legs trussed over a pole carried by two coolies, the eyelids of the pig sewn shut, the pig squealing in agony until it reached the slaughtering place. And then it reappeared as fat slabs of red meat, oozing blood on butchers' counters; or as fly-blown gobbets of gray pork; or as yards-long black-and-brown dust-coated dry sausages hanging from hooks in open stalls, from which the meat merchant would sell from an inch to two feet to any customer. The city repaid the countryside by returning all its bowel movements; collectors emptied the thunder boxes of every home each morning, and padded barefoot down the alley stairs to the riverside, two buckets of liquid muck jiggling from their bamboo staves, until they reached what foreigners delicately styled the 'honey barges'. There, they emptied the excrement into the barges, where rivermen, entirely naked, stirred the muck around at a collection point famous for its stench. From that point, Chungking's gift to the fields was carried upriver to be sold to peasants as fertilizer. From the same river the water-bearers carried up buckets of muddy water, jiggling on the same kind of staves as the honey buckets, to all the homes that could not be reached by Chungking's new, but minimal, piped water supply. The sloshings on the stone steps, up and down the alleys, left them always slippery, and one could never be sure what kind of slime one must avoid.

From the one main motor road in the city, on the crest of the ridge, one descended, as if through centuries, to the past. This main road had the façade of a coastal city; its stores sold bolts of cloth, flashlights, auto parts and canned foods, advertised in neon; its peddlers sold needles, thread, vacuum bottles, imports from down-river. But from the road, the alleys slipped down into darkness. Chungking was always foggy, except for the clear, midsummer bombing months. The alleys were always shadowed, and some were so narrow that a passer could catch the drip from the eaves on both sides with his umbrella. They offered a symphony of smells, fragrant and stinking at the same time—fragrant with the smell of food and spice, the aroma of flowers, roasting chestnuts, incense, the sweetness of opium, yet stinking of uncollected garbage and the urine that ran in the gutters. The noises were a symphony of another kind—of yelling men, screaming women, bawling babies, and squawking hens, which lived with the families in the huts. To which was added the singsong chants of the coolies carrying their buckets or the peddlers carrying wares. Each activity had its own sound. The timbermen, swinging their logs, bellowed. The peddler of cottons announced his journey by clacking rhythmically on a wooden block. The notions dealer carried all his

wares in one great black box and sang his wares with his own particular chant, as the banana man and the fish peddler had on Erie
Street. The night-soil collectors gave out a warning chant peculiar
to them. So, too, did the brassware man, who sold cat's bells,
knives, toothpicks, ear cleaners, back scratchers, all dangling from
a long pole, twirling as in a Calder mobile.

The people in these alleys lived as they always had, responding
sluggishly to the changing times, wrinkling their habits as an animal wrinkles its hide and stirs at a prod. A few had learned to visit
the three missionary clinics that had been established in the town.
But most, when they were ill, visited the herb doctor or the
acupuncture man, and sought medicines unheard of in the West—
moldy bean curd for sore throats, potions of baby urine, powders
ground from crystals of musk or rhinoceros horn. They bought
their virility and fertility aids, their backache and headache cures,
their beauty aids and lotions in their own tradition, seeking the
same elusive magic of life, love and comfort that television adver-
tises with the same futility each day in America. On the ridge of the
motor road were strung the electricity lines that lit the neon of the
storefronts and the offices in which government had found shelter, but down in the alleys, homes were still lit by oil lamps and candles. Paraders bearing green leaves asked the gods for rain in time
of drought; traditional marriage processions followed behind the
red-draped bridal chair, cymbals clanging; at funerals, the people

trooped in white, as they had for millennia, behind the coffin—and sometimes on the body of the corpse mourners still tied a crowing cock to ward off evil spirits.

This Chungking, in the alleys and of the past, needed little of the kind of government of the coastal cities I had seen, where Westerners had planted outposts and seeded industry. Chungking's relation to the countryside was straightforward; its traditional government, though cruel, was simple. Local government policed an orderly place where merchants, moneychangers and shopkeepers could provide a market for the peasants of the valleys; government kept the peace. The merchants paid off to authority—to whomever had the spears, the soldiers, the guns, the power to keep the trading place functioning. Such people had paid their taxes to a millennial succession of imperial civil servants, to mandarins and viceroys and, more recently, to warlords. They might have paid off forever, living undisturbed by any but local predators, except for the war. Not Chungking, but China, as a nation, needed a new kind of government. And I had come to Chungking to serve the government that had only recently taken refuge there.

48

CROSSING THE YANGTZE IN THE MIST

ROBERT PAYNE

During the Sino-Japanese war, Chongqing was filled with foreign journalists, military advisers, spies, and soldiers of all descriptions. Robert Payne was a wanderer, teaching at a series of universities, working as a war correspondent in Spain, and ending up in Singapore where his father was stationed. Just before Singapore fell to the Japanese, he was sent to Chongqing by the Head of British Intelligence in the Far East. He claims he was given no clear brief and spent much of his time involved with the Chinese universities in exile. From childhood China had held a fascination for him, and he had dreamt that he would 'marry a Chinese princess and live in a palace in Peking'. But life in wartime was very different. Although exciting, it was also squalid, dangerous, and full of misery. Yet he found a beauty and dignity there. He translated Chinese poetry, and many of the passages in his diaries are poetry in themselves. This entry was written in 1942.

January 16th—The river is still high, a great turbulent white sheet flowing under a thick mist. It is impossible to see the sky or the clouds, and in this whiteness everything dissolves in patches of mist. This morning, as we crossed the river in the motor-boat, we saw a small sampan gliding past us, caught up in the current, and three or four small brown figures cowering at the bottom of the boat. There was no expression on their faces; they looked neither backwards nor forwards. As sometimes happens in a dream, when the figures suddenly lose colour and great black spiders' webs begin to dissolve the picture, I had the impression that at any moment a black hand would descend from the clouds and carry them away. Our small motor-boat chugged in circles. There was the occasional sound of rocks grating against the iron bottom of the boat; and in the mist the small yellowish-grey sampan was still gliding past us, so slowly that I felt certain that this was a dream. When the sampan was about to disappear from our field of vision, it suddenly stopped and began to sway backwards and forwards, caught against the rocks, swinging like scissors, until suddenly the roar of the river came to our ears and at that moment the sampan broke in two, spilling the occupants into the white river. For two or three seconds—certainly not more than five seconds—we watched three or four small black heads bobbing up and down against the smooth rock; then they disappeared, following the boat which was already disappearing downstream.

I am told that this happens always in time of floods. The rocks are treacherous; and the current so deceptive that the most skilled boatmen have been known to lose their lives in the Yangtse. The river is quite merciless; and though in some places rocks have been dynamited, and though the masts of sampans can be seen protruding above the river at all seasons, every year the river claims its victims. I am beginning to believe that the Yangtse is a living and breathing thing, a smooth turbulent dragon who never relinquishes her claim on the lives of the Chinese who live on her banks. This morning, after we had watched the sampan breaking in two, we were lost in midstream. The mist was as thick as a waterfall. Somewhere a boy was beating a drum on the high rocks, and we heard the continual hooting of motor-cars high up on the rocky cliffs of Chungking. We were continually turning in circles, and once we hit a rock with such a sickening crash of plates that we instinctively made ready to dive overboard; but if we had dived, we would have lived for ten seconds—no more. It was half an hour before we reached the other side of the river, we were drenched with mist and our cigarettes wouldn't light—they were so wet. And as we began to climb the immense reach of steps which leads to the Dragon Gate of Chungking, I looked back and watched the river through a break in the clouds. The river was white and full, swirling along, hurrying, talking to itself, in absorbed intent tones. And the suspicion that it was a dragon, a real dragon, with scales and fins and great golden eyes, with an immense lashing tail and huge hairy arms, with which it could climb on the shore and engulf everything within sight, became so overpowering that I began to understand why at times of high flood there are more suicides in the river than at any other time.

But at night the river is beautiful beyond words. The little black paddle-steamer, with its ghostly oil-lamps, lies reflected in the torrent. Armies of cloud march in rank across the sky, obscuring the mountains with their ragged banners, and through the mist you can see the faint silver lights shining on the south bank and the great red puffs of smoke coming from the bamboo flares on the landing-stage. Sometimes it may take an hour to cross the river, even in the paddle-boat. But once you have arrived on the rocky shore of the south bank, small boys run forward with plaited yellow bamboo flares, and the smoky red flares shining on the granite steps and on the faces of the passengers are so vivid and so consoling that you forget the tedium of the journey and the loneliness in mid-river, when the paddle-boat mills round in a whirlpool or fights against the sheer weight of the current.

49

PAST, PRESENT, & FUTURE

PAUL THEROUX

Sailing the Yangtze on a luxury tourist boat in 1984, travel writer Paul Theroux had little time for the China mystique. Although traces of beauty remain, they cannot mitigate the pollution, poverty, and dearth of wildlife that he sees.

In the 1800s, sportsmen travelling the river found more than enough game to occupy them. British travellers such as Lord Elgin and W. S. Percival wrote of the plentiful wildfowl—geese, pheasants, and duck. The naturalist E. H. Wilson, who travelled the region in 1899, wrote of tigers around Yichang, the 'goral' or wild goat of the Gorges, and the little river deer of the lower reaches, to name but a few of the animals along the Yangtze. In the early 1900s, crewmen aboard American gunboats complained of eating too much venison and pheasant!

But by the time of Theroux's visit, these animals were just a memory. Theroux's view of the Yangtze and its future is bleak indeed.

In 1937 Captain Williamson saw only the city walls of Chang Shou from the river. Today there are no city walls, and Chang Shou (the name means 'Long Life') is one of the nightmare cities of the river. It burst through its old walls and sprawled across the banks, blackening three hillsides with chimneys and factories and blocks of workers' flats. 'Looks like Pittsburgh,' someone said. But Chungking had looked like Pittsburgh, and so did six others downstream. Yellow froth streamed from pipes and posterns, and drained into the river with white muck and oil and the suds of treated sewage and beautifully coloured poison. And on a bluff below the town, there was an old untroubled pagoda, still symmetrical, looking as if it had been carved from a piece of laundry soap.

These pagodas have a purpose. They are always found near towns and cities and, even now in unspiritual China, serve a spiritual function, controlling the *Fengshui* ('Wind-water') of a place: they balance the female influences of the *Yin* ('Darkness') and the male influence of the *Yang* ('Light'). The Chinese say they no longer believe in such superstitious malarkey, but the visible fact is that most pagodas survived the Cultural Revolution. Anything that a fanatical Red Guard left intact must be regarded as worthy, if not sacred. The pagodas on the Yangtze bluffs remain pretty much as they always were.

It was near Chang Shou, about noon on that first day, that I saw a sailing junk being steered to the bank, and the sail struck, and five men leaping onto the shore with tow-lines around their waists. They ran ahead, then jerked like dogs on a leash, and immediately began towing the junk against the current. These are trackers. They are mentioned by the earliest travellers on the Yangtze. They strain, leaning forward, and almost imperceptibly the sixty-foot junk begins to move upstream. There is no level towpath. The trackers are rock-climbers: they scamper from boulder to boulder, moving higher until the boulders give out, and then dropping down, pulling and climbing until there is a reach on the river where the junk can sail again. The only difference—but it is a fairly large one—between trackers long-ago and trackers today is that they are no longer whipped. 'Often our men have to climb or jump like monkeys,' wrote a Yangtze traveller, in the middle of the last century, of his trackers, 'and their backs are lashed by the two chiefs, to urge them to work at critical moments. This new spectacle at first revolts and angers us, but when we see that the men do not complain about the lashings we realize that it is the custom of the country, justified by the exceptional difficulties along the route.' Captain Little saw a tracker chief strip his clothes off, jump into the river, then roll himself in sand until he looked half-human, like a gritty ape; then he did a demon dance, and howled, and whipped the trackers, who—scared out of their wits—willingly pulled a junk off a sandbank.

The trackers sing or chant. There are garbled versions of what they say. Some travellers have them grunting and groaning, others are more specific and report the trackers yelling, 'Chor! Chor!' —slang for 'Shang-chia' or 'Put your shoulder to it'. I asked a boatman what the trackers were chanting. He said that they cried out 'Hai tzo! Hai tzo!' over and over again, which means 'Number!

Number!' in Szechuanese, and is uttered by trackers and oarsmen alike.

'When we institute the Four Modernizations', he added—this man was one of the miniscule number who are members of the Chinese Communist party—'there will be no more junks or trackers.'

One day I was standing at the ship's rail with Big Bob. We saw some trackers, six of them, pulling a junk. The men skipped from rock to rock, they climbed, they hauled the lines attached to the junk, and they struggled along the steep rocky towpath. They were barefoot. . . .

The junks and these trackers will be on the river for some time to come.* Stare for five minutes at any point on the Yangtze and you will see a junk, sailing upstream with its ragged, ribbed sail; or being towed by yelling, tethered men; or slipping downstream with a skinny man clinging to its rudder. There are many new-fangled ships and boats on the river, but I should say that the Yangtze is a river of junks and sampans, fuelled by human sweat. Still, there is nothing lovelier than a junk  with a following wind (the wind blows upstream, from east to west—a piece of great meteorological luck and a shaper of Chinese history), sailing so well that the clumsy vessel looks as light as a waterbird paddling and foraging in the muddy current.

That image is welcome, because there is little birdlife on the Yangtze—indeed, China itself is no place for an ornithologist. It is hard to say if the absence of trees is the reason for the scarceness of birds; or is it the use of powerful insecticides, or the plain hunger of the people who seem to kill anything that moves? Apart from a few kites and hawks, and some feeble sparrows, the only wild ground-dwelling creature I saw in China was a rat, and in twenty-two trips on the Yangtze a Lindblad guide told me he had

---

* In fact there are few junks left today.

only seen one wild thing, a small snake. No wonder the Chinese stared at mink coats and alligator handbags! Abbé David saw very few birds on the Yangtze in the 1860s and, as a naturalist, he was looking hard for them. He put it down to the wilful destruction of animals by the Chinese, and his reflection on this has proved to be prophetic: 'A selfish and blind preoccupation with material interests has caused us to reduce this cosmos, so marvellous to him with eyes to see it, to a hard matter-of-fact place. Soon the horse and the pig on the one hand and wheat and potatoes on the other will replace hundreds of thousands of animals and plants given us by God.'

Down the Yangtze the awful prediction has been fulfilled. You expect this river trip to be an experience of the past—and it is. But it is also a glimpse of the future. In a hundred years or so, under a cold uncolonized moon, what we call the civilized world will all look like China, muddy and senile and old-fangled: no trees, no birds, and shortages of fuel and metal and meat; but plenty of pushcarts, cobblestones, ditch-diggers, and wooden inventions. Nine hundred million farmers splashing through puddles and the rest of the population growing weak and blind working the crashing looms in black factories.

PART 3

THE UPPER REACHES:
BEYOND CHONGQING

Geographers have speculated on the true source of the river ever since the Warring States period, more than 2,000 years ago. Although knowledge of the source has advanced considerably since then, the baffling number of tributaries, together with the difficulties of the terrain which hinder exploration, have kept the debate alive to this day. In the 1970s, a Chinese expedition believed that they had finally traced the source to one of the many headstreams, the Tuotuo. A few years later, however, the explorer How Man Wong identified the source as the Damqu, an even longer tributary than the Tuotuo.

Whatever the definitive source, the Yangtze's main headwaters begin high in the Tanggula Mountains on the Qinghai–Tibet plateau. It is a windswept land of glaciers and permafrost, snow-covered for up to ten months of the year and frequented only by a few hardy Tibetan nomads. The Chinese know the higher reaches of the Yangtze as the Jinsha or River of Golden Sand. But inside Tibet, the Tibetans name it the Dri Chu, or Wild Yak River, since they believe that the source spills from the mouth of an immense female yak, living high in the mountains.

Going upstream along the Jinsha, the river winds along the border between Sichuan and Yunnan, loops deep into Yunnan, back to the border and then runs parallel to itself back into Yunnan once more. As it doubles back yet again towards Tibet, it rushes through the mountains alongside the Salween, the Mekong, and for a short distance, the Irawaddy also. The four great rivers flow side by side through a stretch of land only about 160 kilometres (100 miles) wide.

From the headwaters down to Chongqing is about 3,220 kilometres (2,000 miles), or over half the river's total length. Yet most of this is little known territory, even today. Once beyond the rapids at tiny Xinshizhen, the last possible navigable point on the river, the lands of the Han Chinese are left behind. The traveller enters the wild and sparsely populated realms of minority peoples, which were independent kingdoms until 1949. Here live the Yi, the Naxi, the Lisu, and the Tibetans.

50

THE YANGTSE IN ITS REAL HOME

SAMUEL POLLARD

In Samuel Pollard's time, at the turn of the nineteenth century, the Yi were known as the fearsome 'Mantsz' or 'Lolo', derogatory nicknames given by the Chinese. Today, the Han and the Yi co-exist peacefully, and the Yi have their own autonomous county. Located along the tumbling rapids of the river, it is aptly named Leibo, 'Thunder and Waves'.

A British Protestant missionary, Pollard gave twenty-seven years of his life to the wilds of western China and finally died there. He maintained that those who only ventured as far as Hankou had merely seen the Yangtze's 'company manners', not its true face. 'All the love and tragedy and intrigue and comedy are hidden beyond Yichang, and the traveller that ventures farther gets a sudden rude awakening.' He spoke from bitter personal experience, as he was shipwrecked at Xintan Rapids on his first voyage upriver in 1887. Years later he wrote that anyone who has gone through such an experience will never think lightly of the Yangtze again: 'If, like some of us, he has been wrecked and tossed into the raging waters of the wild rapids and only just escaped with his life, he will never forget the weird, hissing, triumphant song the angry, boisterous waves sang in his ears as he battled for life against a merciless enemy. And when, years after, far inland and away from the great Yangtse, he wakes at night and hears the rain beating on the roof and the hill torrent roaring in the gullies, he will hear once more that weird, hissing song and feel the quiver of the wings of that angry, merciless river demon. Ugh! It is nearly thirty years since he shook and tossed and bit me and I can feel him even now. The merciless brute! The roar of the river will ring in the ears of some of us till the day of the crossing of the great last river.'

But for Pollard, even the rapids of the Three Gorges were not the real home of the Yangtze. For that you must venture further west beyond Chongqing.

But leave Chungking alone. Forget those little, almost impudent gunboats which hold up the flags of several nations before the gaze of the busy farmers and traders of the richest province of all China [Sichuan], and one of the finest countries in the whole world. Do not fancy you have yet seen the real Yangtse. Press on still farther. The greatest mysteries of all lie towards the sunset, and he who would speak to the heart of the mighty river must diligently resist the temptation to stop, and keep on crying: Westward Ho! The houseboats and junks push their way up river for a few weeks more, and in the summer-time, when the waters are swollen high, the perky little gunboats fly their flags a few hundred miles farther west, and give the natives the opportunity of thinking that the vaunted navies of England and Germany are composed of little boats half the size of some of their huge salt junks and drawing only three or four feet of water. No wonder they are never much impressed in these inland provinces with the naval power of the great Western nations.

Now you must go slowly, for you are approaching the real home of the great river, and are getting near the heart, where the secrets are kept closely hidden from all but the closest friends and the mighty hills and the eternal skies.

Away up, two days beyond the farthest point, where the most daring and skilfully navigated of these little Western gunboats have been, twenty miles west of the little town of Fukwan, which from its home in the province of Yunnan faces the big sister province of Szechuan, an enormous rapid, the Oxhide Rapid, stops all junk traffic, and the merry songs of the hard-working boatmen stop here. Reaching this place is almost like reaching the death point of a mighty industry. A few small boats manage to crawl on five miles farther to Mao Shui Kong—'the Hole where the Water rushes out'—but this represents the last feeble efforts of the great boat traffic to conquer the waters of the mighty river. Beyond this the Yangtse is supreme in its own home, and has time to tell its own story and reveal its hidden secrets. . . .

Just near where the junk traffic finally ceases a rock juts out into one of the dangerous rapids. A lot of splendid fish are caught at this point, and the men who live in the vicinity know the advantages of the place for fishing. There is not room, however, for more than one fisher at a time, and if he has a struggle with a twenty-pounder, which he not infrequently has, he is liable to follow the fish into its rough elements, thus causing a complete turn of the tables. To prevent such a calamity the fisher is tied by a rope to the shore, and near by the anchorage a stick of incense is constantly burning. This is not in honour of Wang-ye, the great river god of West China, but is the fisherman's time mark. Each man can stay on the point as long as one stick of incense burns. When it has burnt away a fresh fisherman tries his luck, while a new stick of incense is gradually being consumed.

There being no up-river boats now the traveller has to follow the Yangtse by means of the narrow paths on its banks. Sometimes the road lies on the right bank and sometimes on the left. Every now and again there are ferry boats which cross the stream, and in a few places where there are some miles of fairly smooth waters small boats ply up and down, carrying coolies and travellers at a very reasonable rate. . . .

One missed the boats and the cheery song of the toiling boat-men. Except for the roar of the waters, all was as quiet as an ordinary country-side. The river had all the song to itself, and now and again it was full band and chorus. Passing by one of the many Shin Tans (New Rapids) which the river possesses, one had to stand and marvel at the great waters beating against the rocks in midstream. The white horses and the lovely foam crested the huge waves as I have often seen them crest the waves which have dashed against Cape Cornwall near Land's End; and beyond the roaring breakers the treacherous whirlpools, which twist and turn as if moving in harmony with the maddest of giant dancers. One can never imagine boats trying to negotiate those waters. And yet there are men who have gone down over these wild billows and have lived to tell their thrilling experience.

In many places along by the river-side building wood is very difficult to procure. Farther up river, however, forest land is more plentiful, and planks and beams are cheap. These planks and beams are bound together into strong rafts, and an attempt is made to take them down over the dangerous rapids to the profitable markets lower down river. A Chinaman will risk almost anything for money, and there are some who now and again face these wild waters of the Upper Yangtse.

The raft is allowed to drift most of the way, the adventurous travellers doing nothing to assist it along. Here and there iron rings are driven into the planks, and when nearing the dangerous parts the men lie down, thrust their arms through the rings, and in this position go right through the waters overwhelmed by the great billows again and again. The greatest danger feared by the raft travellers is when the raft approaches a cliff, and instead of being swept on by the swaying waters the head of it is sucked under and the stern of the raft is thrown up against the cliff. When this happens the men on the raft are spoken of as being stuck on the cliff like scrolls are pasted on the door-posts at the New Year time. The danger of becoming a New Year's scroll is the danger most dreaded by these hazardous voyagers. . . .

The white towers dotted all over the country-side mean danger. The district is a borderland district, and there is the constant fear of sudden raids, with their attendant burnings and murders and captures for slavery. If you ask the owners of these towers why they have built them they will invariably answer: 'Fear of the Mantsz.' The dread of the Mantsz exists all over the country-side, and extends into three provinces. The word 'Mantsz' means wildmen, and one wonders at once who these wildmen are, who can so terrorise an enormous district and incidentally alter the architectural appearance of great parts of three provinces. You ask again where is the home of these wildmen, and with protruding chin or pointing finger your informant directs you to the hills north of the Yangtse, right opposite to where you are standing and asking the question.

The hills on that side of the great river look very similar to the hills on this side. The geological formation is precisely the same. Why should there be wildmen on one side of the river and civilised Chinese on the other?

If you understand the language spoken by the people you can easily get the owners of the white towers to talk by the hour about the Mantsz, and blood-curdling are many of the stories. For generations and even centuries there has been constant warfare between the wildmen among the hills north of the Yangtse and the Chinese who have settled near the home of these hardy raiders. . . .

Without warning, the hillmen will burst forth and make a raid on the wealthier Chinese villages and farmsteads. They come with great swiftness, strike, rob, burn, take captive without any hesitation, and in a very few days are back again into their highland homes, safe from pursuit. The raiders cross the Yangtse in small boats at some safe point, and the boats are made inland, far from the gaze of the Chinese who live on the south bank of the river.

It is to the benefit of the hillmen to keep up the feeling of terror which the Chinese have of them. Only in this way can they keep their land safe. Gold and other precious metals, the value of which is well known to the Chinese, are reported to exist in large quantities, and it is a wonder that long ago the more numerous race has not gone in and subdued the people, people who live an almost independent existence among the great hills north of the Yangtse. Nominally they owe allegiance to the Central Government of China, but in reality they enjoy the completest form of home rule.

After our discovery of the white towers we continued to follow the river up for some days, meeting similar towers with great frequency. Day after day we looked across at the land where dwell the so-called Mantsz, the wildmen, and as we did so we wished much to get into that land and lift the veil off one of the remaining mysteries of inland China. The ferries, however, were guarded, and for some time no chance opened out for us. At night all the ferryboats are drawn up on the Chinese bank, so as to prevent the hillmen using the boats for any midnight raid. Apparently the hillmen sleep in peace, never dreaming that the Chinese could cross in these same boats and serve their homes as they have so often served the Chinese homes and farms.

There is a great contrast in the cultivation on the two sides of the river. On the southern side, where the Chinese dwell, the country is like one great, well-cultivated garden, where cotton, sugar-cane, rice, maize, sweet potatoes, monkey nuts, oranges, pomegranates, persimmons, etc., etc., produce bountiful crops. Just across the river, which is often less than a hundred yards wide, in the land which would produce similar crops in equally rich profusion, we saw very few signs of cultivation. Most of the land was neglected jungle. It is a constant eyesore to the Chinese, who before everything else are farmers and who long for the opportunity of extracting from the neglected land the riches it is so willing to give to those who treat it patiently and kindly. A garden on one side of the river and a desert on the other, the soil the same in each case. Some day in the land where these hillmen live there will be a great outlet for the surplus population of the neighbouring provinces, but that day as yet seems a long way off.

One day, while still following the river and looking with longing eyes at the unknown land on the other side, we came to the Hill of Slippery Sand, and found the worst piece of land I had ever travelled over, in nearly twenty years of life in West China. The place has a fearful reputation, and the man who has been over the Hill of Slippery Sand talks about it to the end of his days. The road winds in and out around the face of a long, high cliff, and is sometimes less than a foot in width. There is a sheer cut down to the roaring waters below, and there is no outside protection to the road at all. As one walks or crawls along, the cliff seems to press over and to lean on to one, as if it were some recruiting demon in league with the treacherous waters below, trying to force one into the deeps and destruction. Here and there the road is a little wider, and one can sit down and rest in safety. Different parts of the road are named after the various stations in the Chinese Temple of Hades, and a knowledge of these names did not add to one's feeling of comfort. The King of Hell's Slide, The Gate of Hell, The Last Look at Home, The Place where even the Soul is Lost—these are some of the names given to points on the road over the Hill of Slippery Sand. At one point, about half-way across, someone had built a small shrine, and here used to sit an old woman selling oatmeal. In the Chinese Temple of Hades, after all the many torture chambers have been gone through, the adventurous lost soul approaches the gate of transmigration, and prepares for his re-entrance into the world. At this gate sits an old woman, selling the 'Broth of Oblivion', the Chinese equivalent of the Waters of Lethe. When the soul has drunk of this broth it forgets all about its former existence, and all about its many adventures in Hades, and goes with a clean memory slate into the world once more.

The travellers over the Hill of Slippery Sand dubbed the old lady who sold the oatmeal 'The Lady in charge of the Broth of Oblivion'. When travellers reached this spot it is said that they promptly sat down and repented of ninety-five per cent of all their evil deeds and sins, so that the good spirits might come and help them over the rest of the dangerous path.

When we were near this conscience-awakening spot some travellers told me some stories to keep up our pluck. One of the stories was this: A family was crossing this Hill of Slippery Sand. In front walked the boy of twelve. Next came the mother, carrying the baby on her back, in the usual convenient way. Last of all came the father, bearing some goods. The boy slipped and fell over. The mother shrieked in terror, lost her balance and followed the boy. Fright struck the father likewise, and he also fell into the raging billows. The whole family was gone in a few seconds.

Those who are used to the road go over it as if it were nothing at all unusual. Long before I reached the end of the cliff road my legs were shaking, my heart was beating loudly and I had to strain all nerves to keep at all steady. One of my coolies, who carried my bedding and other things, in two baskets slung from the ends of a pole over his shoulder, went across as if it were great fun, and at the end said: 'I have for long wished to meet and conquer this much-talked-of Hill of Slippery Sand.' . . .

Twenty miles above the Plain of the Great Well is another small market town, notable as the place where the first bridge across the Yangtse, from the mouth up, was built. The river is about thirty yards wide at this place, and across it was built a hawser bridge on the same principle as the transporter bridges. The Chinese name for such a transporter is *liu*. It usually consists of just one big bamboo hawser, fastened to rocks on either side of the river. From the hawser hangs a loop, sometimes merely a loop of rope; sometimes a little board seat is provided as well. These rope transporters are very common over the many rivers of West China. The traveller slips into the loop and slides down to the lowest part of the hawser bridge. Then he pulls himself up, hand over hand, until he reaches the other side. Sometimes he is helped across by men who are stationed on either side, in charge of the transporter. These men pull the loop to either side, by means of a small rope attached to it. The first sensation as the loop is freed and goes down the slope is very strange. If you have any nerves at all they begin to be very jumpy. The slide down is comfortable enough, but what lies underneath is the disturbing factor in the situation. The *liu*s are often over very treacherous stretches of water, with roaring rapids or fierce falls dashing against rocks in midstream. It is what awaits one, should the rope break, or the traveller lose his balance, that disturbs one. If you only think of the rope, and forget the raging waters and jagged rocks below, the experience on the rope bridge is pleasant enough. The first time I crossed one of these I was in company with another missionary, a fine specimen of a sturdy John Bull Englishman. I got safely over without mishap, and laughed at the quivering dance my nerves had set up as I hung over the rapids for a few seconds while the slack-pulling rope was being gathered in. My companion was not so fortunate. He slid down to the centre of the bridge all right, and then the man in charge began to pull up the rope on the other side. Before half the journey up had been completed, the pulling rope broke, and back went the traveller to the centre of the rope bridge, where he remained dangling for some time over the angry waters. It was an awkward position to be in, and did not look at all pleasant to those who were looking on.

Those who are used to this method of crossing rivers soon learn to treat the situation with freedom and carelessness. Sheep and goats are often sent across in the same way, and very rarely does a mishap take place.

This first bridge over the Yangtse, the bamboo transporter, does not now exist. One night a band of the wildmen from the unexplored hills silently crossed over, and while the Chinese in the little market near by were sleeping peacefully the hillmen set fire to the houses and in the confusion stole a number of children and gathered much loot. They were over the *liu* and clean away with their spoils before any steps could be taken to stop them. The day after the market people cut the bamboo transporter, and now the first bridge over the Yangtse is only reached after many hundred miles more have been travelled towards the source of the great river.

51

NAKHI MOUNTAIN WEDDING

PETER GOULLART

Peter Goullart was a White Russian who fled to Shanghai after the Bolshevik revolution. He was sent to Lijiang in 1941 by the Nationalist Government as Depot Master, his main task being to set up industrial co-operatives. One of his big successes was the introduction of the wool-spinning wheel to the Naxi (Nakhi) ethnic group. It became so popular among the women that Lijiang became a great centre of the wool industry. He also ran a simple clinic.

For Goullart, the spectacular scenery and simple people of Lijiang made it a paradise on earth. As he says, however, in spite of its beauty, it was hardly a place that most Westerners would call heaven. There were no such things as hotels or cinemas, and disease was rife. His happiness came from the joy of balancing magnificent surroundings with useful work, together with his belief in God, and the friendship and trust of the people around him.

However, this idyll could not last. After the Chinese Revolution in 1949, there were rumours that he was an 'agent of Western Imperialism'. It was clear that all Westerners were in danger, and so for the second time in his life, Communism forced Goullart to leave his home. He and his mentor, the botanist Joseph Rock, chartered a plane, saying that they were going on a short visit to Kunming; and very reluctantly, they left their paradise forever.

Here he describes a raucous country wedding on the banks of the Yangtze, and the terrors of crossing the river. The passage also illustrates the fighting and tensions between the different racial groups living in close proximity with each other.

A year or so after ... I had to go to my Copper Mining Cooperative on the Yangtze River, run by my friend Hoyei. I liked the visits there but I always dreaded the precipices that I had to pass on the way. The mine was ninety *li* (thirty miles) from

Likiang and it was a long day's journey. As almost everywhere in Likiang district, the trail was one continuous panorama of mountain beauty and grandeur. After sixty *li* of comparatively level marching, we came to a point from which the great river became visible. There she flowed, like a liquid emerald, in the abyss that made my head reel. Like a green dragon she twisted, turned and foamed in gorges that staggered imagination. The trail dropped straight down, at least forty-five degrees, and down we went with our struggling horses. It was more a delayed fall than a regular descent. So steep was the path in some places that I had to break my descent by clinging to wayside trees. It was wonderful to see how our horses took it. Any moment I expected one of them to collapse with broken legs during the hours it took to negotiate this dangerous stretch. Then my real terrors began. A hanging bridge over a roaring stream a hundred feet below had to be crossed, after which the path ran along the wall of a sheer cliff with a fall of a thousand feet on the other side. Although I was led by Hoyei I suffered from nausea and my legs felt like jelly.

The village, where the mine was located, was perched on a small shelf over the roaring river; up to it narrow steps were cut in the rock, but there were no railings or protection at all from a bone-breaking fall. After lunch I was persuaded to visit a new copper mine they had opened somewhere along the river. They said the trip was quite safe and I agreed to go. The path led along a narrow shelf two thousand feet above the river. Cajoled and supported by Hoyei and his friends I somehow walked a mile or so. At one spot the rock shelf had collapsed and the path crossed the gap on the trunks of the trees driven into the face of the cliff. I could see through the crevices the river foaming far beneath my very feet. Then the path abruptly ended on a tiny platform jutting over the river. I became so giddy that I should have fallen off over the precipice had not my friends seized me in time. I collapsed, unable to go forward or backward, and I still do not remember clearly how I was dragged, or carried, back to the village.

The inhabitants of the village were the mountain Nakhi—simple and hospitable folk mostly clad in skin garments. They were quite poor as there was little good soil around. Only down below, where the hissing river made a turn, was there a narrow lunette of green fields and groves of *mitou*—Likiang oranges—hanging like

yellow lanterns on tall, dark trees. This type of orange, or perhaps it was tangerine, was an outstanding fruit of Likiang. It was very large, like a medium-size grapefruit, with a puffy, pimply, and easily detachable skin. It was very juicy and had a very pleasant taste, quite unlike any other orange or tangerine.

Many people came to see me at the Copper Mining Co-operative and, quite unexpectedly, I was handed an invitation to a wedding feast the same evening. I was very glad to accept as I was assured that many strange tribes would attend. The Nakhi customs here were rather different from Likiang and, I thought, it would be interesting to see them.

The bridegroom's house was somewhere by the river and it was quite dark when, *mingtzes* [pine torches] in hand, we descended to the river through the hedges of giant *euphorbias candelabra.* There was another terror in store for me. For at least a thousand yards we had to jump from boulder to boulder, over the dark waters rushing and swirling between. I was quite exhausted when we reached the scene of festivity. The house was on a ledge, just above the river, and the bonfires, lighted on the bank, were reflected in the racing waters. There were crowds of men and women inside and outside as we arrived. The youths, in blue turbans and clad in skin jackets and pants, played on flutes and *houloussehs*—a kind of bagless bagpipe made of bamboo stems with gourds for resonance.

I was heartily welcomed by the family, but this time I had to sit down to the feast together with the old men. Fortunately it was a short meal. Afterwards Hoyei came up to me with the bridegroom.

'There are important guests here to-night,' Hoyei said, 'and we want you to meet them.' I followed them into an upper room. A very dignified lady in a blue skirt and crimson jacket sat at the table with her husband, an oldish man with a long moustache. She must be a Noble Lolo, I thought.

'Please meet the Baroness and her husband,' Hoyei was saying. She rose, smiled and pointed to a place next to her.

'We are from the Black Lissu,' she said, 'and this is my husband.' I bowed.

'We live at the castle on top of that mountain across Yibi (the Yangtze),' she said, pointing. 'Lately we have had much trouble. Those dogs, the wild Lolos, have attacked us and burned three of my people's houses. Luckily we beat them off. I wanted to bring my sons and daughters here to-day but they cannot be spared. They are up at the castle defending it,' she continued in a conversational tone. I sat down. She offered me a bowl of white wine and indicated the dishes of food of which I pretended to eat a little. She was very good-looking for her age which must have been forty-eight or fifty. She wore a high silver collar with a clasp and long silver ear-rings terminating with hollow silver bubbles in the shape of eggs. Her husband's face was quite flushed from drinking and he looked very sleepy. Glancing round the room, I noticed several rifles stacked in the corner.

'These are our arms,' the Baroness said. 'We must always have them handy.' Of course she was right. Only then I realized that the village we were in was just opposite the infamous Siaoliangshan where the outlaw Lolos roamed, plundering and burning: but the Black Lissu were their brothers in spirit and quite a match for them. I wondered how it happened that the bridegroom's family were such good friends with this noble family: arms and opium running, I conjectured, as it was scarcely possible to raise such a question. The Black Lissu wanted arms just as badly as the Black Lolos, and they had the opium which the Chinese wanted. Fair exchange is no robbery, and it was on that principle, I was sure, that the intimate friendship with this dangerous couple was based.

The courtyard, which was very small, was just below the room.

'Let us go and watch the dancing,' said the Baroness. I followed her. The snake-like file of youths and women was already undulating around the fire. There was no singing here but dance music provided by a dozen or so of the mountain boys playing on flutes and *houloussehs*. The music was soft and lilting and in no way different, in its rhythm, from a foxtrot.

'Let us dance!' decreed the Baroness.

'I can follow the music, but I am not sure about the steps,' I protested.

'Never mind. I will show you,' she said, joining the dancers. I followed her with my hands on her shoulders.

'Ouch, you stepped on my toe!' she cried when I made a wrong step; and I apologized.

'Disgraceful,' she murmured. 'Look at that woman fondling that boy. She could be his grandmother,' she added, indicating with her head an elderly woman who was practically hanging on the neck of a handsome mountain boy dressed in skins. The people at this village were certainly uninhibited. Romance was rampant; and girls were dancing as if in a trance, clasping their boy friends around the waist and looking at them with melting eyes as if they were little gods. There was a blast of flutes, pipes and *houloussehs* and the boys rushed into the middle of the courtyard playing their instruments and executing a sort of Cossack dance, throwing their sandalled feet in the air. Then there was another dance which was exactly like the Big Apple, and like little furies the girls jumped on to the boys and were whirled by them until exhausted. It was already very late and everybody was getting drunk. I bowed to the Baroness, who pressed me to visit them across the river where they were returning on the following day.

In the morning we went to see them off. Three rafts waited for them. Each raft consisted of twenty or thirty inflated pigskins, held together by a flimsy bamboo frame. The rafts had been brought as far up the river as was possible. The Baroness and her husband lay down on one raft and their suite occupied the others. The naked men, swimming in the water and holding the raft with one hand, helped to direct its course. The current was terrific, and the rafts twisted and bobbed up and down but soon they touched the other bank at the intended spot. Horses and retainers awaited the party there and they started crawling up the barren side of the mountain towards the forest and their castle.

Such were the marriages in Likiang and round about. For a girl who did not love her husband it was the end of her golden days when, as a *pangchinmei* [maiden], she roamed freely with her friends, boys and girls, dancing and romancing. In Likiang no one really objected to romances between a Nakhi girl and boy, but the people were roused if the romance was with a stranger. The motto was 'The Nakhi girls for the Nakhi boys and nobody else', and everyone was free within the framework of the tribe. A Minkia or Chinese, who tried to flirt with a Nakhi girl, went in danger of his life and, as a matter of fact, many were killed by the jealous Nakhi men. I remember a young Chinese, a refugee from the Japanese, who came to Likiang on business. Attracted by the apparent ease with which *pangchinmei* mixed with men, he started to court a pretty Nakhi girl. Soon afterwards, in broad daylight, he was ambushed by three Nakhi who concealed their faces with handkerchiefs. They shot him in the cheek and said, 'This is the first warning. Next time it will be in the heart.' The man left Likiang in a hurry.

52

SLIPPING INTO TIBET

MARION H. DUNCAN

Veering northwards beyond the lands of the Naxi, the River of Golden Sand forms today's border between Sichuan and Tibet. American Marion Duncan, self-described 'missionary, geographer and explorer' spent from 1921 until the mid-1930s stationed in Batang, a Tibetan town (although on the Chinese side of the river). Batang was so cut-off that letters from America took three to six months to arrive, while the average delivery time for freight packages was two years.

After the fall of the Manchu dynasty in 1911, fighting broke out between China and Tibet. Although a peace treaty was drawn up in 1918, the Chinese refused to ratify it. So the Tibetan government denied permission to Chinese citizens to enter their country, a state of affairs which continued until the death of the thirteenth Dalai Lama in 1933. Since Duncan was living on the Chinese side of the border, Tibet was closed to him. However, in 1931, Batang's resident Western doctor was summoned to Tibet to treat a military official. The visit was such a success that Duncan too was given permission for a short foray into Tibet. Here he describes the first few days of his trip.

The Chinese saying that a thousand days at home are equivalent to one day on the road properly evaluates travel in the Orient as contrasted to the Occident. In the wild lands of the Tibetan Plateau this is exceptionally true. From narrow precarious roads animals now and then plunge into foaming rivers. The accommodations but not the comforts of a hotel must be transported. Cloth tents during thunderstorms and blizzards at high altitudes demand personal attention lest one's quarters fly away. The principal food procurable on the road is *tsamba* (parched barley flour), stale buttered tea and goat steak. However, appetites are not fastidious after rugged mule riding up airless passes and scrambling down stony trails.

We take a full month's supply of food but dispense with the tent as the dry season is near at hand; when no house is available we will sleep in caves or out in the open. Nomad tents are a last resort but too often they are not pitched in the right place for an inn, usually over a high range in another valley, and when found too full of home folks for a large party.

The worst obstacle are the bandits. Rarely does the frequent traveller in these parts escape being stripped clean of clothing and food and having his beasts driven away. Clothing, being so essential in such a frigid climate, is peeled off only at the insistence of a pointing gun. Sometimes the owner of the gun gets too nervous with the trigger (the profession of highwayman is hard on the nerves in this land where cutting off the head is the penalty when caught) and a dead merchant is added to the other losses.

Travelling being a matter of life and death a propitious day must be found. Astrological books and the stars are carefully scanned to discover a lucky day. We have no faith in the stars' prophetic voice but as it is the 29th of the Tibetan month, the day (our October 10th, 1931) is easily arranged. Journeys are not undertaken except on certain (usually the uneven) days of the month and on the days which are auspicious for that direction.

We hire mules from the chief priest of Batang since bandits are less prone to attack the caravan of a high ranking lama. Robbers fear the power of his charms and evil prayers which are said to cause sickness, ill-luck and even death to an offender; such charms being projected through the air from the residence of the priest to the home of an enemy—perhaps the first wireless messages. The priesthood of Tibet is a religious guild in which, if one member is robbed, a representative is sent to the home of the robber to argue the brigand into giving back the goods, if necessary using the bandit's own personal priest as a mediator. Lamas know that it is to the welfare of the monastery for all men to be in deadly fear of their power.

As usual our mulemen want to delay a day at the last minute but an ultimatum that it is now or never is conclusive. The high hire I pay is too good to lose but their customary promised arrival at sunrise (in these high mountains about seven) is converted, as I expected, into a departure about noon. Friends escort us down the road for a half mile or more as is the custom in Tibet when one

takes an extended trip. Our departure is under auspicious circumstances for outside the gate we meet a woman with a full barrel of water,—an empty cask would have been an ill-omen.

Coursing down with the Batang River we climb over the 9,500 foot shoulder pass of Khuyee formed by a mountain spur through which the Batang River is compelled to cut a deep defile in order to reach the Yangtze River which here is about 8,400 feet above sea level, perhaps a hundred feet lower than Batang. This pass is a favorite rendezvous for brigands and its soil is tainted with the blood of many men, including Dr. A. L. Shelton who was assassinated from ambush near the top in 1922. Like all passersby we gaze intently into the bushes scattered amidst countless bowl-shaped resurrection plants, for all know that Tibetan robbers keep themselves well hidden before firing suddenly from behind rocks; either killing, or intimidating travellers, before revealing themselves. We are unarmed but the chief priest has sent along two guns which he thinks are enough to risk losing because guns are valuable.

We go prepared to lose everything at the hands of robbers and figure on the law of averages to retain our lives. Our party is hardened to such eventualities. Brigands had attacked us in 1927 generously leaving the clothes we wore. My Tibetan teacher Atring had lost his father by beheading at the hands of Chao Erh Feng because he was one of the late Prince's chief stewards; in addition, his older brother, some five years previously, had been killed by bandits and his caravan pillaged a half day's journey below the pass we are now crossing. The medical assistant, Shao Pin Sen, is the most nervous as he had only helped my party once put on a bold front to keep us from being attacked by nomads two days west of here in 1925 when we visited a Red Cap shrine at Dorjetroleh. Our guide, Jitsen, is a hardened old sinner who has been trading on this road for many years, losing money to both officials and thieves so that he has to keep on trading to make a living. Last of all our cook, Chohdrah, has been chased by robbers and had his animals stolen, besides being a thief who filched from a former foreign resident of Batang and survived a period in an Oriental jail after having been beaten a thousand strokes on the thighs.

Arriving at Li (Leh) we set the talk in motion for the use of the ferryboat down to Druwalung. We have wisely secured a Chinese official travel pass telling all headmen not to delay us on the road by refusing to grant 'Oolah'—or forced transportation. We have animals to carry our goods but desire to send them empty to Druwalung and avoid the possibility of being held up by robbers at their favorite assaulting place halfway down. Furthermore the boat ride will be quicker and easier and a new experience for me. The boatmen wish naturally to avoid the arduous labor of pulling the boat back against the Yangtze current unless they are paid more than the usual small rate.

'How much will the master give us,' is their opening question as they gather in a group around our teapot over the open fire at the temple.

'You know the custom and this is part of your taxes,' is my answer, knowing full well they wish to hold me up for an exorbitant price.

'If you give us twenty rupees we will take the teacher down,' is their opening offer, settling down for the long harangue.

'You know that the official rate is five rupees and sometimes with officials you do not get that. This is an official pass, and you don't want to ignore that, do you?' I return.

'What will the master give us; it is a long hard trip and you as a teacher of religion should have mercy upon us,' they reply, knowing the weak points of my position.

'Well, I will not state what I will give you but you know that I have always been generous and no foreigner has ever given you less than twice the official rate,' I state, and in spite of their pressure I will not promise what I will give, preferring to let the force of authority rule rather than the force of cash. They have no work to do and whatever they get will be a bonus. So in time they assent to ride us down in the boat the next morning.

Li is built a little above the Yangtze high-water mark, upon one of the numerous alluvial plains formed by a small mountain stream. The Yangtze in this region rises above twenty-five feet in summer and does not expand much beyond its usual width of about three hundred to nine hundred feet. The houses of Li are built of masonry and plastered with soot inside. The inhabitants, human, quadruped and insect, with the last not the least prominent, dwell in lively companionship. However if one has to wrest a living as do these people, from tiny fields, oppressed by robbers, religionists, and rulers, one can understand their poverty and dirt.

The Yangtze is in mid-flood at least fifteen feet above low-water level. Fifteen days previously it was some seven feet higher for the dirty line can be seen on the white yellow sands. September had unusually heavy rains which has piled immense tracts of sand into miniature mountain ranges along the banks. So vast are these sand banks and containing so much gold that the Chinese have named the Yangtze within the Tibetan borderlands the 'River of Golden Sands'. Above this point the Yangtze is better known as the Dri Chu or Female Wild Yak River because of its legendary origin.

The sands are not always beautiful. When the dry season sets in, the steady southwest winds of winter stir up the tiny pellets and hurl them relentlessly upon the unwary traveller. The tightest cases are useless, even those of watches, while the faint-hearted along with the courageous must swallow grit to strengthen them.

Early on the eleventh of October we embark with all our goods on the wooden ferry barge which is preferred to the skin coracles in use in most places. At the coracle ferries animals must swim and the weaker ones are sometimes lost in the swift currents. Our craft is wide, flat-bottomed and heavy. Its length is about sixty feet, its width seven feet and seven compartments divide the hold. The previous one burnt by the Ranalama in 1923 was fifty-one feet long, nine feet wide and the same number of compartments. At the stern is a steering oar twenty-five feet long. On each side are two rowing oars each twenty feet long and manned by three men apiece. Every trip about ten animals and their loads can be carried. The actual crossing is a matter of three minutes but an hour is required for the round trip. The boat must be pulled by hand upstream, for the current in each crossing sweeps the craft down several hundred feet. The Yangtze in this stretch is from two hundred and fifty to three hundred and fifty yards wide.

We sit in the boat enjoying the varied scenery of brushed mountain spurs and alluvial plains created during the ages by the raging torrents from mountain tips. Scarred houses remind us of the Ranalama's raid in 1923 when he led his monastic band to within ten miles below Batang, looting and killing. Later chased back to his monastery three days below us, his own subjects chopped off his head with an axe one dark night, notwithstanding his sanctity as an incarnated saint popularly called a Living Buddha. His killers were men from a rival monastery whose monks he had mistreated and whose relations he had slaughtered. In one and a half hours we arrive in Druwalung but our animals take four hours on the trail.

At Druwalung we board a slightly larger ferry barge to cross the river and then, to continue downstream on that side past the mouth of a tributary river, the Sheh Chu, entering from the west with rain-swollen waters too deep for fording without wetting the loads. This river, whose headwaters we crossed on our return farther north, has carried away the flimsy wooden bridge, which is rebuilt every winter and washed into the Yangtze every summer.

We go ashore and mount our mules, entering a canyon where the fierce rapids, filled with huge boulders, prohibit navigation. Gazing upward on the western range one can see where an immense landslide has carried away half of the mountain into the river, compressing the channel into barely three hundred feet wide. The rains every year wash down great fields of mud and stones which must tax the angry waters to carry it away before the next rainy season.

Most of the Yangtze tributaries are from the east, small torrents formed and fed by springs. The maintenance of streams throughout the year is through numerous powerful springs rather than through the melting of snow. The rainfall of twenty-two to forty-five inches falls mostly during the summer while winter and spring are the dry seasons with scarcely an inch of overall precipitation.

In Batang and along the Mekong and Yangtze rivers the altitude is low enough for two crops a year. The first crop is wheat or barley and after this is cut in July, buckwheat or millet are sown, and harvested in October. One variety of millet called Tri is pulled up by the roots instead of being cut off. Millet and buckwheat are never grown at the higher altitudes, above ten thousand five hundred feet, as buckwheat especially does not stand frosts; furthermore when only one crop can be grown barley and wheat are more valuable.

On our third day we leave the Yangtze to turn south over a high cliff, whose eroded soil, of variegated colors, is said by the Chinese to indicate deposits of gold. The Yangtze yearly eats out great chunks of this rainbow cliff, carrying the gold for deposit in sands farther down where some of it is panned out by washing. From our turning point the mighty river goes southeast into a still more formidable canyon, most of it untrod by men. Savage rapids must tear at the rocks for the altitude here of 8,200 feet drops a half mile during the next one hundred and fifty miles of the river's course.

53

FROZEN

EVARISTE-REGIS HUC

Abbé Huc, a French Lazarist priest, arrived in China in 1841 to join the Mongolian mission. The Pope had divided the territory between different groups, giving Mongolia to the Lazarists, and Manchuria to the Jesuits. In 1844 Huc and Joseph Gabet, another Lazarist, set off from Mongolia to Tibet, looking for new peoples to convert. The two were chosen because they spoke Manchu, Mongolian, and some Tibetan. They got as far as Kumbun Monastery in Qinghai Province (then part of Tibet) where they stayed for eight months. War between the Chinese and the Tibetans made return impossible, so they continued on towards Lhasa, 'the very Rome of Buddhism'.

In this extract from Huc's account, they are on their way to Lhasa. Even for today's explorers, equipped with all kinds of modern supplies, such a trip would be very dangerous and difficult. How much more so for these travellers! Their caravan of camels, horses, and men had to rely on gathering 'argols' (dried horse dung) for fuel, and subsisted only on 'tsampa' (barley-meal) and tea. Before this passage begins, the caravan had just said goodbye to their military escort, as they are about to enter Tibet, where the Chinese and Tartar soldiers could not accompany them. But now their main fear was not that they might be killed by brigands, as before: 'the point was to avoid being killed by the cold'.

It was on Mount Chuga that the long train of our real miseries really began. The snow, the wind, and the cold there set to work upon us, with a fury which daily increased. The deserts of Thibet are certainly the most frightful country that it is possible to conceive. The ground continuing to rise, vegetation diminished as we advanced, and the cold grew more and more intense. Death now hovered over the unfortunate caravan. The want of water and of pasturage soon destroyed the strength of our animals. Each day we had to abandon beasts of burden that could drag themselves on no further. The turn of the men came somewhat later. The aspect of the road was of dismal auspice. For several days we travelled through what seemed the excavations of a great cemetery. Human bones and the carcases of animals presenting themselves at every step, seemed to warn us that, in this fatal region, amidst this savage nature, the caravans which had preceded us had preceded us in death.

To complete our misery, M. Gabet fell ill, his health abandoning him just at the moment when the frightful difficulties of the route called for redoubled energy and courage. The excessive cold he had undergone on the passage of Mount Chuga had entirely broken up his strength. To regain his previous vigour, he needed repose, tonic drinks, and a substantial nourishment, whereas all we had to give him was barley-meal, and tea made with snow water; and, moreover, notwithstanding his extreme weakness, he had every day to ride on horseback, and to struggle against an iron climate. And we had two months more of this travelling before us, in the depth of winter. Our prospect was, indeed, sombre!

Towards the commencement of September, we arrived in sight of the Bayen-Kharat, the famous chain of mountains, extending from south-east to north-west, between the Hoang-Ho [Yellow River] and the Kin-Cha-Kiang [Jinshajiang—the Yangtze]. These two great rivers, after running a parallel course on either side of the Bayen-Kharat, then separate, and take opposite directions, the one towards the north, the other towards the south. After a thousand capricious meanderings in Tartary and Thibet, they both enter the Chinese empire; and after having watered it from west to east, they approach each other towards their mouths, and fall into the Yellow Sea very nearly together. The point at which we crossed the Bayen-Kharat is not far from the sources of the Yellow River; they lay on our left, and a couple of days' journey would have enabled us to visit them; but this was by no means the season for pleasure trips. We had no fancy for a tourist's excursion to the sources of the Yellow River: how to cross the Bayen-Kharat was ample occupation for our thoughts.

From its foot to its summit the mountain was completely enveloped in a thick coat of snow. Before undertaking the ascent, the principal members of the embassy held a council. The question was not whether they should pass the mountain: if they desired to reach Lha-Ssa, the passage of the mountain was an essential preliminary; nor was it the question whether they should await the melting of the snow; the point was simply whether it would be more advantageous to ascend the mountain at once or to wait till next day. The fear of avalanches filled every-one's mind, and we should all have gladly subscribed to effect an assurance against the wind. After the example of all the councils in the world, the council of the Thibetian embassy was soon divided into two parties, the one contending that it would be better to start forthwith, the other insisting that we ought, by all means, to wait till the morrow.

To extricate themselves from this embarrassment, they had recourse to the Lamas, who had the reputation of being diviners. But this expedient did not combine all minds in unity. Among the diviners there were some who declared that this day would be calm, but that the next day there would be a terrible wind, and there were others who announced an exactly contrary opinion. The caravan thus became divided into two camps, that of movement and that of non-movement. It will at once be understood that in our character of French citizens we instinctively placed ourselves in the ranks of the progressists; that is to say, of those who desired to advance, and to have done with this villainous mountain as soon as possible. It appeared to us, moreover, that reason was altogether on our side. The weather just then was perfectly calm; but we knew not what it might be on the morrow. Our party, therefore, proceeded to scale these mountains of snow, sometimes on horseback, but more frequently on foot. In the latter case, we made our animals precede us, and we hung on to their tails, a mode of ascending mountains which is certainly the least fatiguing of all. M. Gabet suffered dreadfully, but God, of his infinite goodness, gave us strength and energy enough to reach the other side. The weather was calm throughout, and we were assailed by no avalanche whatever.

Next morning, at daybreak, the party who had remained behind advanced and crossed the mountain with entire success. As we had had the politeness to wait for them, they joined us, and we entered together a valley where the temperature was comparatively mild. The excellence of the pasturage induced the caravan to take a day's rest here. A deep lake, in the ice of which we dug wells, supplied us with abundance of water. We had plenty of fuel, too, for the embassies and pilgrimages being in the habit of halting in the valley, after the passage of the Bayen-Kharat, one is always sure to find plenty of *argols* there. We all kept up great fires throughout our stay, burning all the burnable things we could find, without the smallest consideration for our successors, leaving it to our 15,000 long-haired oxen to supply the deficit.

We quitted the great valley of Bayen-Kharat, and set up our tents on the banks of the Mouroui-Oussou, or, as the Thibetians call it, Polei-Tchou [Polei-ch'u] 'river of the Lord.' Towards its source, this magnificent river bears the name of Mouroui-Oussou [Murui-usu] 'tortuous river'; further on it is called Kin-Cha-Kiang 'river of golden sand,' and arrived in the province of Sse-Tchouan, it becomes the famous Yang-Dze-Kiang 'blue river.' As we were passing the Mouroui-Oussou, on the ice, a singular spectacle presented itself. We had previously, from our encampment, observed dark, shapeless masses, ranged across this great river; and it was not until we came quite close to these fantastic islets that we could at all make head or tail of them. Then we found out that they were neither more nor less than upwards of fifty wild cattle, absolutely encrusted in the ice. They had no doubt attempted to swim across the river, at the precise moment of the concretion of the waters, and had been so hemmed in by the flakes as to be unable to extricate themselves. Their fine heads, surmounted with great horns, were still above the surface; the rest of the bodies was enclosed by the ice, which was so transparent as to give a full view of the form and position of the unlucky animals, which looked as though they were still swimming. The eagles and crows had pecked out their eyes.

IN PRAISE OF THE RIVER:
A NEW INSPIRATION

54

THE RIVER

TSOU TI-FAN

Compared to the constantly flooding Yellow River, 'China's Sorrow', the Chinese consider the Yangtze to be quite benevolent. Yet it is clear from these extracts that most who have known this powerful river, whether in the lower or upper reaches, have always had reason to regard it with a fearful respect. It is often likened to a dragon, symbol of power, of the Emperor and of China itself; a capricious and unpredictable creature, who could bring wealth one season and destruction and death the next.

This poem, however, represents a profoundly new way of looking at the Yangtze. It was written in June of the terrible year of 1938, only a few months before the fall of Wuhan to the Japanese. The refugees Tsou mentions are fleeing further and further upriver as the Japanese advance. Yet the poem illustrates the beginning of a new spirit among patriotic Chinese of the 1920s and 1930s, an energy later embodied in the poems of Mao Zedong, who gloried not in harmony but in struggle, and who believed that nature's wildness could be harnessed by man and used for his benefit. Tsou compares the Yangtze not to a dragon but to a fiery battle horse, friend of man, its strength and vitality a challenge and an inspiration.

The muddy river swells in summer,
The torrents, dancing and prancing, spreading over ten
thousand acres, A battle horse carrying a full load of wind
and sand,
Gallops down
From the prairie land of the Bayan Kara Mountain;
Having bitten off its rein.
Its red mane defies the restraint of the Three Gorges
As it darts towards a destination faraway.

Eagles scream above
And gibbons in the gulches and creeks scream in unison.
The boatmen with two bright eyes
In a dark brown face,
A pair of dark brown arms,
And a blue turban,
Poles his raft.
He pushes his pole against the rocks,
His body bent double,
In combat with the river.
The spray of the waves fall off the rock,
An eagle lands on it;
And again the waves roll over the rock,
The eagle takes off in surprise.

A stormy rain descends.
More loudly roar the waterfalls on both banks,
The rain boosts the waves,
And the waves, with their sharp tongues
lash against the rocks,
Leaving endless rings of eddies whirling by.
The river calls

And howls
And laughs without restraint.

The river rushes over the grassland of the south,
Whipped by willow trees along the way.
The whistles of river boats
Echo each other.
And the river on its laborious journey,
With its mane and tail flying,
Neighs and gallops on the high wind.

Ah, river—
I love your robust strength
That carries you thousands upon thousands of miles.
No dike can stop your surging billows
From irrigating the land and feeding the people along your course

For thousands of years without end.
Today the fortune of our fatherland is so pitiable.
The refugees fleeing disasters upriver
Are like the flood that rushes downhill.
Ah, river—
You will hear
And see
How those suffering people groan and grieve
All around you.
Ah, river—
I'm grateful for your revelation,
For I too shall offer to our fatherland a bit of service
And a bit of warmth.
I shall mount my battle horse
To gallop after your huge roaring waves without stop,
Leaving a storm of dust that trails my horse's hooves.

BIBLIOGRAPHY

Noel Barber, *The Fall of Shanghai*, New York: Coward, McCann and Geoghagen, 1976.

Isabella Bird, *The Yangtze Valley and Beyond*, London: John Murrary, 1899. Reprinted by Virago Press, London, 1985.

Thomas W. Blakiston, *Five Months on the Yang-tse*, London: John Murray, 1862.

Judy Bonavia, *The Yangzi River*, Hong Kong: The Guidebook Company, 1995.

Chen Shixu, translated by Yu Fanqin, *The Angry Waves*, Part 2, 1984. Reprinted in the *Chinese Literature Quarterly*, Autumn 1985.

Edwin J. Dingle, *Across China on Foot*, London: J. W. Arrowsmith Ltd, 1911.

Cyril Drummond Le Gros Clark, trans., *Selections from the Works of Su Tung-P'o*, London: Jonathan Cape, London, 1931.

Marion H. Duncan, *The Yangtse and the Yak*, Michigan: Edwards Bros., 1952.

Hua-Ling Nieh Engle and Paul Engle, *The Poetry of Mao Tse-tung*, London: Wildwood House, 1973.

William Gill, *River of Golden Sand*, Volume 1, London: John Murray, 1880. Reprinted by Gregg International, Westmead, UK, 1969.

A. C. Graham, trans., *Poems of the Late T'ang*, London: Penguin, 1965.

W. A. Grist & Samuel Pollard, *Pioneer Missionary in China*, London: Cassell and Company. Reprinted by Ch'eng Wen Publishing, Taipei, 1971.

Peter Goullart, *Forgotten Kingdom*, London: John Murray, 1955.

Gregory Haines, *Gunboats on the Great River*, London: Macdonald & Jane's, 1976.

Theodore F. Harris, *Pearl S. Buck: A Biography*, London: Methuen, 1970.

John Hersey, *A Single Pebble*, New York: Alfred A. Knopf, 1956. Reprinted by Corgi, 1966.

Tom Hilditch, 'The Plight of the Baiji', *Sunday Morning Post*

Magazine, 23 October 1994.

Hilda Hookham, *A Short History of China*, New York: Mentor, 1972.

Alexander Hosie, *Three Years in Western China*, London: George Phelps and Son, 1890. Reprinted by Ch'eng Wen Publishing, Taipei, 1972.

Kai-yu Hsu, ed. and trans., *Twentieth-century Chinese Poetry*, New York: Doubleday & Co., 1963

Joan Hua, 'Harnessing the Yangtze', *Window Magazine*, Hong Kong, 5 November 1993.

Evariste-Regis Huc and Joseph Gabet, *Travels in Tartary, Thibet and China 1844–1846*, Volume 2, London: George Routledge, 1928. Original French publication, 1850, English translation by William Hazlett published 1851. Reprinted by Dover Publications, New York, 1987.

Jiang Liu, *China's Longest River*, Beijing: Foreign Languages Press, 1980.

Jing Yan, 'Preserving the Gorge's Plant Life'. *China Daily*, Beijing, 20 September 1994.

Archibald John Little, F. R. G. S., *Through the Yang-tse Gorges or Trade and Travel in Western China*, London: Sampson Low, Marston & Company, 1898. Reprinted by the Ch'eng Wen Publishing Co., Taipei, 1972.

Liu Binwen and Xiong Lei, eds., *Portraits of Ordinary Chinese*, Beijing: Foreign Languages Press, 1990.

Lo Kuan-chung, translated by Moss Roberts, *The Three Kingdoms*, New York: Pantheon, 1976.

Mao Dun, *A Ballad of Algae*, 1936. Published in *Chinese Literature Quarterly*, translated by Simon Johnstone, Beijing, Winter, 1986.

Mao Tsetung, *Poems*, Beijing: Foreign Languages Press, 1976.

A. R. Margary, *The Journal of Augustus Raymond Margary: From Shanghai to Bhamo, and back to Manwyne*, London: Macmillan, 1876.

Franz Michael, *The Taiping Rebellion: History and Documents*, Volume 1, Seattle: University of Washington Press, 1966.

Laurence Oliphant, *Elgin's Mission to China and Japan*, Volume 2, London: William Blackwood and Sons, 1859. Reprinted by Oxford University Press, 1970.

Robert Payne, ed., *The White Pony*, New York: The John Day

Company, 1947.

Robert Payne, *Chinese Diaries 1941–1946*, USA: Weybright & Talley Inc, 1970.

Fred Pearce, 'The Biggest Dam in the World', *New Scientist Magazine*, Australia, 28 January 1995.

William Spencer Percival, *The Land of the Dragon: My Boating and Shooting Excursions to the Gorges of the Upper Yangtse*, London: Hurst and Blackett, 1889.

Samuel Pollard, *In Unknown China*, London: Seeley, Service & Co, 1921.

Harriet Sergeant, *Shanghai*, London: Jonathan Cape, 1991.

Sun Yu, trans., *Li Po: A New Translation*, Hong Kong: The Commercial Press, 1982.

David W. Swift, 'Ninety Li A Day', *Asian Folklore and Social Life Monographs*, The Orient Cultural Service, Taipei, Volume 69, Spring, 1975.

Tan Shi-hua and S. Tretiakov, *A Chinese Testament*, London: Victor Gollancz, 1934.

Paul Theroux, *Sailing through China*, Boston: Houghton Mifflin, 1984.

Colin Thubron, *Behind the Wall*, London: William Heinemann, 1987.

Kemp Tolley, *Yangtze Patrol*, Annapolis MD: Naval Institute Press, 1971.

William Ferdinand Tyler, *Pulling Strings in China*, London: Constable & Co., 1929.

Lyman P. Van Slyke, *Yangtse: Nature, History and the River*, Massachusetts, Addison-Wesley Publishing Co. Inc., 1988.

Arthur Waley, *One Hundred and Seventy Chinese Poems*, London: Constable and Company, 1918.

Arthur Waley, *The Poetry and Career of Li Po, AD 701-762*, London: George Allen & Unwin, 1950.

Burton Watson, *The Old Man Who Does As He Pleases*, New York, Columbia University Press, 1973.

Theodore H. White, *In Search of History: A Personal Adventure*, New York: HarperCollins, 1978.

E. H. Wilson, *A Naturalist in Western China*, London: Methuen & Co., 1913. Republished by Cadogan Books, London, 1986.

How Man Wong, *Exploring the Yangtse*, Hong Kong: Odyssey

Productions Ltd., 1989.

H. G. W. Woodhead, C. B. E., *The Yangtsze and its Problems*, Shanghai: The Mercury Press, 1931.

Thomas Woodroofe, *The River of Golden Sand*, London, Faber, 1936.

H. R. G. Worcester, *Sail and Sweep in China*, London: British Science Museum, 1966.

Xiao Yu, 'Funds Sought to Save Relics', *Sunday Morning Post*, Hong Kong, 16 July 1995.

Yang Xianyi and Gladys Yang, trans., *Poetry and Prose of the Tang and Song*, Beijing: Panda Books, 1984.

Zhang Xinxin and Sang Ye, eds., and Gladys Yang, trans., *Chinese Profiles*, Beijing: Panda Books, 1986.

Zhao Pei, *Water Town*, translated by Song Shouquan, Chinese Literature Quarterly, Winter, 1986.

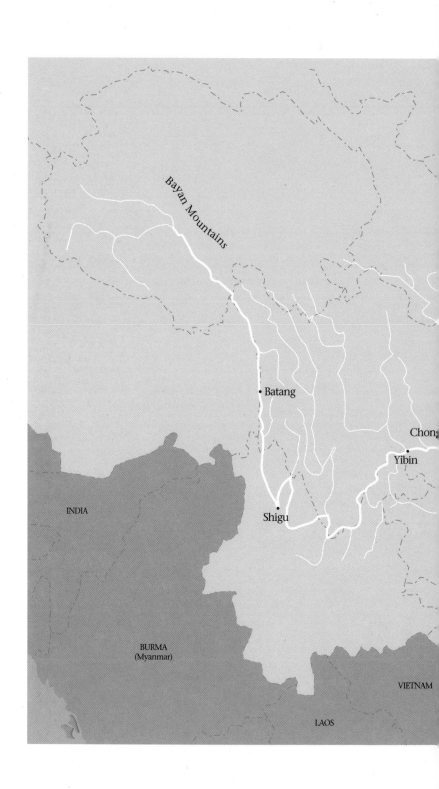